THE LAW OF WAR AND PEACE

A Gender Analysis

THE LAW OF WAR AND PEACE

A Gender Analysis

Vol 1

**Sara Bertotti, Gina Heathcote,
Emily Jones, Sheri Labenski**

BLOOMSBURY ACADEMIC
LONDON • NEW YORK • OXFORD • NEW DELHI • SYDNEY

BLOOMSBURY ACADEMIC
Bloomsbury Publishing Plc
50 Bedford Square, London, WC1B 3DP, UK
1385 Broadway, New York, NY 10018, USA
29 Earlsfort Terrace, Dublin 2, Ireland

BLOOMSBURY, BLOOMSBURY ACADEMIC and the Diana logo
are trademarks of Bloomsbury Publishing Plc

First published in Great Britain in 2021 by Zed Books Ltd, Bloomsbury
Publishing, 50 Bedford Square, London, WC1B 3DP
This paperback edition published by Bloomsbury Academic in 2022

A catalogue record for this book is available from the British Library.

ISBN: HB: 978-1-7869-9668-8
PB: 978-1-7869-9669-5
ePDF: 978-1-7869-9670-1
eBook: 978-1-7869-9671-8

Typeset by Integra Software Services Pvt. Ltd.

To find out more about our authors and books visit
www.bloomsbury.com and sign up for our newsletters.

CONTENTS

AUTHOR BIOGRAPHIES

Sara Bertotti is a Doctoral Researcher and Teaching Fellow at the School of Law, SOAS University of London.

Gina Heathcote is a Reader in Gender Studies and International Law, at the Centre for Gender Studies and the School of Law, SOAS University of London.

Emily Jones is a Lecturer in the School of Law and Human Rights Centre at the University of Essex.

Sheri Labenski is a Research Officer in the Centre for Women, Peace, and Security at the London School of Economics and Political Science, where she works on an ERC-funded project Gendered Peace.

TABLE OF CASES

ABBREVIATIONS

ATCSA	Anti-Terrorism, Crime and Security Act, UK
ATT	Arms Trade Treaty
CEDAW	Convention on the Elimination of All Forms of Discrimination Against Women
CPN-M	Communist Party of Nepal-Maoist
COI	Commission of Inquiry
COIN	Counterinsurgency
DRC	Democratic Republic of the Congo
ECCC	Extraordinary Chambers in the Courts of Cambodia
ECHR	European Convention on Human Rights
ECtHR	European Court of Human Rights
FET	Female Engagement Team
HRA	Human Rights Act, UK
HRC	Human Rights Council
ICC	International Criminal Court
ICCPR	International Covenant on Civil and Political Rights
ICJ	International Court of Justice
ICRC	International Committee of the Red Cross
ICTR	International Criminal Tribunal for Rwanda
ICTY	International Criminal Tribunal for the former Yugoslavia
IMT	International Military Tribunal
IMTFE	International Military Tribunal for the Far East
INGO	International Non-Governmental Organization
ISIS	Islamic State of Iraq and Syria
LAWS	Lethal Autonomous Weapons Systems
LGBT	Lesbian, Gay, Bisexual, Transgender
LGBTQ	Lesbian, Gay, Bisexual, Transgender, Queer
LGBTQIA	Lesbian, Gay, Bisexual, Transgender, Queer, Intersex, Asexual
NATO	North Atlantic Treaty Organization
NGO	Non-Governmental Organization
OHCHR	Office of the United Nations High Commissioner for Human Rights
OTP	Office of the Prosecutor
PLA	People's Liberation Army, Nepal
R2P	Responsibility to Protect
RNA	Royal Nepal Army
SCSL	Special Court for Sierra Leone
STL	Special Tribunal for Lebanon

TADA	Terrorist and Disruptive Activities (Control and Punishment) Act, Nepal
TADO	Terrorist and Disruptive Activities (Control and Punishment) Ordinance, Nepal
UN	United Nations
USAID	United States Agency for International Development
WILPF	Women's International League for Peace and Freedom
WWII	Second World War

INTRODUCTION

...feminism is a mode of analysis, a method of approaching life and politics, a way of asking questions and searching for answers, rather than a set of political conclusions about the oppression of women.[1]

...an exception is made in favour of women and children ...[2]

Peace and war are predominantly understood in opposition to one another; likewise, understandings of security and insecurity or the assumed binary between men and women.

Peace is thus imagined as distinct from war, to be achieved at the end of hostilities and, significantly, given lesser research, resources and attention from international and state institutions. This can also be seen in academic curricula where war studies or strategic studies outnumber peace studies and peace research.[3] This book is one of a two-volume set analysing international laws on peace and war from a gender perspective.

Seventeenth-century scholar Hugo Grotius is famously known for his treatise *De Jure Belli ac Pacis,* or *On the Law of War and Peace,* one of the earliest, and most influential, international legal texts that is often still referenced in international legal scholarship today.[4] Grotius' book delineated the different obligations of states in times of war, which he perceived as an appropriate means to achieve peace,[5] while

1. Nancy Hartsock, 'Feminist Theory and the Development of Revolutionary Strategy' in Zillah R Eisenstein (ed), *Capitalist Patriarchy and the Case for Socialist Feminism* (Monthly Review Press 1978) 58, 59
2. Hugo Grotius, *On the Law of War and Peace* (trans. Archibald Colin Campbell, Anodos Books 2019) 182
3. Carol Cohn, 'Women and Wars: Toward a Conceptual Framework' in Carol Cohn (ed), *Women and Wars: Contested Histories, Uncertain Futures* (Polity Press 2013) 12
4. Grotius, above note 2
5. '... and then war itself will lead us to peace, as to its proper end.' Grotius, above note 2, 11

advancing the notion of an international society.[6] Although Grotius did not conceive of gender as central to international law, his analysis is built on an analogy between the power of the patriarch and the power of the state.[7] As the quote above attests, Grotius saw women and children as a separate class of subjects, defined by an entitlement to protection, during war.[8] In contrast, this book analyses war and peace as interlocking, gender as diverse and fluid, and security as gendered. Our account of the law of war and peace analyses contemporary laws, including collective security, unilateral force and counter-terrorism as well as the legal regimes governing the international humanitarian law of armed conflict and international criminal law. The book, and the forthcoming second volume, approaches peace and war as intertwined while analysing these laws through the lens of gender. Throughout, the text draws in feminist analyses of international law, gender and conflict.[9] While the laws of war and peace have changed in many ways since Grotius' day, we analyse the entrenched assumptions about gender that persist in the law of war and the law of peace. In positioning law in our analysis of gender and conflict, we add to the development of gender and conflict as a field of research through an in-depth study of the relevant legal regimes.[10]

As a gender analysis, our starting point is Duncanson's definition of gender as functioning as an individual identity and as a symbolic system, requiring attention to the embodied realities of gendered lives and the nexus to larger power relations.[11] Duncanson identifies the limitations of perceiving gender as simply an individual identity and the centring of women as a named group that experiences discrimination,

---

6. Hedley Bull, Benedict Kingsbury and Adam Roberts (eds), *Hugo Grotius and International Relations* (Clarendon Press 1992) 6ff

7. Helen Kinsella, 'Gendering Grotius: Sex and Sex Difference in the Laws of War' (2006) 34 (2) Political Theory 170, 171

8. Also, Grotius, above note 2, 191

9. Hilary Charlesworth and Christine Chinkin, *The Boundaries of International Law: A Feminist Analysis* (Manchester University Press 2000); Gina Heathcote, *Feminist Dialogues on International Law: Successes, Tensions, Futures* (Oxford University Press 2019)

10. Cynthia Cockburn and Dubravka Zarkov (eds), *The Postwar Moment: Militaries, Masculinities and International Peacekeeping* (Lawrence and Wishart 2002); Cynthia Enloe, *Maneuvers: The International Politics of Militarizing Women's Lives* (University of California Press 2000)

11. Claire Duncanson, *Gender and Peacebuilding* (Polity Press 2016) 7

which reinforces an essentialist and heteronormative binary account of gender. This approach writes out women's diversity as well as the diversity of gendered lives. Similarly, legal outcomes focused on gender as a marker of identity tend towards liberal feminist framings focused on rights and the individual; the production of quotas for participation; and result in limited means to address heteronormativity, as well as raced and ableist experiences of gender.[12] Through identifying gender as an identity marker while addressing gender as a symbolic system, gender analysis is developed through the examination of systems and structures of meaning as well as institutions.[13] In applying this approach to the study of armed conflict and peace processes, we acknowledge the lived experience of gender as consequence of symbolic structures and systems of meaning, including law.

Studies of gender and conflict have identified the war-peace dichotomy as a false, gendered binary.[14] Our project is to think more deeply, ask more questions and theorize beyond war and peace to consider how war and peace are equally invested in each other: peacetime states are never wholly peaceful and those at war, or – to use the terminology of contemporary international lawyers – in a situation of armed conflict, are also, always, invested in peace.[15] As a consequence, across this book, and the forthcoming second volume, we develop an analysis that interrogates the gendered meanings of peace and armed conflict to understand the persistence of military behaviour and the complexities of peace. Both texts shift between diverse feminist, queer and gender tools as well as locations of violence, from macro to micro sites, to challenge legal boundaries between peace and conflict, security and insecurity, masculine and feminine forms. In analysing peace and war, security and insecurity, the objective is to avoid a tokenistic

---

12. Ratna Kapur, *Erotic Justice: Law and the New Politics of Postcolonialism* (Routledge 2005); Gina Heathcote, 'Participation, Gender and Security' in Gina Heathcote and Dianne Otto (eds), *Rethinking Peacekeeping, Gender Equality and Collective Security* (Palgrave 2014)

13. Carol Cohn (ed), *Women and Wars: Contested Histories, Uncertain Futures* (Polity Press 2013)

14. Cynthia Cockburn, *The Space between Us: Negotiating Gender and National Identities in Conflict* (Zed Books 1998)

15. Dianne Otto, *Rethinking Peace from a Queer Feminist Perspective*, 26 September 2019, Public Lecture at LSE Centre for Women, Peace and Security, London

treatment of peace as an afterthought of armed conflict. If Grotius' writing makes a series of assumptions around the role and persistence of the patriarch in the framing of law, this text takes its starting point from the role and persistence of feminisms as tools for dismantling the legacy of patriarchy in laws. The book, and the forthcoming second volume, adds an important perspective to the study of gender and conflict.

As authors we have different points of view, sometimes with quite radical divergences, on what a feminist analysis might look like. The use of the pronoun 'we' thus holds our disagreements, tensions and conversations – what Cockburn refers to as the 'space between us' – as productive moments in the writing of the text.[16] While Cockburn articulates this as a feminist methodology for creating alliances across (imagined and real) differences in armed conflict, our commitment has been to explore how our differences as authors have the capacity to inflect and change the text via recognition of these 'spaces between us'. More concretely, these differences are reflected in our theoretical choices (from theories of gender and sexuality, queer scholarship to intersectionality and postcolonial theories, from feminist international relations work to feminist legal theories) alongside strongly held commitments to feminist peace activism, to addressing the reality of female violence, to the politics of the everyday and through posthuman and queer feminisms that we have held, drawn in, discussed and sat with across both texts: as such, we ask the reader to regard what we describe as a feminist methodology as one which questions our differences, our assumed knowledges and sometimes our disagreements as authors.

In the following section we introduce the key debates on gender and international law, as well as law and war, before presenting the contours of our methodology, exploring the feminist convergences, conversations and differences that inform our overarching methodology. Throughout the book different components of the methodology – structural bias, intersectionality, queer and postcolonial feminisms, while moving towards a feminist anti-militarism – are explored chapter by chapter. The third section of this chapter introduces the Security Council resolutions on women, peace and security, noting the prominent place that the women, peace and security resolutions hold in the bulk of academic writing on gender and conflict and seeking to both draw on these resolutions as important tools and set forth strategies to develop

---

16. Cockburn, above note 14; Robyn Wiegman, *Object Lessons* (Duke University Press 2012) 13

research on law regulating armed conflict and peace processes beyond the women, peace and security agenda.[17] We hope, as reader, you are able to engage with a range of feminist methodologies via the two volumes, as well as the various international legal regimes that govern war and peace. In the final section of this introductory chapter, we outline the structure of Volume One and provide a short insight into the focus of Volume Two.

Gender in international law, war and peace

This section introduces some of the key terminologies and concepts used throughout the book. One of our goals in the book is to highlight the range of international laws that regulate armed conflict, looking at both *jus ad bellum* and *jus in bello*. The *jus ad bellum,* or the law on resorting to war, governs the decisions of states to use military force. The *jus in bello,* or law in war, governs the conduct of hostilities, incorporating the methods and means of armed conflict, as well as the humanitarian restraints and protections that apply. In Volume One, we also provide an analysis of international criminal law, the key international legal regime for holding individuals accountable for international crimes. In focusing on these legal regimes, our goal is to address a larger gap in the literature on gender and conflict that primarily focuses on a narrow range of international instruments: the Security Council resolutions on women, peace and security, which we discuss below, and the international criminal laws that address gender crimes, which we discuss in Chapter 5.[18] Throughout, we argue for an expansive gender analysis of conflict that addresses international law through the laws that govern war and peace. We commence the project in this volume through an analysis of collective security, unilateral force and counter-terrorism and the relevant legal regimes, followed by a gender analysis of the international humanitarian law of armed conflict and international criminal law. Volume Two provides analysis

17. Sara E Davies and Jacqui True (eds), *The Oxford Handbook of Women, Peace, and Security* (Oxford University Press 2019)
18. Vasuki Nesiah, 'Gender and Forms of Conflict: The Moral Hazards of Dating the Security Council' in Fionnuala Ní Aoláin, Naomi Cahn, Dina Francesca Haynes and Nahla Valji (eds), *The Oxford Handbook on Gender and Conflict* (Oxford University Press 2018)

of military technologies, peace agreements, peacekeeping and peace enforcement, as well as alternative transitional justice mechanisms and feminist peace activism. In both volumes we examine the impact of the various regimes on both peacetime states and states understood to be at war, identifying and disrupting the assumption that peacetime states are not co-opted and affected by global conflicts.

Gender and international law

Charlesworth and Chinkin's work on feminist approaches to international law moves from a focus on the effects of international law on gendered lives to interrogate the ways in which gender structures international law.[19] Elsewhere, Charlesworth analyses the ways in which multiple gendered binaries both underpin and uphold international legal structures. This includes legal perceptions of 'objective/ subjective, legal/political, logic/emotion, order/anarchy, mind/body, culture/nature, action/passivity, public/private, protector/protected'.[20] International law primarily values the first (male) characteristic over the second characteristic, which is deemed to be feminized, thereby not only working to present international law as an inherently masculine structure, but also enforcing gender stereotypes more broadly.[21] Otto explains:

> Dichotomized ideas that are associated with gender, like strength and weakness, are also organized hierarchically so that the masculine option is valued more highly than the feminine. Associating a course of action with weakness immediately gives the alternative course the connotation of strength. Thus gendered dichotomies provide a powerful means of shaping what appear to be "common sense" choices.[22]

This deep structural constraint in law also makes addressing gender beyond a binarized articulation difficult whilst also embedding a

---

19. Charlesworth and Chinkin, above note 9
20. Hilary Charlesworth, 'International Law: a Discipline of Crisis' (2002) 65 (3) Modern Law Review 377, 389–90
21. Ibid.
22. Dianne Otto, 'A Sign of "Weakness"? Disrupting Gender Certainties in the Implementation of Security Council Resolution 1325' (2006) 13 Michigan Journal of Gender & Law 113, 122

heteronormative relation between masculinity and femininity. Gender as an analytical tool thus emerges within international legal scholarship as a means to expose and uncover these deep structural biases.

Race, class, sexuality, ableism and socio-economic status, among other factors, all contribute towards the biopolitical ordering of individuals, as well as contributing to the normative values which underpin international legal frames.[23] Gender must therefore be understood as intersecting with these other organizing structures. Intersectionality as articulated by Crenshaw, who coined the term through drawing on a much longer history of Black feminist approaches, highlights the necessity of understanding gender through an intersectional lens and recognizing 'the "multidimensionality" of marginalized subjects' lived experiences'.[24] While Crenshaw's work on intersectionality was borne from a US anti-discrimination law perspective, it has influenced the way scholars articulate the convergence of identities before the law. Yuval-Davis has expanded the work on intersectionality to include the way political arrangements and concepts such as citizenship (both formal and informal), indigeneity and migration influence the lives of individuals in international and local spaces.[25] While Yuval-Davis' work may not necessarily engage with intersectionality in international law in specific terms, her work illustrates the need for a thorough discussion of identity politics within international discourse, and indeed its presence in human rights and women's rights on a global scale.[26]

Within gender scholarship on international law, intersectionality is foremost identified and analysed in relation to the Convention on the Elimination of All Forms of Discrimination Against Women

23. Michel Foucault, *The Will to Knowledge: The History of Sexuality* Volume 1 (1976, trans. Robert Hurley, Penguin 1998); as a starting point, biopolitics can be understood as a form of positive politico-administrative power over life 'to ensure, sustain, and multiply life, to put this life in order ...'. Foucault, at 138
24. Jennifer Nash, 'Re-thinking Intersectionality' (2008) 89 Feminist Review 1, 2; Kimberlé Crenshaw, 'Demarginalizing the Intersection of Race and Sex: A Black Feminist Critique of Antidiscrimination Doctrine, Feminist Theory and Antiracist Politics' (1989) 1 The University of Chicago Legal Forum 139; Jennifer Nash, *Black Feminism Reimagined: After Intersectionality* (Duke University Press 2019)
25. Nira Yuval-Davis, 'Intersectionality and Feminist Politics' (2006) 13 (3) European Journal of Women's Studies 193
26. Yuval-Davis, ibid.

(CEDAW).[27] Although CEDAW, as an anti-discrimination treaty, does not address intersectionality in its text, its application and interpretation via the CEDAW Committee is regarded as developing an intersectional feminist agenda.[28] The CEDAW Committee, via its General Recommendations, has also broadened the range of the treaty to address violence against women and women in conflict prevention, conflict and post-conflict situations.[29] The CEDAW Committee has also specifically addressed the needs of disabled women, rural women, migrant women and refugee and stateless women.[30] This represents an important effort at gender law reform within international law. Nevertheless, CEDAW's interventions remain circumscribed by the language of women's rights: a legal model that centres liberal ideologies and prioritizing the individual in adversarial legal systems that also underpins neoliberal market logics.[31] Although the development of the

27. Convention on the Elimination of All Forms of Discrimination against Women (18 December 1979) 1249 UNTS 13

28. Meghan Campbell, 'CEDAW and Women's Intersecting Identities: A Pioneering New Approach to Intersectional Discrimination' (2015) 11 (2) Direito GV Law Review 479; Lola Okolosie, 'Beyond "Talking" and "Owning" Intersectionality' (2014) 108 Feminist Review 90

29. Committee on the Elimination of Discrimination against Women, 'General Recommendation No. 35 on gender-based violence against women, updating General Recommendation No. 19' (26 July 2017) UN Doc. CEDAW/C/GC/35; Committee on the Elimination of Discrimination against Women, 'General Recommendation No. 30 on women in conflict prevention, conflict and post-conflict situations' (1 November 2013) UN Doc. CEDAW/C/GC/30

30. Committee on the Elimination of Discrimination against Women, 'General Recommendation No. 18, tenth session, 1991, disabled women' (30 January 1992) UN Doc. A/46/38; Committee on the Elimination of Discrimination against Women, 'General Recommendation No. 26 on women migrant workers' (5 December 2008) UN Doc. CEDAW/C/2009/WP.1/R; Committee on the Elimination of Discrimination against Women, 'General Recommendation No. 32 on the gender-related dimensions of refugee status, asylum, nationality and statelessness of women' (14 November 2014) UN Doc. CEDAW/C/GC/32; Committee on the Elimination of Discrimination against Women, 'General Recommendation No. 34 on the rights of rural women' (7 March 2016) UN Doc. CEDAW/C/GC/34

31. Rosemary Hunter, 'Contesting the Dominant Paradigm: Feminist Critiques of Liberal Legalism' in Margaret Davies and Vanessa Munro (eds), *The Ashgate Research Companion to Feminist Legal Theory* (Ashgate 2013)

CEDAW provisions — its recommendations and reports are an important element of international law, and via General Recommendation 30 are explicitly linked to the women, peace and security agenda — they remain outside the key focus of this book because of the limited mode of intersectionality that we perceive as achievable within a rights framework that, we argue, risks collapsing back into a set of competing identity claims.[32] Nonetheless, in the chapter on collective security we utilize the CEDAW Committee's work on Syria, which has incorporated a multifaceted gender approach to gendered harms. The UN system has largely ignored the need for a gender analysis in their response to the armed conflict in Syria. However, the CEDAW Committee has challenged the Syrian government on their incorporation of the women, peace and security agenda and on a broader politico-socio-economic understanding of gendered harm, which demonstrates the importance of feminist work via the CEDAW Committee. We recognize that while CEDAW can offer a limited rights-based framework at times, it remains an important avenue for engagement within the current international legal order.

We understand intersectionality as a feminist tool that is necessary to identify how power and privilege operate in tandem across dominant categories of gender, race, class, sexuality and ableism. We regard any approach to gender that is isolated from analysis of these co-ordinating sites of privilege as likely to produce gains for women who otherwise match the privilege of those in power. This remains a limitation of gender law reform within international law that has often empowered actors in the global north while seeking to 'save' and 'protect' women in the global south.[33] Both the global and intra-state dynamics of race and the histories of imperialism, we argue, must be addressed within structural bias feminisms through a feminist methodological commitment to seeing gender as produced in intersection with other spaces of power and privilege. Otto describes this as a need to push against,

> the reliance on essentialist and imperial representations of women as pacifying and civilizing influences because these representations, ironically, bear an unsettling resemblance to the gender stereotypes that sustain militarism and women's inequality.[34]

32. Heathcote, above note 9, ch 5
33. Kapur, above note 12
34. Otto, above note 22, 115

Developing the commitment to intersectionality and with a desire to actively respond to the heteronormativity of the gender binary, our work draws on both queer and postcolonial feminist approaches to international law. Queer approaches to international law provide an opportunity to question the hetero/normative underpinnings of the international legal structure. Queer approaches, like feminist approaches, cut across many layers of analysis, from focusing on the lived experiences of LGBTQIA persons, to understanding the ways in which the law applies to LGBTQIA subjects unequally,[35] to approaches which seek to unsettle the normative underpinnings of international legal structures via 'changing meanings, unsettling taxonomies, and inverting conventions'.[36] These two volumes thus draw on both feminist methodologies and queer approaches at different times to understand the gendering of the law and conflict.

Postcolonial feminisms are also drawn on to highlight the colonial histories and imperialism which have structured much of international law and gender law reform. The histories and the present of feminism are interrogated in terms of their co-optation into the denial of alternative histories of knowledge, the dominance of military-capital and the legacies of colonialism in international law and in the

---

35. We have chosen to use the term LGBTQIA, as opposed to LGBT. We regard this as a conscious departing from liberal LGBT rights frameworks through focusing on queer approaches, as well as encompassing a wider range of identities. LGBTQIA standing for lesbian, gay, bisexual, transgender, queer, intersex and asexual. A number of identity categories which we would wish to include are still missing, including, for example, trans people who do not identify as transgender, non-binary and genderqueer people. The semiotic challenge exemplifies one of the core problems with identity politics which seek to label subjects who do not neatly fit into labels or chose not to be labelled. At the same time, we have chosen to use LGBTQIA here as opposed to queer because we are talking about lived subjects who may or may not identify with queer as an all-encompassing anti-identity. For an analysis of LGBTQIA in a legal frame, see Sara Bengtson, Damian Gonzalez-Salzberg, Loveday Hodson and Paul Johnson, 'Christine Goodwin v the United Kingdom' in Loveday Hodson and Troy Lavers (eds), *Feminist Judgments in International Law* (Hart Publishing 2019)

36. Dianne Otto, 'Introduction: Embracing Queer Curiosity' in Dianne Otto (ed), *Queering International Law: Possibilities, Alliances, Complicities, Risks* (Routledge 2018) 2

deployment of military force. For example, to 'save' women in the global south from the violence of local military and political actors.[37] Drawing on Kapur's articulation of peripheral subjects and the construction of victim feminisms, we are mindful of the means through which dominant discourses on gender and conflict within international law deploy global distinctions between gendered empowerment and gendered protection.[38] This informs our framing of Chapters 4 and 5 where the hyperfocus on conflict-related sexual violence in international humanitarian law and international criminal law prompts our study of additional gendered discourses, including female violence, carceral feminisms and feminist posthumanism.

We have purposefully chosen to name these two books 'a gender analysis' so as to encompass all these perspectives, noting the links between multiple feminist and queer approaches.[39] At the same time, we are mindful of the ways in which 'gender' has often been taken up at an international level so as to refer to women only. This narrowing down of the term 'gender' creates a problematic and essentialist version of gender in international law and potentially silences any focus on subjects who do not neatly fit into the gender binary while fostering a lack of focus on the role of masculinities in enforcing the gender binary.[40] Ultimately, this study therefore conceptualizes the nexus between gender and international law as a linchpin that encourages the delving into further analysis on multiple, intersecting identities, lived experiences and structures, bringing in race, class, political economy, sexuality, ableism, geographic location and other factors

37. Chandra Talpade Mohanty, 'Under Western Eyes: Feminist Scholarship and Colonial Discourses' (1988) 30 Feminist Review 61; Vasuki Nesiah, 'The Ground Beneath Her Feet: "Third World" Feminisms' (2003) 4 (3) Journal of International Women's Studies 30; Vasuki Nesiah, 'From Berlin to Bonn to Baghdad: A Space for Infinite Justice' (2004) 17 Harvard Human Rights Journal 75; Vasuki Nesiah, 'Resistance in the Age of Empire: Occupied Discourse Pending Investigation' (2006) 27 (5) Third World Quarterly 903

38. Kapur, above note 12

39. Martha Albertson Fineman, Jack E Jackson and Aman P Romero (eds), *Feminist and Queer Legal Theory: Intimate Encounters, Uncomfortable Conversations* (Ashgate 2009)

40. Dianne Otto 'International Human Rights Law: Towards Rethinking Sex/Gender Dualism' in Margaret Davies and Vanessa Munro (eds), *The Ashgate Research Companion to Feminist Legal Theory* (Ashgate 2013)

to question power and governance and to challenge the normative underpinnings of the international legal order.

A related feminist critique of gender law reform within international law centres on the problematizing of governance feminism, defined as 'every form in which feminists and feminist ideas exert a governing will within human affairs',[41] noting the engagement feminism has with the work of 'state, state-like, and state-affiliated power'.[42] Highlighting that governance feminism has produced many positives in regards to international legal jurisprudence and feminist law reform, Halley also acknowledges that governance feminism has produced 'terrible mistakes', which are important to 'take stock of'.[43] One such example of governance feminism can be seen in the ways in which some feminist actors, alongside other actors, have sought to use military interventions in order to 'protect' women's rights. Such a perspective ignores the impact of military interventions on women's lives while also allowing women's rights to be used to justify interventions that are often about a wider political will. Critiques of governance feminism are careful to point out that not all feminisms are given space within the 'halls of power'.[44] Mindful of the critique of governance feminisms, in these two volumes we seek to critique such modes of engagement while applying analyses that have largely been left outside of the 'halls of power', including, as highlighted above, intersectional, queer and postcolonial gender perspectives. These are feminist approaches that remain on the peripheries of mainstream international legal thought, even with the small erosions into the world of CEDAW via the use of increasingly intersectional approaches. In applying these feminist approaches we seek to imagine an alternative gender approach to international law and conflict that challenges the multiple structural biases that continue to permeate the current international legal order and the regulation of armed conflict, war and peace.

---

41. Janet Halley, 'Preface: Introducing Governance Feminism' in Janet Halley, Prabha Kotiswaran, Rachel Rebouché and Hila Shamir (eds), *Governance Feminism: An Introduction* (University of Minnesota Press 2018) ix

42. Halley, ibid., x

43. Halley, ibid.

44. Janet Halley, *Split Decisions: How and Why to Take a Break from Feminism* (Princeton University Press 2006) 21

In centring diverse feminist methodologies we, on the one hand, clearly exercise a series of choices and, on the other hand, have actively incorporated methodologies that underscore alternative and varying voices from those that dominate dialogues on gender and conflict within global governance. Following Kapur's account of peripheral subjects, this methodology is used to regard actors outside of dominant knowledge frameworks as equally, indeed perhaps better, situated to contribute to understandings of war, peace and law.[45] At the same time our approach to gender as a tool for law reform actively engages intersectional assemblages as a mechanism for thinking about gender's investment in power relations, in particular the production of heteronormativity in law, the privileging of able-ism/normalizing of bodies and western-derived histories of knowledge and law.

Gender and armed conflict

An important contribution to the international legal literature on gender and armed conflict is Charlesworth's account of international law as a discipline of crisis.[46] Charlesworth discusses the roles of men and women in crisis situations, identifying how women are only recognized as being a part of the crisis, and international legal processes post-conflict, when harms are regarded as constituted against women as a social group (e.g. mass rapes and sexual assaults) while systemic and structural violence is perceived as disconnected from conflict-related violence.[47] Charlesworth's analysis exemplifies how men are seen to be active agents, while women enter only as an afterthought to the regulation of armed conflict.[48] At the same time, while men are often seen as defendants or perpetrators in wartime they are also simultaneously the 'saviour' who solves the crisis, rescuing women in the process. This feeds into the crisis mentality of international law limiting the analysis of how international law itself reflects gendered conceptualizations of violence and security. We are mindful that we too are guilty of focusing on these moments of crisis in order to engage with the literature in the area of gender and conflict. This anxiety thus reflects the tension feminists find themselves facing in international

45. Kapur, above note 12, 128–36
46. Charlesworth, above note 20
47. Ibid., 389
48. Ibid.

law, caught between wanting to de-centre mainstream crisis thinking in international law and desiring to have a voice and broaden perspectives. This shifting, between centre and periphery, between speaking to the mainstream in the hope of change and seeking to prioritize peripheral voices and perspectives haunts the two volumes and, we argue, feminist and critical engagements with international law as a whole. We take this theme up in Chapter 4 of this volume which engages with Kouvo and Pearson's understanding of resistance and compliance as dominant modes of feminist approaches within international law.[49]

As a discipline of crisis, armed conflict has been, and in many aspects still is, understood, studied and narrated as a masculine field. The narrative that armed conflict is strategized, fought and resolved by men paints a picture that can look so natural that it might seem undeserving of questioning. Literature on gender and armed conflict has challenged the framing of armed conflict through men's lives, particularly when the voices of feminists from outside of the global north reflect on modes of resistance and participation in the global south.[50] Cohn brings together the insight of decades of feminist scholarship and activism which, grounded in women's diverse experiences of conflict, recognizes that gender and conflict are 'mutually constitutive'.[51] Cohn defines gender as a structural power relation that is 'inflected through, and co-constituting of, other hierarchical forms of structuring power, such as class, caste, race, ethnicity, age, and sexuality'[52] and that rests on an 'ideology' which, at its root, deems one category (men) as biologically – and therefore immutably – more suited for dominant roles.[53] Referring to the conceptual difference between 'sex' and 'gender', Cohn explains how, at a societal level, a series of characteristics are built for men and women which assign them a significantly larger 'set of differences' than those attributable to biological factors alone.[54] It is this very set

---

49. Sari Kouvo and Zoe Pearson, *Feminist Perspectives on Contemporary International Law: Between Resistance and Compliance?* (Hart Publishing 2011)

50. Marguerite Waller and Jennifer Rycenga (eds), *Frontline Feminisms: Women, War, and Resistance* (Routledge 2001)

51. Cohn, above note 3, 1

52. Cohn, ibid., 5

53. Cohn, ibid., 5, 6; also see Judith Gardam 'An Alien's Encounter with the Law of Armed Conflict' in Ngaire Naffine and Rosemary Owens, *Sexing the Subject of Law* (Law Book Company 1997) 250

54. Cohn, ibid., 7

of 'imputed character traits, capacities, strengths, and weaknesses' and their intersection with other systems of power which determine how women and men live and are seen by others before, during and after the conflict.[55] This reasoning provides us with the analytical tools to challenge a series of stereotypical ideas related to gender and armed conflict such as those that naturally see men involved in active combat roles because of a supposed acceptance and inclination to violence, and women as naturally vulnerable subjects.

Feminists have questioned the classical understanding of conflict and peacetime as neatly separable periods. Women's experience shows how in fact violence can be seen as a 'continuum' crossing conflict and peacetime.[56] Waller and Rycenga use the image of the frontline to bring together women's accounts of violence crossing what is conventionally understood as peace and conflict, arguing: '[t]he frontline is not restricted to military locations', it can be anywhere women fight, in diverse and sometimes contrasting ways, to improve their situation.[57] The frontline is, according to Waller and Rycenga, 'ubiquitous whether in war, work, or love'.[58] This is shown through diverse examples such as the shedding of light on the hidden violence of home searches in the context of racism-infused police brutality in the US[59] and the role of women with the Eritrean People's Liberation Front, with the authors paying attention to how such contexts speak to one another.[60] Waller and Rycenga's collection recognizes the diversity of roles that women can assume during armed conflicts through featuring contributions dealing with both nonviolent and not-nonviolent approaches to change.[61] For

55. Cohn, ibid., 7, 8
56. Cockburn, above note 14, 8, 44, 45
57. Marguerite Waller and Jennifer Rycenga, 'Introduction' in Marguerite Waller and Jennifer Rycenga (eds), *Frontline Feminisms: Women, War, and Resistance* (Routledge 2001) xxi
58. Waller and Rycenga, ibid.
59. Nancy Keefe Rhodes, 'Beyond the Baton: How Women's Responses Are Changing Definitions of Police Violence' in Marguerite Waller and Jennifer Rycenga (eds), *Frontline Feminisms: Women, War, and Resistance* (Routledge 2001)
60. Sondra Hale, 'The Soldier and the State: Post-Liberation Women: The Case of Eritrea' in Marguerite Waller and Jennifer Rycenga (eds), *Frontline Feminisms: Women, War, and Resistance* (Routledge 2001)
61. Waller and Rycenga, above note 57, xxii

instance, Shahri, narrating her experience in the National Liberation Army of Iran, gives her account of how women, motivated by a 'need for resistance' progressively became involved in many if not all spheres of the army: '[w]hen the era of peaceful political opposition drew to a close, and the need for resistance became apparent, women members of the Mojahedin took on a variety of responsibilities in the bases'.[62] In a different context, but also challenging the idea of the inherent and essentializing peacefulness of women, Svirsky explains how behind the initial idea of the peaceful protest group Women in Black 'was not a woman's natural predilection for peacemaking, but the ideological commitment of women to a vision of international peace [which] did not come from instinct, but from socializing and educating each other over the years'.[63] Both approaches identify women's active choices, as well as a gendered necessity/compulsion to change (rather than some characteristics innate to women), in order to achieve change not only for what they respectively thought was best for other women, but for society more generally.

Noting the differences between us, one of the tools which we have deployed as authors to bring in these differences, situating them as a strength rather than as in opposition to one another, has been to write these volumes collaboratively. While many co-authors write chapters or sections each, taking independent control over their allocated parts, we have chosen to write these books together. From the outset we agreed we should each be able to edit as we wish, the aim being to create one complete text within which no one person can identify what they wrote. This process has not always been easy. Within this text lie numerous tensions and disagreements between us. However, drawing on feminist methods, we have sought to work these tensions into the body of the text, highlighting the different positions we all take, having discussed each of these tensions and worked to ensure that they are represented in a way in which all authors feel content.

---

62. Sorayya Shahri, 'Women in Command: A Successful Experience in the National Liberation Army of Iran' in Marguerite Waller and Jennifer Rycenga (eds), *Frontline Feminisms: Women, War, and Resistance* (Routledge 2001) 184

63. Gila Svirsky, 'The Impact of Women in Black in Israel' in Marguerite Waller and Jennifer Rycenga (eds), *Frontline Feminisms: Women, War, and Resistance* (Routledge 2001) 234, 235

This is a method which we have drawn on following the participation of three of us in the Feminist International Judgments Project, under which each judgement was written by a chamber or group of several feminist academics.[64] Collaborative feminist writing as a method to address and embrace difference and as a means to write in plural feminism is thus integral to the text.

Ultimately, we are buoyed by the continuing, enlarging focus on gender and armed conflict that addresses many of the themes of our research. We add to that research through a study of the specific legal regimes that, we argue, gender and conflict might also expand its analysis towards. Prior to commencing our study of the contours of international law on war and peace via a gender analysis, we take stock of the tremendous contribution of gender and feminist scholarship on the women, peace and security agenda inspired by Security Council resolution 1325 and subsequent resolutions.[65]

Security Council resolutions on women, peace and security

The UN Security Council's thematic resolutions on women, peace and security, ten at the time of writing, have provided key footholds and possibilities for feminist engagement with the work of the Security Council. The adoption of the first Security Council resolution on women, peace and security in 2000, and the nine subsequent resolutions, fuels ongoing feminist discussions, debates and activism reflecting

---

64. Loveday Hodson and Troy Lavers (eds), *Feminist Judgments in International Law* (Hart Publishing 2019)

65. Security Council Resolution 1325 (31 October 2000) UN Doc. S/RES/1325; Security Council Resolution 1820 (19 June 2008) UN Doc. S/RES/1820; Security Council Resolution 1888 (30 September 2009) UN Doc. S/RES/1888; Security Council Resolution 1889 (5 October 2009) UN Doc. S/RES/1889; Security Council Resolution 1960 (16 December 2010) UN Doc. S/RES/1960; Security Council Resolution 2106 (24 June 2013) UN Doc. S/RES/2106; Security Council Resolution 2122 (18 October 2013) UN Doc. S/RES/2122; Security Council Resolution 2242 (13 October 2015) UN Doc. S/RES/2242; Security Council Resolution 2467 (23 April 2019) UN Doc. S/RES/2467; Security Council Resolution 2493 (29 October 2019) UN Doc. S/RES/2493

many of the tensions within the literature on gender and war.[66] In the two decades after the adoption of resolution 1325, feminist scholars and activists have taken stock of the merits and the limitations of the women, peace and security agenda, as well as of the risks posed by the institutional capture of feminist debates.[67]

After the conflicts of the 1990s, as well as subsequent reports of widespread sexual violence in the Democratic Republic of the Congo (DRC), there has been a skyrocketing of scholarly, civil society and journalistic interest in women, peace and security.[68] In response to this emphasis of literature on the women, peace and security agenda and,

66. Laura Shepherd, *Gender, Violence and Security: Discourse as Practice* (Zed Books 2008) chs 5 and 6; Dianne Otto, 'The Security Council's Alliance of Gender Legitimacy: The Symbolic Capital of Resolution 1325' in Hilary Charlesworth and Jean-Marc Coicaud (eds), *Fault Lines of International Legitimacy* (Cambridge University Press 2010); Amy Barrow, 'UN Security Council Resolutions 1325 and 1820: Constructing Gender in Armed Conflict and International Humanitarian Law' (2010) 92 (877) International Review of the Red Cross 221; Felicity Ruby, 'Security Council Resolution 1325: A Tool for Conflict Prevention?' in Gina Heathcote and Dianne Otto (eds), *Rethinking Peacekeeping, Gender Equality and Collective Security* (Palgrave Macmillan 2014)

67. Dianne Otto, 'Power and Danger: Feminist Engagement with International Law through the UN Security Council' (2010) 32 Australian Feminist Law Journal 97; Gina Heathcote, 'Feminist Politics and the Use of Force: Theorising Feminist Action and Security Council Resolution 1325' (2011) 7 Socio-Legal Review 23

68. For scholarly accounts, see Sara E Davies and Jacqui True, 'Reframing Conflict-Related Sexual and Gender-Based Violence: Bringing Gender Analysis Back In' (2015) 46 (6) Security Dialogue 495; Nicola Henry, 'Theorizing Wartime Rape: Deconstructing Gender, Sexuality, and Violence' (2016) 30 (1) Gender and Society 44; Elisabeth Jean Wood, 'Conflict-related Sexual Violence and the Policy Implications of Recent Research' (2014) 96 (894) International Review of the Red Cross 457. For an activist/NGO approach, see Oxfam International, *Now, the World Is without Me. An Investigation of Sexual Violence in Eastern Democratic Republic of Congo* 15 April 2010, Policy Paper available online at: https://www. oxfam.org/en/research/now-world-without-me (accessed December 2019). For journalistic approaches, see Iain Guest, 'Rape in Congo Is Not a Myth – If Anything, It Is Under-reported' 21 November 2012, *The Guardian* https:// www.theguardian.com/commentisfree/2012/nov/21/rape-congo-not-myth-under-reported (accessed December 2019); Will Storr, 'The Rape of Men: The Darkest Secret of War' 17 July 2011 *The Observer* https://www.theguardian.com/society/2011/jul/17/the-rape-of-men (accessed December 2019)

in particular, on sexual violence, we purposely take a broader approach studying the intersection of gender, war and law beyond the women, peace and security and conflict-related sexual violence agendas. In this section we provide an account of the contours and focus of the various women, peace and security resolutions, commencing with resolution 1325, followed by a review of the five resolutions addressing conflict-related sexual violence, and concluding with an assessment of the four broader resolutions. While we do come back to these tools in the forthcoming chapters, they are not the primary focus of our study. We argue that the centring of the Security Council resolutions on women, peace and security within gender and conflict research has left wider, additionally important legal regimes governing war and peace under-analysed in gender research.

Security Council resolution 1325

UN Security Council resolution 1325 was unanimously adopted on 31 October 2000. Resolution 1325 is a thematic resolution, a resolution focusing on a broad conflict-related 'theme' as opposed to addressing a situation occurring in a specific country. Its adoption marked the first time the Security Council devoted an entire session to debating women's experiences in conflict and post-conflict situations.[69] While it is generally understood that Security Council resolutions adopted under Chapter VI of the UN Charter are not legally binding, this approach has been questioned by scholars taking a view based on the ICJ's *Namibia* Advisory Opinion.[70] Adopting either view, however, it is difficult to maintain that 1325 is *per se* a formally legally binding instrument.[71]

69. Carol Cohn, Helen Kinsella and Sheri Gibbings, 'Women, Peace and Security Resolution 1325' (2004) 6 International Feminist Journal of Politics 130

70. *Legal Consequences for States of the Continued Presence of South Africa in Namibia (South West Africa), notwithstanding Security Council Resolution 276 (1970)* (Advisory Opinion) [1971] ICJ Rep 16; Rosalyn Higgins, 'The Advisory Opinion on Namibia: Which UN Resolutions Are Binding under Article 25 of the Charter?' (1972) 21 (2) International and Comparative Law Quarterly 270

71. For a contrasting view see Kwadwo Appiagyei-Atua, 'United Nations Security Council Resolution 1325 on Women, Peace, and Security – Is It Binding?' (2011) 18 (3) Human Rights Brief 2 https://digitalcommons.wcl. american.edu/hrbrief/vol18/iss3/1 (accessed December 2019)

Nevertheless, as O'Rourke shows, feminist activists have proved resourceful in adopting strategies to make the most of resolution 1325 in spite of obstacles caused by its legal profile.[72] Since its adoption, and despite its status as 'soft' (non-binding) law, Coomaraswamy argues that 'it is hard to think of one resolution that is better known for its name, number, and content'.[73] Otto likewise notes that resolution 1325 proved to be an equally authoritative 'leverage for many grassroots women's groups to claim a role in peace negotiations and postconflict decision making'.[74] Although resolution 1325 has proven a useful tool for feminist activism, it is worth noting that, while 1325 has become a talisman in the realm of gender and conflict research and policy, this remains confined to this specialized realm. There are multiple other resolutions within the mainstream of international legal studies that have received much more attention and traction, which speaks to the marginalization of feminism and gender within the discipline. These resolutions include some of those authorizing the use of force, for example, resolution 1973 which authorized the use of force in Libya.[75] As such, not only has gender and conflict research centred the resolutions on women, peace and security leaving wider legal regimes under-analysed, this focus has tended to obscure the relative invisibility of women, peace and security within mainstream international legal accounts.

Furthermore, while feminist and women's NGO activism were instrumental in the passing of this first resolution, we are mindful of the challenges connected with entrusting the Security Council 'an undemocratic group, only partially representative of the international community' with the women, peace and security agenda.[76] Motivated by the will to spur implementation of the Women in Armed Conflict chapter of the 1995 Beijing Platform for Action, NGOs involved in the 1998 Commission on the Status of Women came up with the idea to

72. Catherine O'Rourke, 'Feminist Strategy in International Law: Understanding Its Legal, Normative and Political Dimensions' (2017) 28 (4) European Journal of International Law 1019, 1033–5

73. Radhika Coomaraswamy, *Preventing Conflict Transforming Justice Securing the Peace: A Global Study on the Implementation of United Nations Security Council Resolution 1325* (UN Women 2015) 28 https://reliefweb.int/sites/reliefweb.int/files/resources/UNW-GLOBAL-STUDY-1325-2015.pdf (accessed December 2019)

74. Otto, above note 66, 240

75. Security Council Resolution 1973 (17 March 2011) UN Doc. S/RES/1973

76. See Heathcote, above note 67, 26

advocate for a UN Security Council resolution to take up this issue.[77] These efforts were moved in the context of the Security Council's attempt to regain legitimacy through thematic resolutions in the aftermath of its contested post-Cold War expanding mandate.[78] Importantly, an NGO Working Group (facilitated by the Women's International League for Peace and Freedom – WILPF) was involved in drafting and setting the ground for the passing of this resolution; but in doing this, they had to come to terms with the constraints linked to inter-state negotiations. In order to present a common position among the Working Group's participants, and to make the proposal more acceptable to states, WILPF had to preventatively accept not to put forward its historical forte of disarmament and anti-militarism.[79] Then, given that states retain the last word on the content of UN resolutions, the drafting group of NGOs had to accept changes made by states to their initial proposal.[80] It appears that the opportunity of kickstarting the Security Council women, peace and security framework came at the cost of having to entrust its later development to the discretion and whims of the Security Council's political interests. This point was drawn out in 2019 when the US Trump administration challenged the inclusion of sexual and reproductive health in the women, peace and security framework.

Resolution 1325 urges states to 'ensure increased representation of women at all decision-making levels … for the prevention, management, and resolution of conflict',[81] calling also for a gender perspective to be further integrated when thinking through peace agreements and post-conflict reconstruction.[82] Resolution 1325 has the historical merit of rebalancing the Security Council's approach to women in conflict by emphasizing their active roles in peacemaking. However, this has not been enough to challenge the essentialist approach that, as a result, grants women a seat at the table because of their innate peacefulness.[83] This approach is not only oblivious to the fact that women assume diverse roles during conflict, including as combatants and perpetrators of violence, it also reinforces the idea that

---

77. Cohn et al., above note 69, 131
78. Otto, above note 66, 253
79. Otto, ibid., 255
80. See Ruby, above note 66, 173–84; Otto, above note 66, 261, 262
81. S/RES/1325 paragraph 1
82. S/RES/1325 paragraphs 8, 8(a)
83. Otto, above note 66, 256, 274

men are inevitably and naturally prone to conflict and violence, which in turn can be used to excuse violence as normal.[84] In addition, as Cohn notes, '[p]rotecting women *in* war, and insisting that they have an equal right to participate in the processes and negotiations that *end* particular wars, both leave *war* itself in place'.[85] The war and militarist model of solving disputes remains unchallenged by formal equality strategies that uncritically aim at increasing the number of women within pre-existing structures. Furthermore, the liberal feminist approach visible in resolution 1325 of adding women to traditionally masculine structures fails to understand women's diversity and ends up privileging formal equality over substantive gains. This approach assumes that the similarities among women are more important than their differences (for instance, in terms of class and race). By emphasizing sameness this approach leaves uninterrogated the privilege that allows only certain women to access power through liberal feminist approaches.[86] Despite these critiques, resolution 1325 has had significant purchase in the transformation of feminist scholarship, policy and activism: influencing the development of a vast discourse that engages different actors and different levels of law as a means to challenge the gendered contours of conflict. Although the most well-known of the Security Council resolutions on women, peace and security it is, in fact, the first of ten resolutions that the Council adopted in the period from 2000 to 2019.

Security Council resolutions on conflict-related sexual violence

Security Council resolutions 1820 (2008), 1888 (2009), 1960 (2010), 2106 (2013) and 2467 (2019) are characterized by a common focus on conflict-related sexual violence. Four of these resolutions were adopted under either US or UK presidency of the Security Council, while the 2019 resolution was adopted under the presidency of Germany and

---

84. Ibid.

85. Carol Cohn, 'Mainstreaming Gender in UN Security Policy: A Path to Political Transformation?' in Shirin M Rai and Georgina Waylen (eds), *Global Governance: Feminist Perspectives* (Palgrave Macmillan 2008) 198 (emphasis in the original)

86. Gina Heathcote, 'Security Council Resolution 2242 on Women, Peace and Security: Progressive Gains or Dangerous Development?' (2018) 32 (4) Global Society 377, 378

attracted significant opposition from the US, China and Russia.[87] Feminist critique has observed how the focus on sexual violence works to restrict the wider approach that was present in resolution 1325 to a narrow emphasis on sexual violence, which risks overshadowing other kinds of gender-related harms connected to conflict, as well as women's initiatives for peace.[88]

Resolution 1820, the first of this set of resolutions, notes that 'women and girls are particularly targeted by the use of sexual violence, including as a tactic of war'.[89] Significantly, this resolution links conflict-related sexual violence with peace and security. First, the Security Council 'expresses its readiness … to … adopt appropriate steps to address widespread or systematic sexual violence' since it, under specific circumstances, 'may impede the restoration of international peace and security'.[90] Second, it states that 'steps to prevent and respond to such acts' can instead 'significantly contribute to the maintenance of international peace and security'.[91] This can be seen as related to the tendency to expand the category of threats to the peace. Furthermore, the language of *maintaining* and *restoring* international peace and security directly echoes the wording of Article 39 and Article 42 of Chapter VII of the UN Charter. Therefore, through this language, resolution 1820 seems to be setting the ground for the possibility of deploying force to 'save women'.[92] Missing in this account is a gender analysis of how force is legally justified and/or authorized.

Resolution 1888 mainly echoes 1820 starting from restating the connection between sexual violence and peace and security.[93] This resolution provided the basis for the establishment of specific figures including the UN Special Representative of the Secretary General on sexual violence in conflict.[94] While resolution 1960 presents

---

87. What's in Blue, 'In Hindsight: Negotiations on Resolution 2467 on Sexual Violence in Conflict' 2 May 2019, *What's in Blue* https://www.whatsinblue.org/2019/05/in-hindsight-negotiations-on-resolution-2467-on-sexual-violence-in-conflict.php (accessed December 2019)

88. Gina Heathcote, above note 86, 380

89. S/RES/1820 preamble

90. S/RES/1820 paragraph 1

91. S/RES/1820 paragraph 1

92. Gina Heathcote, *The Law on the Use of Force: A Feminist Analysis* (Routledge 2012) 50, 51

93. S/RES/1888 paragraph 1

94. S/RES/1888 paragraphs 4, 8

many aspects of 1325, 1820 and 1888, paragraph 3 of resolution 1960 establishes a 'naming and shaming mechanism' as a way to operationalize implementation of the previous resolutions.[95] Feminist analysis has highlighted the limits of this provision due to its narrowness in adopting naming and shaming as a response to sexual violence rather than more sophisticated strategies tackling 'the nexus between harmful understandings of gender difference that contribute to the prevalence of, and impunity for, sexual violence globally in both conflict and non-conflict communities'.[96] This kind of response originates in the Security Council's responsiveness to US radical feminist approaches and a focus on sexual harm which obscures deeper intersectional understandings of conflict-related harm. In doing so, the Security Council, rather than putting at the centre of its analysis the experiences and needs of women in conflict and post-conflict situations, reflects the presumptions and ideas that many global north (gender) analysts retain and, as a result, it is set to fail to bring about significant change.[97]

Different from the previous resolutions, Security Council resolution 2106 was preceded by the April 2013 G8 *Declaration on Preventing Sexual Violence in Conflict*, an initiative led by the UK.[98] The G8 Declaration touches upon different aspects of conflict-related sexual violence, such as the rehabilitation of victims and the recognition of the need for better protection for human rights defenders, but largely focuses on the lack of accountability for sex-related crimes during armed conflict. This initiative paved the way for resolution 2106 which was adopted under the UK's presidency of the Security Council. Resolution 2106 reiterates the call for the implementation of previous resolutions. The participation aspect is not completely absent from this resolution, but it centres participation in the field of sexual violence prevention.[99]

95. S/RES/1960 paragraph 3; Gina Heathcote, 'Naming and Shaming: Human Rights Accountability in Security Council Resolution 1960 (2010) on Women, Peace and Security' (2012) 4 (1) Journal of Human Rights Practice 82–105

96. Heathcote, above note 95, 86

97. Heathcote, above note 95, 87, 88

98. Declaration on Preventing Sexual Violence in Conflict (11 April 2013) https://www.gov.uk/government/uploads/system/uploads/attachment_data/file/185008/G8_PSVI_Declaration_-_FINAL.pdf (accessed December 2019)

99. For instance, the first paragraph of resolution 2106 retraces the wording of paragraph 1 in resolutions 1820, 1888 and 1960, but here the paragraph's concluding sentence is replaced by the Security Council stressing 'women's participation as essential to any prevention and protection response'. But see also paragraphs 5, 16

This reflects what Heathcote has identified as 'a protective participation model' which can undermine the complexity of women's experiences in armed conflict.[100] As such, the over-emphasis on sexual violence in these resolutions has been criticized for being narrow and reductive. Not only does it reflect just one strand of feminist thought – US radical feminism – but it also focuses on only one of the four pillars initially envisaged in resolution 1325.[101] This has the effect of putting women as victims of sexual violence at the centre-stage of international attention while linking the possibility of the use of force to rescue women from it.[102] Throughout these two volumes our goal is to look beyond this framing to engage law's authorizing and justifying, regulating and prosecuting, armed conflict and post-conflict under international law.

The fifth resolution on conflict-related sexual violence, resolution 2467, demonstrates further the risks of engaging the Security Council, ultimately an unrepresentative and unaccountable political institution with the capacity to make law, to bring forward an agenda on gender and conflict. Germany's initiative as president of the Council was to propose a draft for 2467 that incorporated a wider understanding of victim-survivor needs in post-conflict communities, including addressing sexual and reproductive health in post-conflict communities. However, the conservative US administration, under the Presidency of Donald Trump, refused to support the drawing in of sexual and reproductive health due to a fear of abortion rights being expanded. In the end, agreed language on sexual and reproductive health from resolution 2106 proved to be unacceptable to the US administration and was redacted from the draft as a way to secure US support for the resolution.[103] Furthermore, both China and Russia abstained from voting even in spite of the concessions on the proposed expanded role on sexual violence in conflict to be assigned to the Informal Expert Group on Women, Peace and Security (mentioned below). The final text of the resolution does focus on victims and survivors, including

---

100. Gina Heathcote, 'Participation, Gender and Society' in Gina Heathcote and Dianne Otto (eds), *Rethinking Peacekeeping, Gender Equality and Collective Security* (Palgrave Macmillan 2014) 48–69
101. Heathcote, above note 95, 93, 94; Nicola Lacey, 'Feminist Legal Theory and the Rights of Women' in Karen Knop (ed), *Gender and Human Rights* (Oxford University Press 2004) 23–4
102. Heathcote, above note 67, 20
103. What's in Blue, above note 87

male victims, but has been described as 'overly simplistic and [as failing] to recognize that conflict-related sexual violence is itself an expression of masculinity and dominance'.[104] While not devoid of significance, we argue that these debates have occupied feminist scholars working in the field of gender and conflict at the cost of other, important legal and political engagements.

Security Council resolutions 1889, 2122, 2242 and 2493

In general, resolutions 1889 (2009), 2122 (2013), 2242 (2015) and 2493 (2019) have taken a broader approach to women, peace and security than those discussed in the previous section. In contrast to the group of resolutions focused on conflict-related sexual violence, these resolutions have been adopted under, respectively, Vietnamese, Azeri, Spanish and South African presidencies of the Security Council. Resolution 1889, started building 'a model of substantive participation' for the women, peace and security agenda.[105] Resolution 1889 acknowledges that 'women in situations of armed conflict and post-conflict situations continue to be often considered as victims and not as actors in addressing and resolving situations of armed conflict'[106] and is attentive to the socio-economic dimension in post-conflict and peacebuilding.[107] However, it took until the seventh women, peace and security resolution, resolution 2122, to find evidence of recognition of diversity among women in the text of the resolutions. In a passing, yet significant, mention the resolution '[r]equests the Secretary-General's Special Envoys and Special Representatives to United Nations missions, from early on in their deployment, to regularly consult with women's organizations and women leaders, *including socially and/or economically excluded groups of women*'.[108] While this paragraph is not directed at UN member states and it is therefore circumscribed in its scope, as Heathcote notes 'the language of consulting diverse groups of women ... is of considerable importance and presents an opening for women who feel unrepresented within international

104. 'UN Security Council Adopts Resolution 2467' (2019) *Global Justice Center* http://globaljusticecenter.net/press-center/press-releases/1117-un-security-council-adopts-resolution-2467 (accessed December 2019)

105. Heathcote, above note 86, 380

106. S/RES/1889 preamble

107. S/RES/1889 paragraphs 1, 10, 15

108. S/RES/2122 paragraph 7(a) (emphasis added)

security discourse.[109] Ultimately, however, resolution 2122, like its predecessors, fails to recognize 'women's mobilisation for peace ... as security work.'[110]

The preamble of resolution 2122 does acknowledge the adoption of the Arms Trade Treaty (ATT). Although addressed in a limited manner and only in relation to the ATT (which deals only with issues of the arms trade and not general disarmament), in recognizing the ATT resolution 2122 can be seen as an entry point for future discussion and advocacy on disarmament. Furthermore, through resolution 2122 the Security Council requested the Secretary General to commission the Global Study on the implementation of resolution 1325 ahead of the fifteenth year since the adoption of that resolution, which led to the adoption of resolution 2242 with increased input of feminist and women's NGOs.[111]

Resolution 2242 (2015) was adopted in the context of the stocktaking exercise that marked the fifteenth anniversary of the adoption of resolution 1325. For the first time, the Security Council agreed on a substantive decision: in paragraph 5(b) the Council '[d]ecides to integrate women, peace and security concerns across all country-specific situations on the Security Council's agenda.'[112] While this language is qualified by the notion of 'taking into account the specific context of each country', this formulation is fairly unequivocal in its intent and has the characteristics to bind the Council itself for future action. In the next chapter we undertake an evaluation of this decision with respect to Syria and show that the Security Council in that respect failed to adhere to its own commitments. Following resolution 2242 the Informal Expert Group on Women, Peace and Security was instituted in 2016. The group was created 'to facilitate a more systematic approach to Women, Peace and Security within [the] work [of the Council] and enable greater oversight and coordination of implementation efforts.'[113] More research is needed at this stage to establish whether this group has achieved substantive results in changing the approach to women, peace and security.

The existence of women who participate in combat or commit crimes has received limited representation within the Security Council's women, peace and security framework where the image of women

109. Heathcote, above note 86, 381
110. Heathcote, ibid., 382
111. S/RES/2122 paragraph 16
112. S/RES/2242 paragraph 5(b)
113. S/RES/2242 paragraph 5(a)

as victims has comparatively retained primacy. While resolution 2242 mentions the need to conduct research on what leads to the radicalization of women – therefore admitting that women can be involved in extremism and terrorism – it also suggests that women's participation in extremism is not entirely voluntary, but rather it is the result of 'drivers' specific to women.[114] This approach reiterates the assumption that – for women – to participate in extremism, terrorism or indeed violence, there must be a reason that is in some way connected to their gender. However, women's reasons for participating in violent extremism are often similar to men's. Sjoberg and Gentry highlight how the field of terrorism studies has tended to see the women who participate in violence as a result of extremist views as a product of women's maternal and nurturing characteristics.[115] This means that women's 'innate' ability to nurture is seen as so powerful it even extends to participating in terrorism, if only for the need to be needed. Not only does this understanding limit women's ability to be agents in their own lives, but it reaffirms stereotypical characteristics as inevitable. Therefore, while resolution 2242 presents some advances in terms of openings to recognition of differences among women and attention to 'gender perspectives',[116] the juxtaposing of the anti-terrorism and women, peace and security agenda presents the risk of the latter 'being co-opted into the civilising tropes that surround the work of countering terrorism and violent extremism'.[117] As explained by Ní Aoláin, this 'does not mean that women will be included in defining what constitutes terrorism', women are more likely to be added to pre-existing counter-terrorism frameworks (notoriously shaped in a non-feminist way) that would be strengthened through improved gender legitimacy, in turn resulting in women, peace and security 'becoming harnessed to the pursuit of broader military and ideological goals'.[118]

114. S/RES/2242 paragraph 12
115. Laura Sjoberg and Caron E Gentry, *Mothers, Monsters, Whores: Women's Violence in Global Politics* (Zed Books 2007) 33
116. Heathcote, above note 86, 385
117. Heathcote, above note 86, 387
118. Fionnuala Ní Aoláin, 'The "War on Terror" and Extremism: Assessing the Relevance of the Women, Peace and Security Agenda' (2016) 92 (2) International Affairs 276, 278

The most recent Security Council resolution, 2493, is a general resolution that is focused on mobilizing a renewed pledge from states and international institutions in implementing the women, peace and security agenda. While making some references to women's participation in peace talks and in mechanisms to monitor peace agreements (including 'context-specific approaches'),[119] resolution 2493 remains a rather unambitious text. One of the bars to more progressive provisions seemed to have been the continuing controversy over the inclusion of language on sexual and reproductive health that had already characterized the adoption of resolution 2467. After the adoption of 2493, the US Ambassador to the UN stated that the US 'cannot accept references to sexual and reproductive health or any references to safe termination of pregnancy or language that would promote abortion or suggest a right to abortion'.[120]

Positive and negative impacts of the women, peace and security agenda

The women, peace and security agenda presents evidence of a problem that, in another UN context, has been identified as 'ritualism'.[121] Namely, a posture where the Security Council produces resolutions and reports of activities while retaining 'an indifference to or even reluctance' to actually bringing about significant change.[122] This is a problem that O'Rourke and Swaine note, with respect to new women, peace and security resolutions often featuring provisions that are mainly directed at the UN system or merely reiterative of previous women, peace and security language, allowing states to claim they are 'doing something'

119. S/RES/2493 paragraphs 3, 9(a)

120. Record of the 8649th meeting of the UN Security Council (29 October 2019) UN Doc. S/PV.8649, remarks of US Ambassador Kelly Craft; Michelle Nichols, 'U.S. Pitted against Britain, France, South Africa, Others at UN over Abortion' *Reuters* 29 October 2019 https://www.reuters.com/article/us-women-rights-usa-un/us-pitted-against-britain-france-south-africa-others-at-un-over-abortion-idUSKBN1X829K (accessed December 2019)

121. Hilary Charlesworth and Emma Larking, 'Introduction: The Regulatory Power of the Universal Periodic Review' in Hilary Charlesworth and Emma Larking (eds), *Human Rights and the Universal Periodic Review: Rituals and Ritualism* (Cambridge University Press 2015) 10, 21

122. Ibid., 10

while doing very little.[123] This tendency seems to be the natural evolution of what Otto, at the time of the inception of the women, peace and security agenda, had identified as the Security Council's attempt to regain legitimacy through gender after its shortcomings in facing the humanitarian crises of the 1990s.[124] Evidence of gender ritualism can also be found in the fact that women, peace and security language remains confined to thematic resolutions (considered a 'softer' area of work), with the Council seemingly being reluctant to seriously consider women, peace and security concerns in country-specific resolutions, or as Ní Aoláin has observed, in new wars contexts.[125]

At the same time, as noted above, there is a tension for feminists with working with/in the Security Council. Thus, while the lack of reference to women, peace and security in binding Security Council measures can be seen as a problem of enforceability on the one hand, on the other, the actual *use* of women, peace and security as a binding mechanism would be problematic, potentially exacerbating the core issues around representation and intersectionality, the hypervisibility of sexual violence and masking the other silences in the agenda.[126] Rather than advancing a policy point about the content of country-situation resolutions, we are concerned with highlighting the absence of women, peace and security from certain areas of the Council's work because it is symptomatic of the permanence of a gendered bias in the functioning of the institution. Highlighting the Security Council's failure to follow through with its own decision on women, peace and security – while at the same time resisting understandings of use of force as a solution to complex socio-economic-politico-cultural problems – further helps us to question, once again, the appropriateness of the Security Council as a site for progressive work on gender and conflict.

So far feminist engagement through the women, peace and security agenda has not been successful in delivering a fundamental change in the logics and power structures of the Security Council. On the contrary,

123. Catherine O'Rourke and Aisling Swaine, 'CEDAW and the Security Council: Enhancing Women's Rights in Conflict' (2018) 67 International and Comparative Law Quarterly 167, 182

124. Otto, above note 66, 240

125. Ní Aoláin, above note 118, 277; Mary Kaldor, *New and Old Wars: Organized Violence in a Global Era* (Polity Press 1999)

126. Dianne Otto, 'Women, Peace and Security: A Critical Analysis of the Security Council's Vision' in Fionnuala Ní Aoláin et al. (eds), *The Oxford Handbook of Gender and Conflict* (Oxford University Press 2018) 105–18

Otto shows how long-standing feminist agendas on disarmament and militarism had to be dropped while the Council gained a share of 'gender legitimacy'.[127] While resolution 2122, as noted above, does mention disarmament, thus nodding to the feminist activism behind much of the women, peace and security agenda, it does so only in reference to the ATT which is much less about general disarmament and is, rather, about the arms trade and ensuring that arms do not get into the hands of the 'wrong people'.[128] Stavrianakis observed how in the ATT 'language and regulatory bureaucratic practices of risk assessment are embedded in Western, liberal regimes'.[129] The ATT also risks legitimating particular types of arms trade through law by giving the impression that arms trade can be 'ethical' as opposed to seeking to removing arms trade all together. This argument can be linked to the wider critique of how international humanitarian law, in its attempt to 'humanize' war, has also fostered the idea of the possibility of 'humane' wars. We explore this argument in Chapter 4. It is therefore interesting that the moment when the women, peace and security resolutions do finally mention disarmament – despite disarmament having been core in the feminist lobbying on women, peace and security well before 1325 – refers to the ATT as opposed to, for example, the question of the ethics of making, selling and using arms at all.

The problems with the women, peace and security agenda have led scholars such as Kapur to state that the agenda is an expression of

---

127. Dianne Otto, 'Contesting Feminism's Institutional Doubles: Troubling the Security Council's Woman, Peace and Security Agenda' in Halley et al. (eds), *Governance Feminism: Notes from the Field* (University of Minnesota Press 2019) 200–29. To note, while the word 'disarmament' is mentioned in paragraph 13 of resolution 1325, this refers to programmes of disarmament, demobilization and reintegration of former combatants

128. Otto, above note 126

129. Anna Stavrianakis, 'Legitimising Liberal Militarism: Politics, Law and War in the Arms Trade Treaty' (2016) 37 (5) Third World Quarterly 845; Cooper states: 'Arms control as governmentality denotes a context where mechanisms of proscription *and* permission operate as technologies of social control designed to manage which populations can legitimately use what kinds of weapons.' Neil Cooper, 'Race, Sovereignty, and Free Trade: Arms Trade Regulation and Humanitarian Arms Control in the Age of Empire' (2018) 3 (4) Journal of Global Security Studies 445 (emphasis in the original)

what Halley terms 'governance feminism'.[130] The women, peace and security resolutions – with their emphasis on women as victims or peaceful agents who require representation – present a largely radical or liberal feminist version of feminism. It is these versions of feminism which the Security Council and other international legal standard-setting institutions have embraced the most, often even turning these already limited viewpoints on feminism into 'shadowy versions' of themselves.[131] In this understanding, women's active participation in armed conflict or in igniting revolt and armed action is dismissed as minor and as a deviation from the 'normal' role of women. Through such narratives of inclusion and exclusion, gendered and essentializing stereotypes about both men and women are upheld. Importantly, these understandings leave uninterrogated the association of war and violence with masculinity and the idea of a violent response as effective in times of crisis. The wider causes of insecurity are also left untouched by these discussions.

Kapur states that there is a need to understand women's experiences on the peripheries as a method to challenge the normative assumptions that inform gender and sexuality discourses within law.[132] Kapur's discussion of the 'authentic victim subject' highlights the tendency for international women's rights movements to focus on a particular ideal of the 'Third World woman', which excludes the existence of localized or personal everyday harms and rather focuses solely on women's experience of sexual violence in armed conflict.[133] The importance of identifying the hypervisibility of women as victims of sexual violence in armed conflict reaffirms the need to see women in armed conflict as having crucial knowledge on peacebuilding that disrupts both victimhood and the perception that women's insecurity post-conflict is merely a result of harmful cultural practices. Rather, there needs to be greater interrogation of social, political and economic structures that create sites of precarity before, during and after conflict.

While remaining critical of the women, peace and security agenda, we are also wary of dismissing the agenda as merely an expression of

---

130. Ratna Kapur, *Gender, Alterity and Human Rights: Freedom in a Fishbowl* (Edward Elgar 2018) 104

131. Otto, above note 127, 203, referring to Nancy Fraser, 'Feminism, Capitalism and the Cunning of History' (2009) 56 New Left Review 97

132. Kapur, above note 12, 131

133. Kapur, ibid., 115

governance feminism, as to do so risks erasing the framework's origins in women's peace activism. As mentioned above, one of the often-hailed outcomes of the resolutions has been their use as an instrument in local projects for inclusion of women in peace agreements and post-conflict institutions.[134] This has had, however, both positive and negative impacts. For example, while funding has been funnelled through the women, peace and security agenda supporting feminist grassroots groups, these groups have also noted that, since resolution 2242 and the focus on counter-terrorism, much of the funding for grassroots feminist groups working on conflict-related issues is now also tethered to combatting terrorism, which narrows down the focus of such groups and forces them to work on issues which they do not necessarily believe are of priority.[135] An example of the mixed impact of the agenda can be seen when looking at the aftermath of the internal armed conflict in Nepal (1996–2006). Some Nepali women's organizations used resolution 1325 to lobby the UN to uphold the resolution's standards during its work in Nepal and to support the campaign for inclusion of diverse women in the peace process.[136] After the conflict ended however, Sthapit and Doneys have observed the lack of substantive change for rural women in Nepal. In their field research with former female combatants of the People's Liberation Army (PLA), Sthapit and Doneys have found how for these women 'the ground reality remains unchanged'.[137] In the words of one of the combatants: 'These [resolutions] are for the high-ranking fighters and leaders and richer people, for us it makes no difference. We have not felt it trickling down to us, yet.'[138] This 2012 statement clearly highlights how the

134. Otto, above note 67, 105

135. Sophie Giscard d'Estaing, 'Engaging Women in Countering Violent Extremism: Avoiding Instrumentalisation and Furthering Agency' (2017) 25 (1) Gender and Development, 103, 115

136. Open letter from Women Peace Alliance, PEWA to Mr. Ian Martin, Personal Envoy of the UN Secretary General to Nepal for inclusive, proportionate representation and women sensitive peace process, 12 December 2006 https://www.nepalresearch.com/crisis_solution/papers/pewa_061212.pdf (accessed December 2019)

137. Lorina Sthapit and Philippe Doneys, 'Female Maoist Combatants during and after the People's War' in Åshild Kolås (ed), *Women, Peace and Security in Nepal: From Civil War to Post-Conflict Reconstruction* (Special Nepal Edition, Routledge 2018) 43

138. Ibid.

resolutions risk remaining superficial instruments if not accompanied by broader intersectional change, for instance, in the reduction of economic inequality and of the divide between rural and urban Nepal. Incidentally, this is a further clue that encourages us to look beyond law to achieve transformative change. The remarks on 1325 expressed by former female PLA combatants are not surprising if seen in the light of long-standing criticism advanced by Tamang of how foreign development donors were key in creating the figure of 'an essentialized "Nepali woman"' as a 'single over-arching category' and 'homogenized and agency-less' individual.[139] Contextualized in this way, the women, peace and security agenda appears as yet another essentializing western instrument that serves limited inclusion purposes for women from conflict-affected countries. Apart from the timid and belated reference to women's diversity in resolution 2122, the women, peace and security resolutions have not done much to avoid this criticism.

Despite the vast amounts of space and resources dedicated to women, peace and security, 'the continued silence about homophobic and transphobic violence targeting lesbian, gay, bisexual, transgender and queer (LGBTQ) individuals in conflict-related environments is alarming'.[140] Focusing on sexual and gender-based violence, Hagen critiques the 'heteronormative assumptions in the framing of the [women, peace and security] agenda',[141] noting how 'gender' is often equated to 'women,' silencing the experiences of queer survivors of sexual and gender-based violence.[142] This heteronormative focus on women as the paradigm victims and men as the paradigm perpetrators has also been critiqued by Paige when analysing Security Council debates generally (i.e. not just the women, peace and security agenda) highlighting how the lack of focus on queer subjects is prevalent

139. Seira Tamang, 'The Politics of Conflict and Difference or the Difference of Conflict in Politics: The Women's Movement in Nepal' (2009) 91 Feminist Review 61, 65, 66

140. Jamie J Hagen, 'Queering Women, Peace and Security' (2016) 92 (2) International Affairs 313

141. Ibid.

142. Ibid., 318

throughout collective security frameworks.[143] Furthermore, as Hamzić shows, where LGBT[144] subjects are seen within collective security, this is often done through a standard of civilization lens, with the killing of LGBT people by ISIS, for example, being used by the Security Council to highlight the barbarianism of the Islamic 'other'.[145]

The narrow, heteronormative framing of gender within collective security and women, peace and security, however, is problematic not only in terms of which subjects it excludes but also in terms of where gendered voices are visibilized. While the women, peace and security framework remit centres issues such as sexual violence and women's participation, discussions on military technologies, on authorizations for the use of force or the mandate for Security Council authorized missions occur in the Security Council and other international institutions without examination of the gendered contours of these debates. While this lack of focus may be justified, at one level, through the idea that the women, peace and security framework focuses on women's lives, such an argument ignores the gendered impact of military technologies, from the role of gender identification in targeting decisions to the biases present in the use and design of all technologies.[146] At the same time, the spaces in which these technologies are discussed tend to then ignore gender as a useful analytical framework altogether, gender once again being seen as about women as victims or their numeric representation. This is despite the fact that gender provides an extremely useful analytical tool through which to think through

143. Tamsin Phillipa Paige, 'The Maintenance of International Peace and Security Heteronormativity' in Dianne Otto (ed), *Queering International Law: Possibilities, Alliances, Complicities, Risks* (Routledge 2018)

144. The use of LGBT here reflects the Security Council's own framing; see above note 35

145. Vanja Hamzić, 'International Law as Violence: Competing Absences of the Other' in Dianne Otto (ed), *Queering International Law: Possibilities, Alliances, Complicities, Risks* (Routledge 2018)

146. Lauren Wilcox, 'Embodying Algorithmic War: Gender, Race, and the Posthuman in Drone Warfare' (2017) 48 (1) Security Dialogue 11; Lorna McGregor, Daragh Murray and Vivian Ng, 'International Human Rights Law as a Framework for Algorithmic Accountability' (2019) 68 (2) International and Comparative Law Quarterly 309

these issues.[147] The framing of collective security thus binds the women, peace and security agenda to a limited account of gendered approaches to conflict, not only in terms of the conflict-affected subjects it excludes, but also in terms of topics, perpetuating the idea that gender is about sexual violence and participation alone. Women, peace and security, for example, could look extremely different if it were to include feminist perspectives on military technologies, from experiences of living under drones,[148] to the consideration of the ways in which data collection is used post-conflict to invisibilize men of colour as refugees when it comes to resource distribution and aid,[149] to noting the ways in which military technologies are used to uphold and perpetuate gendered, racialized, ableist and humanist norms.[150]

After examining the Security Council women, peace and security framework, it appears that while it has opened opportunities, it also presents serious limitations and challenges. Many of these are connected to the Security Council shaping discourse and policy on women and gender in conflict and post-conflict situations. Importantly, we believe feminist analysts and activist attention on legal and institutional instruments on gender and conflict should not be limited to this forum. This book, noting that much work on gender and conflict since 1325 has been framed in terms of women, peace and security, seeks to move beyond the agenda, taking feminist methodologies as the central point through which to think about gender and conflict as opposed to the women, peace and security agenda and thereby situating feminists as the central voice on gender and conflict as opposed to the Security Council. While we are aware that in outlining the women, peace and security agenda in this introduction we have, already, in some ways centred the agenda in this book, we have done this more to outline the

147. Emily Jones, Sara Kendall and Yoriko Otomo, 'Gender, War and Technology: Peace and Armed Conflict in the 21st Century' (2018) 44 (1) Australian Feminist Law Journal 1

148. Helene Kazan, 'The Architecture of Slow, Structural, and Spectacular Violence and the Poetic Testimony of War' (2018) 44 (1) Australian Feminist Law Journal 119

149. Kristin Sandvik, 'Technology, Dead Male Bodies, and Feminist Recognition: Gendering ICT Harm Theory' (2018) 44 (1) Australian Feminist Law Journal 49

150. Gina Heathcote, 'War's Perpetuity: Disabled Bodies of War and the Exoskeleton of Equality' (2018) 44 (1) Australian Feminist Law Journal 71

inclusions and exclusions from the start to allow us, as authors, to move beyond the agenda throughout the rest of the text.

Introduction to Volume One

This book analyses areas of international law focused on armed conflict including the *jus ad bellum*, the collective security structure and the international humanitarian law of armed conflict, alongside an account of counter-terrorism and countering violent extremism in peacetime states and the everyday, lived realities of insecurity within those states. The final chapter examines international criminal law to think about the role of law and the claim of shifting from armed conflict towards peace through prosecutions. Throughout the text we continue to analyse and draw in the women, peace and security framework. Nevertheless, our primary focus is the international laws on armed conflict, its regulation, authorization and consequences, and the laws governing the transition to peace. Throughout we examine the impact of the laws on armed conflict on states experiencing conflict, peacetime and post-conflict states to disrupt the assumption of war and peace as geographically and temporally distinct experiences.

Chapter 1 uses gender theories to examine the potential and the limitations of collective security structures. The chapter commences with an introduction to the collective security system. That is, the role of the UN Security Council and its powers under Chapter VI and Chapter VII of the UN Charter. To analyse the placing of militarized enforcement measures at the apex of international law, the chapter engages an account of law and violence to illuminate law's persistent violence as well as the conundrum of using military force to halt military force. The chapter reviews the Security Council's resolutions in response to the conflict in Syria since 2011 to demonstrate the limited impact of the women, peace and security agenda and the troubled positioning of feminist approaches within the work of the Security Council. As such, we interrogate the consequences of supporting the work of the Security Council via the women, peace and security framework. The use of and the failure to authorize military intervention raise important, unanswered questions for feminist scholars. The chapter concludes that feminist activism needs to provide wider, and deeper, analysis of the range of collective security endeavours that are bolstered by the institutional turn to the Security Council via the women, peace and security agenda.

Chapter 2 introduces the mechanisms that states use to justify the use of military force, in particular, international law on self-defence and humanitarian intervention, as well as state arguments for the protection of nationals abroad and the use of force with the consent of the host state. The chapter commences with an introduction to these unilateral justifications for military force. The chapter also introduces existing feminist scholarship, largely structural bias feminisms, on unilateral force. The chapter offers an analysis of two forms of unilateral force: self-defence and humanitarian intervention. The chapter argues that the analysis of unilateral force would benefit from further structural bias feminist analyses while also calling for the development of intersectional feminist methods. This approach incorporates the space to analyse gendered livelihoods as well as macro dimensions of power that inform the structures, institutions and contours of international law. The study of power relations, via an intersectional feminist commitment, challenges macro-level manifestations of power and inequality that stem from the everyday to the international. We argue that unilateral force undertaken by states outside of the collective security system is a manifestation of gendered power relations and ultimately distracts scholars from the consequences and lived insecurities that stem from military force, whether justified, authorized or illegal.

Chapter 3, on countering terrorism, identifies the increased convergence of women and counter-terrorism agendas in the work of the Security Council and traces the gendered effects into the domestic policy of states, including peacetime states. The chapter draws in queer perspectives on terrorism, feminist work on everyday violence in the war on terror and postcolonial feminist perspectives to analyse the impact of counter-terrorism laws. The chapter analyses the means through which gender, sexuality, race and Islamophobia, among other factors such as class, play out in the biopolitical and necropolitical ordering of life through law in the era of counter-terrorism.[151] The chapter identifies

---

151. Necropolitics is a concept coined by Mbembe to indicate the 'contemporary forms of subjugation of life to the power of death' in Achille Mbembe, 'Necropolitics' (2003) 15 (1) Public Culture 39. Necropolitics has been understood by Allinson as 'the arrogation of ... the sovereign's command of death, but within the apparatuses of surveillance, auditing, and management which characterize "biopower"', Jamie Allinson, 'The Necropolitics of Drones' (2015) 9 International Political Sociology 114

the lack of focus from feminist and gender theorists on the attrition of international law, particularly international humanitarian law and human rights laws in the era of global war against terrorism. Furthermore, we identify lawfare, that is, the use of the law to justify military force, in counter-terrorism agendas as of interest to future feminist accounts.[152] Throughout Chapter 3 we examine the placement of counter-terrorism strategies at the margins of legality, while impacting most directly on racialized, queer and classed subjects.[153] Through the analysis of UK and French counter-terrorism laws we complicate the assumption that peace and conflict are distinct experiences, demonstrating how peacetime states have used counter-terrorism agendas to produce insecurities.

Chapter 4 offers a feminist analysis of the international humanitarian laws of armed conflict. Through providing an analysis of the Geneva Conventions (including the Additional Protocols) and the Hague Conventions, the chapter draws in existing feminist scholarship on the gendered contours, and effects, of the regulation of the methods and means of armed conflict and attempts at humanitarian constraints on military activities. We identify how discourses of victimization and protection develop within the law as though they are inevitable elements of an armed conflict. The chapter offers a more complex version of wartime subjectivities that seeks to disrupt the heteronormativity of the gender binary that is embedded in international humanitarian law. The chapter problematizes the framework of international humanitarian law identifying the acceptance of the inevitability of armed conflict as troubling for feminist approaches, such that existing feminist analysis of the tensions between resistance and compliance within critical feminist projects are drawn on. The chapter concludes by arguing that the gender binary sits not only in the foundations of international humanitarian law of armed conflict but also that a sole focus on this binary risks ignoring new developments on the battlefield, from new wars and asymmetrical conflicts to the development of new forms of military technologies. The chapter concludes with a call for

152. Eyal Weizman, 'Legislative Attack' (2010) 27 (6) Theory, Culture and Society 11; David Kennedy, 'Lawfare and Warfare' in James Crawford and Martti Koskenniemi (eds), *The Cambridge Companion to International Law* (Cambridge University Press 2012) 158
153. Jasbir K Puar, *Terrorist Assemblages: Homonationalism in Queer Times* (Duke University Press 2007)

posthuman feminist understandings that keep abreast of and challenge feminist thinking beyond the gendered narratives of victimization and protection. This is a theme that re-emerges in Volume Two in our study of military technologies and their capacity to traverse the war and peace dichotomy, re-directing a focus and funds from tackling (gendered) harms and re-producing insecurity in new forms.

The analysis of international criminal law provides the focus of Chapter 5. This chapter introduces the history of international criminal law, in the Nuremberg and Tokyo tribunals, the development of the *ad hoc* tribunals, hybrid courts and the International Criminal Court as an entry into our analysis of international criminal law. We argue that even with the gender law reforms that are apparent from the 1990s, these foundations constrain the scope and possibilities of international criminal law. Following the account of international humanitarian law and the production of gendered victims through legal regulation, this chapter identifies the hypervisibility of crimes of sexual violence against women in international criminal law. This is contrasted with the law's response to female perpetrators prosecuted in international criminal institutions. The chapter interrogates the possibilities and limitations of international criminal law: from local structures that usher the transition to peace after war to alternative modes of listening and developing artefacts for the memories of violence, armed conflict and transition. In this chapter we look to modes of law that work to undo the gendered legacies of the current structures and the gendered legacies of armed conflict while arguing for a mode of gender analysis that incorporates Wright's notion of 'becoming human' as a sentiment for holding difference as a means to frame alternative human futures.[154] These themes of memory and listening will be drawn on again in Volume Two in our discussion of transitional justice processes and feminist theories of justice.

Throughout this first volume we examine the laws *on* war and the laws *in* war while simultaneously identifying and noting the gendered insecurities produced within peacetime states through military thinking and strategies. We note how international criminal law functions as a bridge away from armed conflict, a space of recording and remembering

154. Shelley Wright, 'The Horizon of Becoming: Culture, Gender and History after September 11' (2002) 71 Nordic Journal of International Law 215

the excesses of violence and a space where the gendering of this violence can be thought through.

By concluding the text with an account of international criminal law, we open the space for Volume Two which further examines the period understood as post-conflict. Volume Two also introduces further spaces of gender analysis, drawing on transnational feminisms, feminist peace activism, anti-militarism and disarmament projects, as well as critical disability studies/crip theory and posthuman feminisms alongside indigenous theories of law and justice. In analysing the role of international law in post-conflict we return to reflecting upon the intertwined reality of war and peace, highlighting the militarism of peacekeeping, the gendered insecurities prevalent in peacebuilding missions and the dominance of military actors in peace agreements. The second volume then concludes with a study of transitional justice processes, beyond international criminal law, and of military technologies to question what constitutes peace and to demonstrate how specific, western, liberal, knowledge structures frame and inform international law. This opens the discussion to a study of the inclusion of a wider understanding of insecurity that addresses environmental, health and gendered insecurities that traverse conflict and peacetime states in a global fashion. Volume Two thus complements this volume, which argues for a gender analysis of the law of war and peace commencing with difference and drawing in the work of multiple feminist perspectives, including intersectional, structural bias, posthuman and queer scholars. This is an approach that interrogates law at a structural level and undoes the dominant legal narratives of gender equating to women, and women as vulnerable, as defined by her sexuality and requiring protection.

Chapter 1

COLLECTIVE SECURITY

In this chapter we analyse collective security, seeking to adopt a wider outlook than currently exists in most contemporary approaches to gender, law and conflict. We examine how collective security has so far proven impermeable to feminist change, while at the same time incorporating some feminist initiatives through contingent recognition. Examining the UN Security Council's engagement in Syria, we highlight the thin impact that two decades of women, peace and security work has had on the dominant logics of collective security and the authorization of military force. We question the potential for change via approaches based on the idea of 'adding' women to pre-established mechanisms for collective security that, far from being gender-neutral, are of themselves deeply gendered.

To move beyond the women, peace and security agenda and the hypervisibility of conflict-related sexual violence as the primary sites of feminist engagement with international peace and security, we interrogate collective security from the standpoint of feminist approaches that are invested in feminisms as a methodology rather than just shorthand for 'asking the woman question'.[1] The apparent preoccupation with gender asserted by the Security Council through the women, peace and security agenda is quickly abandoned or displaced when matters are perceived as being more urgent or more important on the Security Council's agenda. Through demonstrating how the law and politics around collective security have remained resistant to women, peace and security, and even more so to feminist ideas outside of the women, peace and security agenda, we conclude by arguing for the continued necessity of a multi-layered feminist engagement attending to the gendered dimensions of insecurity. A multi-layered feminist engagement requires analysis of the spectrum of insecurity experienced in the everyday as equally as in international affairs.

1. Katharine T Bartlett, 'Feminist Legal Methods' (1990) 103 (4) Harvard Law Review 829

The chapter commences with an introduction to the collective security system, followed by an account of law and violence and feminist approaches as offering a lens through which to understand the collective security structure. The chapter then turns to the ongoing conflict in Syria to demonstrate the limited impact of the women, peace and security agenda on the decision-making processes of the Security Council and the fraught positioning of feminist approaches. Having implicitly endorsed the work of the Security Council and the legal-political framework underpinning it through feminist engagement with the women, peace and security agenda, we note how it then seems 'natural' to call for action from the Council when a 'crisis' of insecurity emerges. However, when that action takes the shape of military intervention, this raises questions with respect to the consequences of feminist support for the collective security agenda. At the same time, the years of inaction, or partial action, by the Security Council in relation to the violence in Syria also draws feminist criticism due to the gendered impact of failures of the collective security system.

We contrast the limited interest of the Council in its own women, peace and security agenda in Syria with the approach taken by the CEDAW Committee which – mindful of the continuities with pre-conflict gender insecurity – appears as the UN body undertaking a multifaceted approach by adopting a broader politico-socio-economic understanding of gendered harm in Syria. We illustrate how some feminist accounts have shown the positive potential that CEDAW's approach can have when 'travel[ling] to the periphery of rights and empathically engag[ing] with marginal actors'.[2] Nevertheless, we conclude that international law remains a constrained framework for controlling violence and a potentially dangerous ally of feminist activism because, while it offers opportunities, it also remains inextricably linked to violence.

To shift beyond the inherent limits of law – and of military force – in the conclusion we argue in favour of a focus on the manifestations of social injustices in the everyday during conflict and in peacetime, linked to gender, race and class. We highlight the ongoing heated debates on sexual and reproductive health in the Security Council, and we demonstrate that when reproductive and sexual health are drawn into conversation with collective security new questions regarding the

2. Loveday Hodson, 'Women's Rights and the Periphery: CEDAW's Optional Protocol' (2014) 25 (2) European Journal of International Law 578

gendered nature of collective security – and of peace – are brought into focus.[3] As such, the chapter provides a gender analysis of collective security that examines the relationship between law and violence, to argue in favour of feminist methodologies that shift away from the hyperfocus on the Security Council as the key site of feminist energies.

Collective security at the Security Council

The creation of the UN Security Council with its five permanent members has shaped international understandings of conflict, peace and security since 1945. Security Council resolutions have authorized the use of force,[4] enacted sanctions,[5] established international criminal tribunals,[6] organized peacekeeping operations[7] and promoted the recognition of women's experiences in armed conflict and peacetime.[8] We examine the tribunals in Chapter 5 of this volume and a study of peacekeeping operations appears in Volume Two.

Chapter I of the UN Charter enshrines the purposes and principles of the United Nations. Within Chapter I, Article 2 states the principles according to which the member states of the UN agree to behave in the pursuit of the purposes of the organization, the first purpose being the maintenance of international peace and security. Article 2(3) states that all UN member states 'shall settle their international disputes by peaceful

3. Rola Yasmine and Catherine Moughalian 'Systemic Violence against Syrian Refugee Women and the Myth of Effective Intrapersonal Interventions' (2016) 24 (47) Reproductive Health Matters 27
4. For instance, Security Council Resolution 1973 (17 March 2011) UN Doc. S/RES/1973 authorizing military force in Libya
5. For instance, Security Council Resolution 1306 (5 July 2000) UN Doc. S/RES/1306 paragraph 1; Security Council Resolution 1718 (14 October 2006) UN Doc. S/RES/1718 paragraph 8
6. Security Council Resolution 827 (25 May 1993) UN Doc. S/RES/827 establishing the International Criminal Tribunal for the former Yugoslavia; Security Council Resolution 955 (8 November 1994) UN Doc. S/RES/955 establishing the International Criminal Tribunal for Rwanda
7. The first peacekeeping operation was a military observer mission in Palestine, see Security Council Resolution 50 (29 May 1948) UN Doc. S/RES/50
8. Security Council Resolution 1325 (31 October 2000) UN Doc. S/RES/1325 on women, peace and security (see further the introduction to this volume)

means' and Article 2(4) prohibits the use of force in international relations.[9] The prohibition on the use of force is regarded as a principle of customary international law and has also been interpreted as having *jus cogens* status.[10] Article 2(4) was a considerable improvement when compared to the Covenant of the League of Nations which did not prohibit the use of force. Nevertheless, two key exceptions are provided for in the UN Charter to the prohibition on the use of force stated in Article 2(4). These are: the actions authorized by the UN Security Council referred to as 'collective security' (Chapter VII of the UN Charter), and the right to self-defence (Article 51).

Article 2(3) and Chapter VI of the Charter provide the legal bases for the pacific settlement of disputes likely to endanger peace. It is generally understood that resolutions adopted by the Security Council under this section of the Charter are non-legally binding. However, the ICJ *Namibia* Advisory Opinion suggests that the distinguishing factor for ascertaining binding force is when a resolution (or a part of it) constitutes a Security Council 'decision' as per the meaning of Article 25 of the Charter.[11] It is important to note here that the measures mandated for by Article 2(3) and Chapter VI are comparatively less developed in the Security Council's practice than those regarding collective security.

Chapter VII of the UN Charter contains the provisions that compose the system of collective security. Article 39 sets the threshold for collective security actions; it confers on the Security Council the power to 'determine the existence of any threat to the peace, breach of the peace, or act of aggression'.[12] This determination is crucial as it sets

9. Art 2(4) of the Charter of the United Nations (hereafter UN Charter) states: 'All Members shall refrain in their international relations from the threat or use of force against the territorial integrity or political independence of any state, or in any other manner inconsistent with the Purposes of the United Nations'

10. See 'Report of the International Law Commission on the work of its eighteenth session' (4 May–19 July 1966) UN Doc. A/6309/Rev.1; *Military and Paramilitary Activities in and against Nicaragua (Nicaragua v United States of America)* (Merits) [1986] ICJ Rep 14 paragraph 190; but see, James Green, 'Questioning the Peremptory Status of the Prohibition on the Use of Force' (2011) 32 Michigan Journal of International Law 215

11. *Legal Consequences for States of the Continued Presence of South Africa in Namibia (South West Africa) notwithstanding Security Council Resolution 276 (1970)* (Advisory Opinion) [1971] ICJ Rep 16 paragraphs 113, 114

12. UN Charter Art 39

up the possibility for the Security Council to make recommendations or to decide on measures short of force under Article 41.[13] Or, if Article 41 measures are deemed inappropriate the Security Council can decide on measures involving the use of force under Article 42 in order to 'maintain or restore international peace and security'.[14]

Once a determination under Article 39 has been made the Security Council can adopt non-forcible measures according to Article 41. These have often taken the shape of economic sanctions and arms embargoes, but have also been used in the aftermath of conflict to establish the ICTY and ICTR.[15] Article 42 instead allows the Security Council to respond to an Article 39 determination through 'such action by air, sea, or land forces as may be necessary to maintain or restore international peace and security'.[16] At the time of drafting the UN Charter, measures under Article 42 were intended to be carried out by forces under the standing command of the UN. However, given that a UN force was never constituted in practice, Article 42 is given substance through Security Council authorizations of force directed at coalitions of states willing to intervene militarily. Any use of force which occurs outside the parameters of Chapter VII (which incorporates Article 51 self-defence) constitutes a unilateral action and is in violation of the Charter.[17] Importantly, the UN Charter does not define criteria to identify what constitutes a 'threat to the peace' within the meaning of Article 39. This has led to what constitutes a threat to international peace and security becoming defined through the Security Council's discretionary and often selective practice.[18] In fact, for a determination in accordance with Article 39 to take place, all five permanent members of the Security Council must not disagree.[19] As the lack of adequate

---

13. Note that a decision is binding upon the UN member states according to Article 25 of the UN Charter

14. UN Charter Art 39

15. ICTY Appeals Chamber, *Prosecutor v Tadić*, Decision on the Defence Motion for Interlocutory Appeal on Jurisdiction, Case IT-94-1, 2 October 1995, paragraphs 31–40

16. UN Charter Art 42

17. Nonetheless, international law recognizes the right of governments to invite foreign military intervention; *Nicaragua*, above note 10, paragraph 246

18. Antonio Cassese, *International Law* (2nd edn, Oxford University Press 2005) 347

19. This is the 'veto' power; UN Charter Art 27(3); note that a practice has developed for which abstentions do not stop a Security Council resolution from going through

attention in response to the conflict in Syria illustrates, the Security Council has a history of selective focus on particular conflict situations resulting in comparable contexts escaping attention due to alliances with powerful actors.

While the veto power of the permanent members of the Security Council has been used to block action, a gradual expansion of the circumstances of application of Article 39 for what concerns the existence of threats to peace has been observed.[20] In particular, the Security Council has increasingly deployed this category with regard to internal situations – traditionally considered within the remit of the territorial state – for their consequences at the international level.[21] Early instances of expansion were coupled with language highlighting the exceptional nature of Security Council intervention into internal conflicts; however by 2011, with the authorization of military force in Libya the Security Council had removed such qualifying language.[22] While not directly referring to the 'threat to peace' category, women, peace and security resolutions 1820, 1888, 1960 and 2106 can be seen as part of this expansive tendency given that they connect widespread and systematic conflict-related sexual violence against civilians to international peace and security.[23] The expanding of the category 'threat to the peace' – underpinned by the ever-present spectre of last-resort forcible measures in the background – has been the Security Council's way to assume a responsive posture towards conflicts and tensions since the end of the Cold War. However, as we explain below, from a feminist perspective the idea of collective security shaped around the deployment of military force as an ultimate response to threats or

20. Cassese, above note 18, 347; Gina Heathcote, *The Law on the Use of Force: A Feminist Analysis* (Routledge 2012) 40–2

21. Examples include: the worsening conflict situation in Liberia, Security Council Resolution 788 (19 November 1992) UN Doc. S/RES/788; and the 'challenges to the political, social and economic stability of Haiti' which were deemed 'to constitute a threat to international peace and security in the region', Security Council Resolution 1542 (30 April 2004) UN Doc. S/RES/1542

22. Security Council Resolution 1973 (17 March 2011) UN Doc. S/RES/1973

23. Security Council Resolution 1820 (19 June 2008) UN Doc. S/RES/1820 paragraph 1; Security Council Resolution 1888 (30 September 2009) UN Doc. S/RES/1888 paragraph 1; Security Council Resolution 1960 (16 December 2010) UN Doc. S/RES/1960 paragraph 1; Security Council Resolution 2106 (24 June 2013) UN Doc. S/RES/2106 paragraph 1

breaches of peace[24] potentially undermines the Charter's foundational promise to 'maintain international peace and security' and, in the words of Charlesworth, fosters international law as a 'discipline of crisis'.[25]

Law's violence and feminist approaches to collective security

This section offers an interrogation of the relationship between law and violence. This allows us to expand feminist analysis of collective security through questioning the possibility of feminist strategies for reform. The connection between law and violence has been observed as taking place at different levels: at the foundational (constituent) moment of a legal order, it then persists through the law's enforcement dimension, through the language of law's sharp categories by way of which that order is maintained, and by positioning extra-legal violence as the reason for which law is necessary.[26] As Hamzić stresses, the link between law and violence is deceptively 'denied by law' which instead is couched with the characteristics of 'justice, peace and security'.[27] Here we build on Hamzić's account of the Security Council as 'perhaps the most potent symbol of legally sanctioned state violence in international relations' to expand the feminist analysis of collective security, use of force and law.[28] In particular, we want to highlight the connection between law and violence as it allows us to expose collective security's

24. Although rarely used, breaches of the peace and acts of aggression are also included in Article 39 as grounds for triggering Chapter VII (authorized military) action

25. UN Charter Art 1(1); Hilary Charlesworth, 'International Law: A Discipline of Crisis' (2002) 65 (3) Modern Law Review 377

26. Austin Sarat and Thomas R Kearns, 'Introduction' in Austin Sarat and Thomas R Kearns (eds), *Law's Violence* (University of Michigan Press 1992) 4; Robert Cover, 'The Supreme Court 1982 Term; Foreword: Nomos and Narrative' (1983) 97 Harvard Law Review 4, 40; Jacques Derrida, 'Force of Law: The "Mystical Foundation of Authority"' (1990) 11 Cardozo Law Review 920; David Kennedy, *Of War and Law* (Princeton University Press 2006) 22, 167

27. Vanja Hamzić, 'International Law as Violence: Competing Absences of the Other' in Dianne Otto (ed), *Queering International Law: Possibilities, Alliances, Complicities, Risks* (Routledge 2018) 78

28. Hamzić, ibid., 79; Kennedy has spoken of the Charter system as 'a new legal order that inaugurated a new law of war' and as 'constitutionalization of the law of force'; above note 26, 77, 82

duplicity in relation to non-violence as, on the one hand, it promises to maintain international peace (which should include the absence of violence) and, on the other hand, the ultimate way in which that is done is through legally sanctioned force.

The connection between law and violence is evident in the collective security framework. The origins of collective security are deeply connected to the Second World War and the Security Council's working practice was then shaped by the Cold War's incipient dynamics. The UN collective security framework's creation is intertwined with the establishment of a new order by the victorious powers: the five permanent members of the Security Council (P5). Speaking directly after this foundational moment, the connection between law and violence in relation to collective security is made clear in Kelsen's 1948 definition: '[w]e speak of collective security when the protection of the rights of the states, the reaction against the violation of the law, assumes the character of a collective *enforcement* action.'[29] As noted by Derrida, 'enforceability' carries in itself the direct connection between law and its application through force.[30] The link between legally binding Security Council decisions and military force constitutes a foundational component of the UN, marking its enforcement power as distinct from the comparatively weaker powers of the League of Nations. Chapter VII resolutions are the legal means through which violence authorized by a Council decision is deployed as the ultimate means to resolve international disputes and, increasingly, violence within a state.

Originally, military deployment was to take place through a UN standing force (Article 43), highlighting how deep the relationship between collective security law and violence was intended to be. While this did not happen,[31] Cassese notes how the practice that substituted the deployment of a standing UN armed force under Article 43 (i.e. the Security Council's authorization to states or coalitions to use force) has in fact 'broaden[ed] the scope of Chapter VII of the Charter'.[32] While the

29. Hans Kelsen, 'Collective Security and Collective Self-Defense under the Charter of the United Nations' (1948) 42 (4) American Journal of International Law 783 (emphasis added)

30. Derrida, above note 26, 925

31. The absence of a UN standing force has been described by Shaw as a weakening factor for Article 42 (forcible measures); Malcolm N Shaw, *International Law* (8th edn, Cambridge University Press 2017) 958, 959

32. Cassese, above note 18, 350

core of the collective security system was 'that the use of force is kept in the hands of a central body ... the new system hinges on the idea of that such force [being] spread out among States, that is, is "decentralized", albeit upon authorization of that body'.[33] Clearly, the link between a legally binding Security Council decision and military force persisted and then expanded even if a UN army was never created. Nevertheless, centring armed responses disregards the continuum of violence and feminist accounts of how insecurity persists after armed interventions.[34]

In the same way in which law seems impossible to abandon as a system for control, order and security domestically, collective security also appears unavoidable as a method to contain illegal violence internationally. However, as noted by Sarat and Kearns, the relationship between law and violence is not a balanced one: 'we can never ourselves imagine that law could finally conquer and undo force, coercion, and disorder; its best promise is a promise to substitute one kind of force – legitimate force – for another'.[35] Hence the paradox of Article 2(4) and collective security: through Article 2(4) states committed to renounce violence as a method of international dispute settlement while at the same time agreeing to a collective structure that uses force to resolve disputes.

The fact that the Security Council's composition is enshrined in Charter law contributes to the preservation of the P5's power and status as the ultimate deciders on collective security action. Some commentators have attempted to circumvent the problem of the Security Council's inaction due to deadlock by suggesting that the General Assembly and 'properly constituted regional organisations' should be allowed to authorize the use of force particularly in cases of genocide and crimes against humanity.[36] However, it should be noted that, even in the case of the adoption of a majority-based system (for example

33. Cassese, ibid.

34. Cynthia Cockburn 'The Continuum of Violence: A Gender Perspective on War and Peace' in Wenona Giles and Jennifer Hyndman (eds), *Sites of Violence: Gender and Conflict Zones* (University of California Press 2004) 39–44; Cynthia Cockburn and Dubravka Zarkov (eds), *The Postwar Moment: Militaries, Masculinities and International Peacekeeping* (Lawrence and Wishart 2002)

35. Sarat and Kearns, above note 26, 6

36. Nicholas Tsagourias and Nigel White, *Collective Security: Theory, Law and Practice* (Cambridge University Press 2013) 133

through the removal of the veto power) or regional devolution,[37] this would not *per se* delink collective security from force. While the system could arguably be more democratic, it would still be focused on force. Devolving the power to authorize force could theoretically overcome the Security Council's selectivity and offset its 'legalised hegemony'[38] and its 'indifference or halfhearted responses to armed conflicts.'[39] Still, while a system of this kind would not be so frequently blocked by the veto system, it would consequently have the potential to authorize force more often. Furthermore, proposals to devolve to regional organizations the capacity to decide on the use of force assume that regional intergovernmental bodies and regional hegemons will not be driven by particularistic interest in their decisions. Expansive approaches are risky not only for the expanded 'dangers of abuse'[40] and the proliferation in justifications for use of unilateral force that is likely to follow, but also because regional organizations are likely to continue to centre armed intervention as a solution, fostering a crisis mentality.[41] Crucially, while extending the power to authorize force would make such force *legal*, it would guarantee that violence remains at the heart of the system instead of developing methods of conflict prevention through 'attention to social and economic inequalities both within and across states.'[42]

As such, restricting the ability to internationally sanction the use of force to the Security Council includes both accepting the legality of its deployment of force to 'solve' situations of conflict and insecurity, and accepting its deadlock in cases of disagreement. The collective security structure under the UN responds only to the violence that the Security

37. See discussion in Tsagourias and White, ibid.; Ikechi Mgbeoji, *Collective Insecurity: The Liberian Crisis, Unilateralism, and Global Order* (UBC Press 2003) 144

38. Gerry Simpson, *Great Powers and Outlaw States: Unequal Sovereigns in the International Legal Order* (Cambridge University Press 2004) 187

39. With specific reference to conflict 'in Sudan, Zaire, Angola, Chad, Ethiopia, Eritrea, Guinea-Bissau, Sierra Leone, Uganda, Somalia, Burundi, and other flashpoints in Africa' in Mgbeoji, above note 37, 144

40. Mgbeoji, above note 37, 144; Christine Gray, *International Law and the Use of Force* (4th edn, Oxford University Press 2018) 434

41. Charlesworth, above note 25

42. Gina Heathcote, 'Feminist Perspectives on the Law on the Use of Force' in Marc Weller (ed), *The Oxford Handbook of the Use of Force in International Law* (Oxford University Press 2015) 125

Council (and within it the P5) identifies as constituting a situation. This consideration is crucial as it can be seen as lying at the root of a number of recurrent problematic aspects of collective security, including: first, the problem of the Council's selectivity which allows only certain situations to receive attention while others remain unrecognized; second, the fact that the language of collective security – notably the expanded reading of Article 39 – has been replicated by states to justify unilateral force which, again, often goes unchallenged by the collective security mechanism; and third, the fact that only a certain type of violence and insecurity gets on the radar of the Security Council leaving other types of harm, and the relation between these and international insecurity, uninterrogated.[43] Examples that are not recognized as violence by the law on collective security include, for instance, the private harm suffered by women and LGBTQIA communities globally, not just in terms of violence but also in terms of wider inequality; or the extended insecurity caused by pressure to adopt neoliberal models of governance in states in the global south.

By centring law's relationship with violence, the underlying reasons for the collective security mechanism's failure to satisfactorily realize the goal for which it was created – maintaining international peace and security – become apparent. Law's relationship with violence ultimately betrays law's promise to eliminate violence and reveals its deceptive claim of being an ally of non-violence. To use Hamzić's words, this results in a 'crisis of violence spilling everywhere, of violence that no longer seems containable even by most violent acts of law'.[44] This image of violence spilling uncontrollably through the nets of collective security speaks to Heathcote's argument about the expansion of the Article 39 category 'threat to the peace' and the targets of Security Council sanctions (Article 41) having together 'enhanced state claims for legitimate humanitarian interventions and the legality of targeted strikes against terrorist actors' ultimately reinforcing the idea 'that military action can provide security'.[45] This has taken place via imitation, in that states have supported the legality of forcible actions *not* authorized by the Security Council using similar grounds as those articulated by the Council to justify its own actions through expanded

---

43. Heathcote, above note 20, 51
44. Hamzić, above note 27, 90
45. Heathcote, above note 20, 35

interpretation of its powers under the Charter.[46] This is most evident regarding humanitarian interventions.[47]

Economic sanction regimes under Article 41 have been criticized by feminist scholars for their damaging effects on the civilian population and for their disregard for the consequences of sanctions on women.[48] Moreover, feminist scholars have observed how non-forcible actions under Article 41 should be understood as 'bolster[ing] the appearance of Article 42 force as a viable solution to the increased range of threats' falling under Article 39.[49] Part of the justification for the use of military force in Iraq in 2003 included the notion of 'implied authorization', founded on the perceived non-compliance of the Iraqi state with the existing Article 41 sanctions regime.[50] Similarly, US justifications for targeted strikes against terrorists have been shown to mimic 'developments under the authority of the Security Council in the construction of targeted sanctions under Article 41'.[51]

Feminist analysis has shown how armed intervention often (re)produces rather than eliminates gender inequality, contributing to the continuing of violence and insecurity.[52] This can be seen, for example, in the emergence of exploitative sex trafficking industries adjacent to UN military and peacekeeping bases.[53] The relationship between this recurrent phenomenon and violent forms of masculinity,

46. Heathcote, ibid., 51

47. Heathcote, ibid.; see Chapter 2 in this volume

48. Anne Orford, 'The Politics of Collective Security' (1996) 17 Michigan Journal of International Law 373, 379–81; Hilary Charlesworth and Christine Chinkin, *The Boundaries of International Law: A Feminist Analysis* (Manchester University Press 2000) 302–4; Nadje Al-Ali, 'Women, Gender Relations, and Sanctions in Iraq' in Shams Inati (ed), *Iraq: Its History, People and Politics* (Humanity Books 2003)

49. Heathcote, above note 20, 53

50. Heathcote, ibid., 53, 57

51. Heathcote, ibid., 55

52. Nadje Al-Ali and Nicola Pratt, *What Kind of Liberation? Women and the Occupation of Iraq* (University of California Press 2009); Cynthia Enloe, *Maneuvers: The International Politics of Militarizing Women's Lives* (University of California Press 2000)

53. Samantha Godec, 'Between Rhetoric and Reality: Exploring the Impact of Military Humanitarian Intervention upon Sexual Violence – Post-conflict Sex Trafficking in Kosovo' (2010) 92 (877) International Review of the Red Cross 235

which have been historically encouraged within the military, is not examined as foundational to armed interventions, but rather, it has often been tolerated or dismissed. Zero tolerance policies – the UN official response to sexual exploitation and abuse connected to its missions – are often unconcerned with wider insecurity factors (such as extreme poverty, discrimination and international economic inequality at the basis of peacekeeping economies) that contribute to create the conditions for the 'complex mix of coercion, agency and survival' at the basis of this phenomenon.[54] A feminist examination of the relationship between militarized violent masculinities and gender violence could instead be used to question the very notion of deploying military force as a response to insecurity.

Overall, the expansions of Article 39 and Article 41 categories have enabled justifications for the deployment of force instead of limiting it. This expansion has been unaffected by longstanding feminist critique that has noted how the deployment of force is an unsophisticated method to collectively 'solve' complex situations of conflict and insecurity.[55] Furthermore, as Orford has shown, this crisis mentality – trapped in the dilemma 'to intervene or not to intervene' – tends to construct conflict as particularistic and local, detached from the broader economic and geopolitical context which would instead interrogate the role of, for example, powerful states in setting the conditions for insecurity.[56] The discourse on humanitarian intervention, understood as the use of force to 'save others', risks falling in the footsteps of colonialist narratives as it is underpinned by a gendered, 'white saviour' mindset that legitimates the use of force while, again, concealing the complicity of the global north in the historical root causes of many contemporary conflicts.[57] We reflect at length on humanitarian intervention and the cycles of violence connected to it in the next chapter.

As observed by Heathcote, '[t]he prohibition on the use of force is the lynchpin of the international relationship between law and violence.'[58]

---

54. Dianne Otto, 'Making Sense of Zero Tolerance Policies in Peacekeeping Sexual Economies' in Vanessa Munro and Carl Stychin (eds), *Sexuality and the Law: Feminist Engagements* (Routledge 2007) 266

55. Charlesworth, above note 25

56. Anne Orford, *Reading Humanitarian Intervention: Human Rights and the Use of Force in International Law* (Cambridge University Press 2003) 17, 18, 87–96

57. Orford, ibid., 34, 47, 48

58. Heathcote, above note 42, 128

Restricting the power of legally sanctioning the use of force to the collective security system included acceptance of the consequences of its inaction in case of P5 disagreement. That is, the system created by Article 2(4) and its collective security exception was born having inscribed within itself not only legally sanctioned state violence as a 'solution' to international insecurity, but also the possibility of the 'literal violence of war', which takes place during the Council's silences and deadlocks.[59] The case of Syria – discussed below – shows how in the absence of collective security, all the key actors (including the P5) found other ways to pursue their individual 'security' objectives, often providing legal or pseudo-legal justifications for their actions. This came at an enormous human cost for the Syrian population.

We argue that while the shortcomings of the system of collective security are ingrained in its structure and in the law/violence nexus, they are particularly illuminated by a gendered reading of the Charter that has historically privileged use of force responses over centring, instead, the primacy of Article 2(3), demilitarization and disarmament. Instead, its thematic agenda (including the women, peace and security resolutions) helped the Council to regain legitimacy after the failures of collective security in the 1990s[60] and, more recently, 'enhance[d] the work of the Security Council as an international institution with the capacity to authorise the use of military force'.[61] To this end, Heathcote has spoken of 'a misunderstanding deeply embedded in feminist advocacy within the collective-security arena'; this is the forgetting of the fact that 'the Council's primary work is about collective action not women's livelihoods'.[62] Similarly, Hamzić is sceptical of the thin recognition offered to marginalized groups through engagement with the Security Council and, in general, international law. He questions the value of strategic alliances as he stresses how 'LGBT organisations and individuals … should be aware of the circumstances in which their temporary, contingent and informal "recognition" before the Security

59. Hamzić, above note 27, 88
60. Dianne Otto, 'The Security Council's Alliance of Gender Legitimacy: The Symbolic Capital of Resolution 1325' in Hilary Charlesworth and Jean-Marc Coicaud (eds), *Fault Lines of International Legitimacy* (Cambridge University Press 2010)
61. Gina Heathcote, 'Women and Children and Elephants as Justification for Force' (2017) 4 (1) Journal on the Use of Force and International Law 83
62. Heathcote, ibid.

Council had become possible'.[63] Without wanting to detract from the efforts of feminist advocacy at the Security Council, the Syrian case explored in the next section demonstrates the thin impact that years of feminist engagement with the Security Council have so far achieved in changing the Council's deeply engrained understanding of security.

Case study: Syria

In this section we examine the Security Council's response to the ongoing violence in Syria. This analysis shows how, in addition to the horrific ongoing physical violence, there is another layer of violence found in the absence of effective measures to stop the violence of the conflict. Furthermore, a close description of the Security Council's engagement on Syria shows how its attention to women – let alone gender – remains patchy if not altogether absent. While this kind of analysis is useful to illustrate the fraught positioning of feminist approaches to collective security, we note how it tends towards a narrative that reflects the limited and essentialized way in which the Council understands women and gender as synonyms. Nevertheless, we propose this as a heuristic method to understand the dearth of impact that (non-liberal, non-radical) feminisms have had on collective security despite narratives of feminist victories and governance feminism.[64] This case study is useful to reflect on how the failure of collective security to attend to violence in Syria forces us to retreat our analysis, and to flatten it over searching for references to women, peace and security in the Council's work on Syria. This sidelining of projects which seek to foster peace works to paint a picture in which such projects are seen as overly utopian, a luxury we cannot afford to talk about. This narrows the scope through which feminists can make propositions in relation to the conflict, forcing them to advocate for more urgent, but less ambitious, protection objectives and silencing conversations about eradicating violence and non-military alternatives.

The conflict in Syria began in March 2011 with the increasingly violent repression by the Syrian state forces of popular protests. The

---

63. Hamzić, above note 27, 90
64. Catherine Powell, 'How Women Could Save the World, if Only We Would Let Them: From Gender Essentialism to Inclusive Security' (2017) 28 Yale Journal of Law & Feminism 271

revolution – as only few refer to it anymore[65] – was separate but linked to the wider Arab Spring movements. The UN reports that 'the first wide-scale military operation' by the Syrian armed forces took place in April 2011 and was soon followed by other major military operations.[66] It is estimated that in a period of around eight months from the beginning of the conflict the state forces killed at least 3,500 civilians.[67] Instead of quelling the revolt however, the state's violent repression resulted in the formation of different armed opposition forces and in the escalation of the conflict. It is important to recognize the wide origins of the conflict, including in the leadership's decision to reduce the socio-economic role of the state by liberalizing the economy, the negative effects of which fell mostly on rural and poor-urban populations whose protests – fuelled by the Arab Spring and environmental aspects – were met with repression instead of political openings.[68]

The situation in Syria was first debated at the Security Council in April 2011 and since then the Council has been briefed regularly by UN chief officials, including on the humanitarian, human rights and refugee situation in the country.[69] For instance, as early as August 2011, the then High Commissioner for Human Rights, Pillay spoke of a 'pattern of widespread or systematic human rights violations by Syrian security and military forces'.[70] Nevertheless, in a configuration that would be repeated several times, in October 2011 Russia and China imposed a veto on a Security Council resolution that would have '[s]trongly condemn[ed] the continued grave and systematic human rights violations and the use of force against civilians by the Syrian authorities, and expresse[d] profound regret at the deaths of thousands

---

65. Laila Alodaat, 'The Armed Conflict in Syria and Its Disproportionate Impact on Women' (2014) Focus Gender InfoBrief 10, on file with authors

66. Human Rights Council, 'Report of the Independent International Commission of Inquiry on the Syrian Arab Republic' (23 November 2011) UN Doc. A/HRC/S-17/2/Add.1 paragraph 28

67. Human Rights Council, ibid.

68. Shamel Azmeh, 'Syria's Passage to Conflict: The End of the "Developmental Rentier Fix" and the Consolidation of New Elite Rule' (2016) 44 (4) Politics & Society 499. See also Peter H Gleick, 'Water, Drought, Climate Change, and Conflict in Syria' (2014) 6 Weather, Climate, and Society 331

69. Security Council, 6524th meeting (27 April 2011) UN Doc. S/PV.6524

70. Security Council Report, 'Monthly Forecast: September 2011' (2011) *Security Council Report* https://www.securitycouncilreport.org/monthly_forecast/2011-09 (accessed December 2019)

of people including women and children'.[71] This posture remained largely unchanged even when the first report of the UN Human Rights Council Independent International Commission of Inquiry (COI) on Syria made it clear that the Syrian government was responsible for crimes against humanity.[72]

The prolonged division among the permanent members of the Security Council was temporarily overcome in the aftermath of a chemical weapons attacks in a rebel-controlled area east of Damascus on 21 August 2013. The attack involved the use of Sarin nerve agent and resulted in around 1,400 civilian deaths.[73] After initial statements by the US, UK and France pointing to the possibility of retaliatory unilateral action and several rounds of negotiations, in September 2013 the Security Council agreed on resolution 2118.[74] As part of the compromise achieved between the US and Russia, the resolution

71. Security Council draft resolution sponsored by France, Germany, Portugal and United Kingdom of Great Britain and Northern Ireland (4 October 2011) Un Doc. S/2011/612 paragraph 1

72. Human Rights Council, above note 66; The scale of violence in Syria being cause of concern, in August 2011 the Human Rights Council had established a COI during its 17th Special Session. See Human Rights Council Resolution S-17/1 'Situation of human rights in the Syrian Arab Republic' paragraph 13, in Human Rights Council, 'Report of the Human Rights Council on its Seventeenth Special Session' (18 October 2011) UN Doc. A/HRC/S-17/2

73. General Assembly and Security Council, 'United Nations Mission to Investigate Allegations of the Use of Chemical Weapons in the Syrian Arab Republic: Final Report' (13 December 2013) UN Doc. A/68/663–S/2013/735; see also Martin Chulov, Mona Mahmood and Ian Sample, 'Syria Conflict: Chemical Weapons Blamed as Hundreds Reported Killed' 22 August 2013, *The Guardian* https://www.theguardian.com/world/2013/aug/21/syria-conflcit-chemical-weapons-hundreds-killed (accessed December 2019)

74. Paul Lewis and Spencer Ackerman, 'US Set for Syria Strikes After Kerry Says Evidence of Chemical Attack Is "Clear"' 31 August 2013, *The Guardian* https://www.theguardian.com/world/2013/aug/30/john-kerry-syria-attack-clear-evidence; Oliver Wright, 'The Heir to Blair: PM Makes "Moral Case" for Attack on Syria' 28 August 2013, *The Independent* https://www.independent.co.uk/news/uk/politics/the-heir-to-blair-pm-makes-moral-case-for-attack-on-syria-8786783.html; France 24, 'France Ready to "Punish" Those behind Syria Gas Attack' 27 August 2013, *France 24* https://www.france24.com/en/20130827-france-punish-syrian-chemical-attack-hollande (all links accessed December 2019)

determined 'that the use of chemical weapons *anywhere* constitutes a threat to international peace and security', suggesting that any use of chemical weapons automatically triggers an Article 39 determination.[75] Then, without identifying who was behind the August attack, the resolution condemned the recourse to chemical weapons in Syria and requested the destruction of the Syrian chemical weapons programme.[76] The Council did not authorize the use of force and avoided language that could lend itself to future interpretation implying use of force authorization, but rather it decided 'to impose measures under Chapter VII' in case 'of non-compliance' with the terms of the resolution.[77] The resolution restated 'that Member States are obligated under Article 25 of the Charter of the United Nations to accept and carry out the Council's decisions'.[78]

While the text of the resolution did not directly bring in any women, peace and security-specific concerns, the Council endorsed the 2012 Geneva Communiqué in the second Annex of resolution 2118 and called for all parties attending upcoming talks on Syria to 'be fully representative of the Syrian people'.[79] The Communiqué, a result of the Geneva I Conference on Syria, was announced by then Special Envoy Kofi Annan at the end of the conference attended by the Action Group for Syria uniting several UN and Arab League states. The Communiqué has remained a key reference framework during negotiations while at the same time being interpreted divergently by the US and Russia regarding the future permanence of Assad.[80] The Communiqué set some principles for a Syrian transition, with one aspect being that '[w]omen

75. Security Council Resolution 2118 (27 September 2013) UN Doc. S/RES/2118 paragraph 1 (emphasis added)

76. S/RES/2118 paragraphs 2, 3

77. S/RES/2118 paragraph 21

78. S/RES/2118 preamble

79. S/RES/2118 paragraphs 16, 17

80. For instance, the COI referred to this in its report: Human Rights Council, 'Report of the Independent International Commission of Inquiry on the Syrian Arab Republic' (16 August 2013) UN Doc. A/HRC/24/46 paragraph 198: 'There is no military solution to this conflict. Those who supply arms create but an illusion of victory. A political solution founded on the tenets of the final communiqué of the Action Group for Syria (the Geneva communiqué) is the only path to peace'; Security Council Resolution 2139 (22 February 2014) UN Doc. S/RES/2139 preamble; Security Council Resolution 2165 (14 July 2014) S/RES/2165 paragraph 9

must be fully represented in all [its] aspects.'[81] The resolution also failed to refer to the increasingly worsening humanitarian situation in Syria, with the only mentions to the need for the Syrian government to grant 'full humanitarian access' being confined, again, to the annexed Geneva Communiqué. A largely inconsequential Security Council presidential statement was issued shortly after urging 'the Syrian authorities to take immediate steps to facilitate the expansion of humanitarian relief operations.'[82] The statement further condemned 'all acts of sexual and gender-based violence and abuse.'[83]

In the following period, however, the Security Council failed to extend the convergence that delivered resolution 2118 to adopt measures to facilitate the conflict's resolution or improve the devastating humanitarian situation on the ground. The COI had in the meantime continued to document the systematic imposition of sieges, large-scale crimes against humanity, war crimes and forcible displacement.[84] According to the COI '[t]he violations and abuses committed by anti-government armed groups did not … reach the intensity and scale of those committed by government forces and affiliated militia.'[85] In January 2014, ahead of the Geneva II negotiations, a closed doors Arria formula Security Council meeting was held in New York on women's participation in solving the conflict. The meeting was attended by Syrian women's networks not affiliated with the parties to the conflict who pointed out 'that neither the government nor the opposition sufficiently represent the Syrian people and the integrity of the talks would be undermined if women and civil society were excluded.'[86] However, this meeting did not translate into effective participation as, when the negotiations started in Geneva, women's diverse voices were not given

81. S/RES/2118 Annex II

82. Statement by the President of the Security Council (2 October 2013) UN Doc. S/PRST/2013/15

83. Ibid.

84. Human Rights Council, 'Report of the Independent International Commission of Inquiry on the Syrian Arab Republic' (18 July 2013) UN Doc. A/HRC/23/58; Human Rights Council, 'Report of the Independent International Commission of Inquiry on the Syrian Arab Republic' (16 August 2013) UN Doc. A/HRC/24/46

85. Human Rights Council, ibid., A/HRC/23/58

86. Security Council Report, 'Monthly Forecast: February 2014' (2014) 18 *Security Council Report* https://www.securitycouncilreport.org/monthly_forecast/2014-02 (accessed December 2019)

meaningful space.[87] Activists' accounts show how Syrian women were not seen as a legitimate party to the peace talks.[88]

In parallel to the Geneva II negotiations (January–February 2014), the Security Council was able to agree upon resolution 2139. After three years of armed conflict, and an ever-worsening humanitarian situation, the Council finally agreed on a text focusing on humanitarian access. The resolution '[s]trongly condemn[ed] the widespread violations of human rights and international humanitarian law by the Syrian authorities, as well as the human rights abuses and violations of international humanitarian law by armed groups, including all forms of sexual and gender-based violence'.[89] The text called upon all parties to lift sieges and stop the use of barrel bombs and other forms of indiscriminate attacks against civilians.[90] The resolution further emphasized that without a political solution the humanitarian situation was doomed to worsen and in that respect it stressed 'that rapid progress on a political solution should include full participation by all groups and segments of Syrian society, including women'.[91] Nevertheless, the Geneva II negotiations proved extremely difficult and failed to achieve concrete results, as disagreement regarding the future position of Assad remained. Ahead of the negotiations the Syrian government had 'framed the purpose of the talks strictly as a forum to discuss counter-terrorism'[92] and during the talks it 'refused to discuss any political transition until … a halt to terrorism' was achieved.[93] In order to overcome the

87. Committee on the Elimination of Discrimination against Women, 'Concluding Observations on the Second Periodic Report of the Syrian Arab Republic' (24 July 2014) UN Doc. CEDAW/C/SYR/CO/2 paragraph 13(b)

88. Madeleine Rees, 'Syrian Women Demand to Take Part in the Peace Talks in Geneva' (2014) *Open Democracy* https://www.opendemocracy.net/en/5050/syrian-women-demand-to-take-part-in-peace-talks-in-geneva/ (accessed December 2019)

89. Security Council Resolution 2139 (22 February 2014) UN Doc. S/RES/2139 paragraph 1. See also paragraph 11 demanding 'the release of all arbitrarily detained persons starting with women and children …'

90. S/RES/2139 paragraphs 3, 5

91. S/RES/2139 paragraph 15

92. Security Council Report, above note 86

93. Security Council Report, 'Monthly Forecast: March 2014' (2014) 7 *Security Council Report* https://www.securitycouncilreport.org/monthly_forecast/2014-03 (accessed December 2019)

deadlock related to Assad's position, the UN-Arab League negotiator Brahimi proposed that government and opposition representatives declared their commitment to all of the three key negotiation areas: the formation of a transitional governing body, ending of violence and terrorism. However, '[w]hile the opposition agreed to discuss terrorism and the formation of a transitional government in parallel, the government refused, instead insisting that terrorism be dealt with before any discussion of a transition'.[94] As such, the sole channel open for dialogue on behalf of the Syrian government was that of the fight against terrorism, which Russia indicated as 'the urgent and most pressing [problem]' over 'the establishment of a transitional governing body'.[95] The definition of terrorism remained the prerogative of the Syrian government who, towards the end of the talks, decided to add the negotiators representing non-state actors in Syria to a 'terrorist list'.[96]

In April 2014 High Commissioner for Human Rights Pillay briefed the Security Council stating that 'the government was responsible for

94. Security Council Report, 'Monthly Forecast: April 2014' (2014) 17 *Security Council Report* https://www.securitycouncilreport.org/monthly_forecast/2014-04; UN News, 'UN-Arab League Envoy Apologizes to Syrian People over Stalemate in Peace Talks' 15 February 2014, *UN News* https://news.un.org/en/story/2014/02/461922-un-arab-league-envoy-apologizes-syrian-people-over-stalemate-peace-talks (all links accessed December 2019)

95. Associated Press, 'Syrian Peace Talks in Geneva Reach Impasse after Five Days of Sparring' 14 February 2014, *The Guardian* https://www.theguardian.com/world/2014/feb/14/syrian-peace-talks-impasse-five-days-sparring (accessed December 2019)

96. Khaled Yacoub Oweis, 'Syria Adds Opposition Peace Talks Delegates to "Terrorist List"' 15 February 2014, *Reuters* https://www.reuters.com/article/us-syria-crisis-blacklist/syria-adds-opposition-peace-talks-delegates-to-terrorist-list-idUSBREA1E0QI20140215; Anne Barnard and Nick Cumming-Bruce, 'After Second Round of Syria Talks, No Agreement Even on How to Negotiate' 15 February 2014, *The New York Times* https://www.nytimes.com/2014/02/16/world/middleeast/after-second-round-of-syria-talks-no-agreement-even-on-how-to-negotiate.html (all links accessed December 2019). See further discussion in Chapter 3 in this volume

most violations and that her office could identify the perpetrators in the case of an ICC referral'.[97] This had been the route advocated by the COI and that enjoyed the support of a fairly large group of states led by Switzerland and expressing themselves mainly through the UN Human Rights Council (HRC).[98] Later in May 2014 France tabled a draft Chapter VII resolution taking up this course of action. However, the resolution was vetoed by Russia and China. The text of resolution 2165 instead managed to gather support; adopted on 14 July 2014, the resolution authorized access to humanitarian aid in Syria without the consent of the government.[99] This resolution came in the aftermath of a UN report stating that the government had been denying 'basic and widely accepted humanitarian commodities [as] a deliberate tactic of war'.[100]

From mid-2014, after the capture of Mosul and the escalation of its activities, ISIS increasingly gained the attention of the Council in its discussions of the Syrian conflict.[101] By August 2014 ISIS dominated the international media's attention due to the atrocities against the Yazidi

97. Security Council Report, 'Monthly Forecast: May 2014' (2014) 16 *Security Council Report* https://www.securitycouncilreport.org/monthly_forecast/2014-05 (accessed December 2019)

98. See 'Letter dated 14 January 2013 from the Chargé d'affaires a.i. of the Permanent Mission of Switzerland to the United Nations addressed to the Secretary-General' (16 January 2013) Un Doc. A/67/694–S/2013/19

99. This appears to be a decision pursuant to Article 25 of the Charter. Security Council Resolution 2165 (14 July 2014) UN Doc. S/RES/2165 paragraph 2. The resolution includes preambular references to sexual and gender-based violence. The humanitarian access terms of this resolution were extended periodically. At the time of writing the latest extension was until 10 January 2020. See Security Council Resolution 2449 (13 December 2018) UN Doc. S/RES/2449

100. Security Council, 'Report of the Secretary-General on the Implementation of Security Council Resolution 2139' (20 June 2014) UN Doc. S/2014/427 paragraph 48

101. See the presidential statement on oil trade involving terrorist groups in Syria and Iraq. Statement by the President of the Security Council (28 July 2014) Un Doc. S/PRST/2014/14. 'ISIS' indicates the so-called Islamic State of Iraq and Syria, also known as ISIL, IS or Daesh

population and the beheading of western journalists and aid workers.[102] In September the US – which was already supporting Iraq in its territory to fight ISIS – extended its air strikes into Syria to target the terrorist group with the support of an anti-ISIS coalition. This was justified with a request for support from Iraq and through Article 51.[103] Showing a measure of agreement that had been comparatively much harder to find for other texts on Syria, within a period of around six months, the Security Council agreed on two resolutions on ISIS dealing, respectively, with recruitment of foreign fighters and funding of terrorism through illicit activities including commerce of oil and cultural heritage.[104]

As described so far, and as exemplified by resolution 2139, gender and women have not been at the centre of the Security Council's attention and received only occasional consideration, as victims of gender-based violence or through isolated and inconsequential mentions in favour of their participation in negotiations. Interestingly however, while the Security Council did not adequately engage with women, peace and security in Syria, the CEDAW Committee took it upon itself to challenge the Syrian government on the women, peace and security agenda during its review in July 2014. Citing resolution 1325, the CEDAW Committee noted the importance of 'the meaningful and inclusive participation of women at all stages of peace and reconstruction processes, as well as in transitional justice' and reconciliation.[105] It expressed concern

---

102. Martin Chulov, '40,000 Iraqis Stranded on Mountain as Isis Jihadists Threaten Death' 7 August 2014, *The Guardian* https://www.theguardian.com/world/2014/aug/07/40000-iraqis-stranded-mountain-isis-death-threat; see also news items related to the deaths of James Foley, Steven Sotloff, David Haines and Alan Henning. For instance, Brian Stelter, 'James Foley Remembered as "Brave and Tireless" Journalist' 21 August 2014 *CNN* https://edition.cnn.com/2014/08/20/us/james-foley-life/index.html (all links accessed December 2019)

103. See 'Letter dated 20 September 2014 from the Permanent Representative of Iraq to the United Nations addressed to the President of the Security Council' (22 September 2014) UN Doc. S/2014/691; see also 'Letter dated 23 September 2014 from the Permanent Representative of the United States of America to the United Nations addressed to the Secretary-General' (23 September 2014) UN Doc. S/2014/695

104. Security Council Resolution 2170 (15 August 2014) UN Doc. S/RES/2170; Security Council Resolution 2199 (12 February 2015) UN Doc. S/RES/2199

105. CEDAW, above note 87, paragraph 13(c)

at the fact that the Syrian government's own activities on women in peacebuilding and reconstruction had not been inclusive.[106] The CEDAW Committee also expressed a similar concern at the fact that 'the diverse voices of women have been marginalized when it comes to actively and meaningfully participating in peace negotiation efforts' such as the Geneva II talks.[107] Furthermore, the Committee noted '[c]onsistent reports indicating that most of the women activists have been detained under terrorism charges' and urged Syria to 'disclose the number of women detained on grounds of terrorism' and amend its terrorist legislation.[108] While the Committee advanced several recommendations regarding peace negotiations and violence, it also raised political and economic rights, such as education, employment and health, including sexual and reproductive health.[109]

The CEDAW Committee, which often draws on civil society reports in its observations,[110] was mindful of the continuum of violence, of how pre-existing gendered harm and insecurity intersect and is worsened by the conflict.[111] Alodaat similarly notes how laws and conditions that were harmful for women before the conflict are exacerbated by the violence of war and stresses the importance of tackling these for achieving positive peace.[112] The Committee's recommendations are closer to the understanding offered by Alodaat than the Security Council's limited focus. While the CEDAW Committee's work has also been the object of feminist criticism, its strength has been identified in its position 'simultaneously at the centre and at the periphery of international law'.[113] From a legal point of view, this is interesting because the CEDAW Committee is a quasi-judicial body which has worked in developing its remit through soft law (General Recommendations and

106. CEDAW, ibid., paragraph 13(a)

107. CEDAW, ibid., paragraph 13(b)

108. CEDAW, ibid., paragraphs 29(b), 30(d) and (f)

109. CEDAW, ibid., paragraphs 39, 40, 41

110. Joint report submitted to the CEDAW in response to the report submitted by Syria: MADRE, CUNY Law School and WILPF, 'Seeking Accountability and Demanding Change: A Report on Women's Human Rights Violations in Syria before and during the Conflict' (July 2014); the report states that it was compiled in collaboration with Syrian women's organizations and activists

111. CEDAW, above note 87, paragraphs 39(a), 41

112. Alodaat, above note 65

113. Hodson, above note 2, 561

Concluding Observations) beyond the exact letter of the law enshrined in the CEDAW text. While its work has been informed by attention to women's experiences, we note that the expansion of the CEDAW's agenda happens at the margin of what is perceived to be 'real' law – the division between soft and hard law being, of course, a gendered one. Provided that the Committee expands its intersectional approach and that its unquestionable 'association with the human rights centre does not become a permanent fixation that leaves it voiceless',[114] the unique position of the Committee and its expansive and non-formalist approach can be viewed as elements challenging – at least in part – law's prevalent 'vertical' dimension; in Davies' words, 'flattening' law.[115]

From the point of view of intra-UN institutional dynamics, CEDAW's Concluding Observations on Syria are useful to observe that the Committee is following through on its General Recommendation 30 in which it requested states to report on their women, peace and security commitments during their CEDAW periodic reviews (arrogating itself the right to monitor country implementation of this Security Council agenda).[116] The case of Syria shows that instead of 'constructive cross-regime dialogue and inter-regime accountability',[117] we observe the CEDAW Committee being more attentive than the Security Council to women, peace and security being applied to situations of conflict. This is even more significant as it happened at a

114. Hodson, ibid., 576

115. Margaret Davies, 'Feminism and the Flat Law Theory' (2008) 16 (3) Feminist Legal Studies 281; Hodson suggested that the CEDAW committee undertakes: 'voyages to the periphery in order to expand its frame of reference'; above note 2, 577; on the possibility of redefinition of legal categories through peripheral contributions in another UN human rights process, see Sara Bertotti, 'Separate or Inseparable? How Discourse Interpreting Law and Politics as Separable Categories Shaped the Formation of the UN Human Rights Council's Universal Periodic Review' (2019) 23 (7) The International Journal of Human Rights 1140, 1150–1

116. Committee on the Elimination of Discrimination against Women, 'General Recommendation No. 30 on Women in Conflict Prevention, Conflict and Post-conflict Situations' (1 November 2013) UN Doc. CEDAW/C/GC/30

117. Catherine O'Rourke and Aisling Swaine, 'CEDAW and the Security Council: Enhancing Women's Rights in Conflict' (2018) 67 (1) International & Comparative Law Quarterly 199

time in which other UN bodies' attention became focused on ISIS, as in the experience of the HRC described below.

Comparatively, the HRC had been more attentive to women, peace and security concerns than the Security Council. However, it is striking to observe how – in conjunction with the US decision to target military action against ISIS in September 2014 and the peak of media focus on ISIS atrocities – the HRC dropped all references to women, gender and women, peace and security from its regular resolution on Syria. After some texts that included mainly protective references,[118] in March 2014 the HRC adopted language on Syria encouraging the 'full participation of women in political talks as envisaged ... by the Security Council in its resolutions 1325 ... and 2122'.[119] Similar language was adopted during the following regular session.[120] However, all references to the women, peace and security agenda were dropped in the September 2014 text on Syria.[121] Though not in an overwhelming number, and otherwise focusing prevalently on the COI, this resolution includes new references to ISIS informed by contemporary events. While it is impossible to determine with certainty why the women, peace and security language was left out, it is difficult not to suspect that in September 2014 women, peace and security language had to make space for the references to

118. For instance, HRC Resolution 22/24 'Situation of human rights in the Syrian Arab Republic' (12 April 2013) UN Doc. A/HRC/RES/22/24. This resolution contains mostly protective language but also 'calls for the involvement of women at decision-making levels in conflict resolution and peace processes'; see also HRC Resolution 23/26 'The deterioration of the situation of human rights in the Syrian Arab Republic, and the need to grant immediate access to the commission of inquiry' (25 June 2013) UN Doc. A/HRC/RES/23/26

119. HRC Resolution 25/23 'The continuing grave deterioration of the human rights and humanitarian situation in the Syrian Arab Republic' (9 April 2014) UN Doc. A/HRC/RES/25/23 paragraph 16

120. HRC Resolution 26/23 'The continuing grave deterioration in the human rights and humanitarian situation in the Syrian Arab Republic' (17 July 2014) UN Doc. A/HRC/RES/26/23 paragraph 26

121. HRC Resolution 27/16 'The continuing grave deterioration in the human rights and humanitarian situation in the Syrian Arab Republic' (3 October 2014) UN Doc. A/HRC/RES/27/16. But note a reference to sexual violence in government detention centres in paragraph 7. The references to women, peace and security reappeared in the text on Syria at the following HRC session

ISIS. The other side of the scarce consideration given to gender when international bodies are confronted with situations that require 'strong' responses is that of using gender as a legitimizing tool. This is Hamzić's reading of the August 2015 Arria-formula meeting on the targeting of LGBT people by ISIS. Provocatively, Hamzić argues that the meeting merely conferred only "'contextual" (victim-based) recognition' to 'conjure up the good from across the political divide in order to make the evil of ISIS more palpable, more personal, more punishable'.[122] Consequently, he urges LGBT groups to be aware of the 'circumstances in which their temporary, contingent and informal "recognition" before the Security Council had become possible'.[123]

After the November 2015 Paris terrorist attacks, the Security Council adopted resolution 2249. The resolution is an exercise in 'constructive ambiguity'[124] as it uses language close to what is typically associated with Security Council language authorizing the use of force without actually authorizing any specific collective security action.[125] Resolution 2249 states that ISIS is 'a global and unprecedented threat to international peace and security'.[126] Then it:

> calls upon Member States that have the capacity to do so to take all necessary measures, in compliance with international law, in particular with the United Nations Charter, as well as international human rights, refugee and humanitarian law, on the territory under the control of ISIL also known as Da'esh, in Syria and Iraq, to redouble and coordinate their efforts to prevent and suppress terrorist acts committed specifically by ISIL also known as Da'esh as well as ANF, and all other individuals, groups, undertakings, and entities associated with Al Qaeda, and other terrorist groups, as designated by the United Nations Security Council ...[127]

122. Hamzić, above note 27, 89, 90
123. Hamzić, ibid., 90
124. Dapo Akande and Marko Milanovic, 'The Constructive Ambiguity of the Security Council's ISIS Resolution' (2015) *EJIL: Talk!* https://www.ejiltalk. org/the-constructive-ambiguity-of-the-security-councils-isis-resolution (accessed December 2019)
125. Gray, above note 40, 385; Hamzić, above note 27, 87 fn 62; Akande and Milanovic, above note 124
126. Security Council Resolution 2249 (20 November 2015) UN Doc. S/RES/2249 preamble
127. S/RES/2249 paragraph 5

The resolution however was not explicitly adopted under Chapter VII. Nevertheless, the Security Council called upon states to carry out actions ('all necessary measures') that are in line with international law to suppress ISIS' terrorist acts.[128] The Council supported all independently lawful actions against ISIS, but it did not *per se* authorize any new ones or explicitly prohibit force. As noted by Gross, however, the resolution's language of eradication of ISIS' safe havens is difficult to be interpreted 'in any way other than authorizing military force'.[129] Furthermore, while resolution 2249 was not referred to as the legal authorizing ground for use of force against ISIS in the official correspondence the UK and Germany sent to the Security Council,[130] France, Germany and – most clearly – the UK had mentioned the resolution at different times in relation to the use of force against ISIS in Syria.[131]

Confirming the trend that saw the Council find a measure of agreement only on terrorism, through resolution 2249 the Security Council foregrounds the violence of ISIS while leaving the violence of the Syrian state unaddressed. The violence that is recognized by the Council coincides with the occasion in which ISIS' violence managed to reach the west directly through the dimension of the ISIS attacks on Paris (prompting France's initiative), while the violence taking place in Syria at the hands of the state is left largely unquestioned by the Security Council. This despite, in a report covering the period from March 2011 to November 2015, the COI describing how the Syrian government had committed a systematic extermination of individuals in detention:

128. Gray, above note 40, 386. See also Akande and Milanovic, above note 124

129. Oren Gross, 'Unresolved Legal Questions Concerning Operation Inherent Resolve' (2017) 52 (2) Texas International Law Journal 234

130. Gray, above note 40, 386 fn 214

131. See Gross, above note 129, 234, 235. It should be noted that Turkey referred to this resolution to justify its use of force in Syria in October 2019: 'This operation is essential also within the context of the responsibility attributed to States Members of the United Nations in the fight against terrorism through Security Council resolutions 1373 (2001) … 2249 (2015)'. See 'Letter dated 9 October 2019 from the Permanent Representative of Turkey to the United Nations addressed to the President of the Security Council' (9 October 2019) UN Doc. S/2019/804

It is apparent that the Government authorities administering prisons and detention centres were aware that deaths on a massive scale were occurring. The accumulated custodial deaths were brought about by inflicting life conditions in a calculated awareness that such conditions would cause mass deaths of detainees in the ordinary course of events, and occurred in the pursuance of a State policy to attack a civilian population. There are reasonable grounds to believe that the conduct described amounts to extermination as a crime against humanity.[132]

Furthermore, the November 2015 resolution does not address any concerns within the women, peace and security agenda and, again, a Security Council resolution regarding force remains unconcerned with the framework put in place by the same Council via resolution 1325. This is particularly striking as resolution 2249 was adopted just over a month after the Security Council had passed its latest women, peace and security resolution (resolution 2242). As we explained in the previous chapter, through that resolution the Council decided to integrate women, peace and security 'across all country-specific situations on the Security Council's agenda'.[133] Despite all the 'celebration and self-congratulation on display' when resolution 2242 was adopted, it is clear that when matters that are viewed as being of greater importance are considered, women, peace and security concerns continue to be superseded.[134] This demonstrates that, so far, the women, peace and security agenda has been ineffective in changing the dynamics at the heart of collective security and of choices regarding the use of force. Analysing the Security Council authorization to use force in Libya in 2011, Heathcote has observed how – in spite of women, peace and security being part of the established agenda of the Council for over a decade – 'decisions with respect to the use of force remain untouched by the women, peace, and security framework'.[135] Explicitly acting

132. COI report: Human Rights Council, 'Out of Sight, Out of Mind: Deaths in Detention in the Syrian Arab Republic' (3 February 2016) UN Doc. A/HRC/31/CRP.1 paragraph 97

133. Security Council Resolution 2242 (13 October 2015) UN Doc. S/RES/2242 paragraph 5(b)

134. Fionnuala Ní Aoláin, 'The "War on Terror" and Extremism: Assessing the Relevance of the Women, Peace and Security Agenda' (2016) 92 (2) International Affairs 275

135. Heathcote, above note 42, 115

under Chapter VII, the Security Council in resolution 1973 authorized 'all necessary measures ... to protect civilians and civilian populated areas'.[136] The resolution did not consider any of the 'normative and organizational requirements of resolution 1325, in particular the need for women's participation in the decision to authorize force'.[137] Women, peace and security concerns were only relatively and partially integrated once the Security Council moved to the post-conflict phase. This is symptomatic of the permanence of a gendered power imbalance entrenched in the heart of the UN. Importantly, rather than advocating in favour of an integration of women, peace and security language in use of force resolutions, this analysis is useful to expose the superficiality of approaches centred on gender mainstreaming which function by 'adding' gender to already established international structures.

The Security Council failed to prevent the further militarization of the conflict, for instance the Aleppo offensive led by Syrian and Russian forces. The COI found that during the battle for Aleppo 'Syrian and Russian forces carried out daily air strikes, claiming hundreds of lives and reducing hospitals, schools and markets to rubble'.[138] Overall, after more than eight years the conflict in Syria has caused hundreds of thousands of deaths and even more injured and displaced people. Deadlock in the Security Council has allowed for this violence to be largely unchecked, has slowed humanitarian assistance and has worked to support the Syrian regime regaining control over territory. At the time of writing prospects for peace remain uncertain. Resolution 2254 traced a roadmap for peace in Syria setting a timeline for transition (including elections, a new constitution and governance). The resolution is not an ambitious text in terms of women, peace and security concerns. It calls on the parties to release arbitrarily detained people 'particularly women and children' and, in the preamble, merely *encourages* 'the meaningful participation of women in the UN-facilitated political process for Syria'.[139] The most recent incarnation of the peace process is a Constitutional Committee featuring 150 members (50 each backed

136. S/RES/1973 paragraph 4

137. Heathcote, above note 42, 118

138. Human Rights Council, 'Report of the Independent International Commission of Inquiry on the Syrian Arab Republic' (2 February 2017) UN Doc. A/HRC/34/64

139. Security Council Resolution 2254 (18 December 2015) UN Doc. S/RES/2254 preamble, paragraph 12

by Assad, the opposition and civil society), almost 30 per cent of which are women. The Committee was launched in Geneva at the end of October 2019, but prospects for success remain slim as the government side insists on issues which led to the floundering of previous peace talks, such as the discussion of terrorism ahead of any discussion of constitutional matters.[140] Furthermore, Assad has recently stressed that while the government delegation 'represents the viewpoint of the Syrian government ... the Syrian government is not part of these negotiations';[141] therefore instilling doubts on whether any outcome of the talks will be considered a commitment officially undertaken by the state.[142] In the meantime, the Russian-backed Syrian government's offensive continues.[143]

Conclusion: Towards a feminist approach to collective security

Overall, the Security Council remains organized along the lines set by the Charter which accepts authorized military action as a means of conflict resolution, as well as the Council's silence on the use of military force when it is unable to intervene or respond. Alternative

140. Security Council Report, 'Monthly Forecast: January 2020' (2019) 5 *Security Council Report* https://www.securitycouncilreport.org/monthly_forecast/2020-01 (accessed December 2019). When the 2017 talks collapsed the UN chief mediator blamed the Syrian government for rejecting any discussion of 'two of the major potential agenda items – a constitutional process and presidential elections – insisting instead it would only discuss terrorism.' See Patrick Wintour, '"Golden Opportunity" Lost as Syrian Peace Talks Collapse' 14 December 2017 *The Guardian* https://www.theguardian.com/world/2017/dec/14/golden-opportunity-lost-as-syrian-peace-talks-collapse (accessed December 2019)

141. As reported in Security Council Report, ibid.

142. See Lara Seligman and Colum Lynch, 'As Assad Gains Ground, New Syria Talks Offer Little Hope of Peace' 12 November 2019, *Foreign Policy* https://foreignpolicy.com/2019/11/12/as-assad-gains-ground-new-syria-talks-offer-little-hope-of-peace/ (accessed December 2019)

143. Suleiman Al-Khalidi, 'Russian-backed Forces Gain Ground in Rebel-held Northwest Syria' 22 December 2019, *Reuters* https://www.reuters.com/article/us-syria-security-idlib/russian-backed-forces-gain-ground-in-rebel-held-northwest-syria-idUSKBN1YQ0DB (accessed December 2019)

non-violent avenues for the resolution of conflict which are mindful of the experience of marginalized local populations remain minimal. As shown above, the strategic successes obtained through the women, peace and security agenda have been insufficient to change the Security Council's work on the use of force, its authorization and deployment. We question the very possibility of 'reform' of structures that – things thus standing – are so entrenched and so powerful at absorbing women's agentic action for peace towards their own ends.

The link between sexual health and women's insecurity highlights the importance of drawing out both macro and micro complexities. As the most recent debates on women, peace and security in the Council have demonstrated, the shifting political will in the US is ultimately gagging the Security Council in its capacity to respond to the needs of survivors of conflict-related sexual violence.[144] As highlighted in the previous chapter, the language on sexual and reproductive health for survivors of conflict-related sexual violence was removed from the draft of resolution 2467 following the threat of veto by the US motivated by fears such language 'normalizes sexual activity and condones abortion'.[145] The subsequent resolution, 2493, is silent on conflict-related sexual violence; however, after the adoption of the text, the US ambassador to the UN further emphasized the US commitment to a continued silence on sexual and reproductive health and safe terminations in the women, peace and security agenda highlighting the commitment of the US government to overturning the prior approach.[146] This is a further demonstration that entrusting feminist change to the Security Council might be underpinned by a fundamental misjudgement regarding the

144. Security Council Resolution 2467 (23 April 2019) S/RES/2467; Security Council Resolution 2493 (29 October 2019) S/RES/2493

145. Robbie Gramer and Colum Lynch, 'How a U.N. Bid to Prevent Sexual Violence Turned into a Spat Over Abortion' 23 April 2019, *Foreign Policy* https://foreignpolicy.com/2019/04/23/united-nations-bid-end-sexual-violence-rape-support-survivors-spat-trump-administration-sexual-reproductive-health-dispute-abortion-internal-state-department-cable/ (accessed December 2019)

146. Record of the 8649th meeting of the UN Security Council (29 October 2019) UN Doc. S/PV.8649, remarks of US Ambassador Kelly Craft; Michelle Nichols, 'U.S. Pitted against Britain, France, South Africa, Others at UN over Abortion' 29 October 2019, *Reuters* https://www.reuters.com/article/us-women-rights-usa-un/us-pitted-against-britain-france-south-africa-others-at-un-over-abortion-idUSKBN1X829K (accessed December 2019)

Council's ultimate functions, composition and objectives.[147] Only the violence recognized as such by the P5 can be given legibility through the language of resolutions – and that limited legibility might still come at the price of enhancing the Security Council's legitimacy, *not* progressively changing the collective security structures.

Not only does the US insistence on the removal of references to sexual and reproductive health underline the political contingencies that are the reality of Security Council practice, it also demonstrates how the women, peace and security agenda remains one of asking for the inclusion of women, or 'adding women', to a pre-existing security agenda. Yasmine and Moughalian, in their study of refugee women, observe how '[t]he experience of Syrian refugee women in Lebanon … is often lost in a reductive analysis of women in war and gender-based violence' and adopt instead a 'social ecological model' to better understand and respond to the causes of their poor sexual and reproductive health.[148] This model is useful to our analysis of security because it refuses single-cause explanations and strategies:

> Within this framework, violence is perpetuated through four multilayered factors. The first is the *intra-individual level*, or one's personal history, which influences one's health behavior. The second is the *microsystem*, or one's immediate context, such as interactions with friends, family, and partners. The third is the *exosystem*, which in this case includes all the formal and informal institutions that influence Syrian refugee women's health behavior, such as their work context, social networks, UNHCR and the humanitarian aid system, the police, and the policies adopted by the Ministry of Health and municipalities in Lebanon. Finally, the fourth factor is the *macrosystem*, which represents the views and attitudes predominant in the culture.[149]

This approach speaks to O'Rourke's notion of 'web of gender-based harms'[150] which shows the multifaceted interconnections between 'different though complexly related public and private harms' in contexts

147. Heathcote, above note 61, 83
148. Yasmine and Moughalian, above note 3, 27, 28
149. Yasmine and Moughalian, ibid., 28 (emphasis in the original)
150. Catherine O'Rourke, *Gender Politics in Transitional Justice* (Routledge 2013) 37

of conflict and political violence.[151] What these approaches highlight is the importance of feminist interventions that are mindful and reflective of this complexity and of the interconnections between these different layers of insecurity analysis. These are tools useful to look beyond the 'crisis moment' of violent conflict to the larger insecurities a state faces that can ultimately lead to violence, such as economic instability and poverty, as well as the importance of material conditions that are often overlooked in security discourse. These tools are also useful in disrupting distinctions between responses to insecurities during conflict, in post-conflict spaces and peacetime, identifying instead the layers of gendered insecurity that persist in both war and peace.

Syrian women have been engaged in creating spaces of peace in the midst of the conflict, an effort that so far the official peace process has struggled to recognize adequately. As explained by Alodaat women have created:

> grassroots, sustainable and non-violent peacebuilding, even as conflict rages on. In 2011, some 2,000 Syrian women and children blocked a main road in northeastern Syria to demand the release of hundreds of imprisoned men. [In 2015] 470 Syrian women in the city of Zabadani risked their lives to publicly sign a statement demanding the Syrian army, Hezbollah and the Sunni Ahar a-Sham militant group stop attacks. Women in Syria's Atmeh camp for internally displaced persons led a successful campaign to control small arms after an argument in the camp lead to the death of civilians. National and international advocacy groups rarely see this level of success when it comes to controlling the use of arms. Syrian women are working to provide essential medical relief and food to a starving population, and have established safe spaces for women and children. Some living in ISIS controlled territory have even been able to negotiate the opening of temporary schools for children denied a regular education since war began.[152]

While we are not renouncing the advantages law can offer, we are wary of the limits and of the duplicity of law as a method to eradicate

---

151. O'Rourke, ibid., 38

152. Laila Alodaat, 'No Women, No Peace in Syria' 9 December 2016, *The Huffington Post* https://www.huffpost.com/entry/no-women-no-peace-in-syri_b_8762904 (accessed December 2019)

violence as discussed in this chapter.[153] As a result, we argue in favour of the importance of *non-legal* feminist enterprises to deliver change, such as health interventions, social, cultural and political interventions, education and the arts: all strategies often deployed and nurtured via transnational feminist spaces. Heathcote identifies this as a need for 'non-legal feminist action as a legitimate and important component of future dialogues on international law; exploring how protest and micro-level interventions must be rendered present in feminist approaches to global governance to shift from strategies for gender law reform to dialogues on feminist methodologies'.[154] These are feminist strategies that need not wait for conflict to be mobilized as a mechanism for undoing insecurity.

Given the present impossibility of organizing law, peace and security along a completely new system of thinking, any solution offered through the engagement with the current system can only be palliative at best. Instead, we propose an approach that moves away from crisis mentality and militarized answers to security problems in order to focus on social justice – meaning gender, race and class justice – in the everyday, in peacetime as in conflict. The following chapter takes this up through the lens of intersectionality as a feminist analytical tool and through the use of structural bias feminisms. We engage peace as a project that happens concurrently – and throughout – armed conflict as opposed to understanding it as an afterthought. While feminist peace approaches have historically been dismissed as 'a sign of weakness',[155] we argue in favour of this approach not based on alleged women's 'natural predilection' for peace but informed by an 'ideological commitment ... to a vision of international peace' which is also based on the rejection of militarism as a security solution.[156]

153. Heathcote, above note 42, 126
154. Gina Heathcote, *Feminist Dialogues on International Law: Successes, Tensions, Futures* (Oxford University Press 2019) 175
155. Dianne Otto, 'A Sign of "Weakness"? Disrupting Gender Certainties in the Implementation of Security Council Resolution 1325' (2006) 13 Michigan Journal of Gender & Law 113
156. Gila Svirsky, 'The Impact of Women in Black in Israel' in Marguerite Waller and Jennifer Rycenga (eds), *Frontline Feminisms: Women, War, and Resistance* (Routledge 2001) 234, 235

Chapter 2

UNILATERAL FORCE

In this chapter we focus on unilateral force to consider the urgent need for a feminist analysis of the legal regulation of war, beyond the collective security regime and beyond the women, peace and security framework. Under international law, unilateral force refers to any military force undertaken on the territory of another state outside of the collective security apparatus. That is, it may still be the act of multiple states working in concert; as the term 'unilateral' is used, in international legal contexts, to refer to states acting outside of the agreed form of collective military force as established in Chapter VII of the UN Charter. Although many aspects of gender and conflict have received increased attention after the creation of resolution 1325, the study of the legal justifications for military force has not benefitted from continued feminist analysis.[1] This chapter reviews the key feminist contributions to further a gender analysis of military force undertaken by states outside of the Security Council: unilateral force.

We highlight two categories of unilateral force in the chapter: self-defence and humanitarian intervention, with adjunct discussions on the protection of nationals abroad and the consent of the host state. This develops the account of law and violence provided in the previous chapter and questions the adjunct power structures that are brought into view when a gender analysis of unilateral force is undertaken. The chapter thus draws feminist approaches into dialogue with the study of unilateral force, to demonstrate the 'nexus between global inequalities, gendered understandings of violence, and [the need for a] ... diversity of feminist approaches,'[2]

---

1. Gina Heathcote, *The Law on the Use of Force: A Feminist Analysis* (Routledge 2012)

2. Gina Heathcote, 'Feminist Perspectives on the Law on the Use of Force' in Marc Weller (ed), *The Oxford Handbook of the Use of Force in International Law* (Oxford University Press 2015) 125

so as to argue for accounts of unilateral force that do not collapse back into justifications for great power privilege.[3] We argue for intersectionality as a methodology and as an essential component of feminist and gender projects because of the mechanisms it brings to a gender analysis to 'see' the embedded nature of gender in additional power structures.[4] In this chapter we examine feminist intersectional, postcolonial and structural bias feminist methods as a means to rethink the continued acceptance of unilateral force as within, rather than outside, of normal, legal, state acts, while in the following chapters we introduce a range of feminist approaches, alongside dominant legal feminisms, to avoid settling on a meta-narrative or invocation of a single feminist account.

In the following section, the chapter commences with an introduction to unilateral justifications for military force, and the relevant feminist scholarship on unilateral force, which can largely be described as coming from a structural bias feminist standpoint which sees the bias in the overarching structures of the law and politics. In the third section, the chapter provides a longer analysis of two modes of unilateral force: self-defence and humanitarian intervention. The chapter also examines state practice on consent to use force on the territory of another state, as Russia argues in relation to its military endeavours in Syria, and the use of force to rescue nationals abroad.[5] We conclude that the analysis of unilateral force, as with collective security authorizations, benefits from a structural bias feminism that is attentive to intersectional feminist methods and postcolonial analyses. We argue that gender analysis requires a movement

---

3. Gerry Simpson, *Great Powers and Outlaw States: Unequal Sovereigns in the International Legal Order* (Cambridge University Press 2004)

4. Dubravka Zarkov, 'From Women and War to Gender and Conflict?: Feminist Trajectories' in Fionnuala Ní Aoláin, Naomi Cahn, Dina Francesca Haynes and Nahla Valji (eds), *The Oxford Handbook of Gender and Conflict* (Oxford University Press 2018)

5. Onur Güven and Olivier Ribbelink, 'The Protection of Nationals Abroad: A Return to Old Practice?' in Christophe Paulussen, Tamara Takács, Vesna Lazić and Ben Van Rompuy (eds), *Fundamental Rights in International and European Law* (T.M.C. Asser Press 2016)

between the particulars of women's and gendered lived experiences alongside an interrogation of the macro dimensions of power that inform the structures, institutions and contours of international law. A gender analysis without the larger study of power relations risks perpetuating macro-level manifestations of power and inequality that stem from the everyday to the international. We conclude the chapter highlighting different feminist approaches, in particular, intersectionality, postcolonial and structural bias, as offering a means to think differently about unilateral force and as a mechanism for the study of gender and conflict.

Unilateral force: International legal developments and feminist interventions

Despite the existence of the prohibition on the threat or use of force contained in Article 2(4) of the UN Charter, the unilateral use of force on the territory of another state has been a persistent element of the Charter era. States attempt to justify the use of force with arguments for self-defence, on humanitarian grounds and as 'under' the threshold of force established in Article 2(4). International law retains the possibility that states can use military force on the territory of another state if that state has consented, or invited, the foreign state to intervene. States have also argued that they have the right to protect their nationals abroad without violating Article 2(4). Self-defence is enshrined in the UN Charter in Article 51. Feminist and gender analysis of these acts or the accompanying legal arguments from states remains limited. In this section we examine the range of unilateral force and existing feminist and gender scholarship.

Post-millennium unilateral military acts by Russia – in Crimea in 2014 and South Ossetia and Abkhazia in 2008 – are illustrative of the status quo of international law, where unilateral force is at once prohibited, condemned and yet seemingly tolerated by the international community. The power of the permanent member veto in the Security Council protects the five permanent member states from any collective response to the mobilization of unilateral military force. In 2014 unilateral force occurred when Russian military forces entered the territory of Ukraine and annexed the Autonomous Republic of Crimea. Subsequently, a referendum was held on 16 March 2014, in which participants voted to secede from Ukraine and become part of the Russian Federation.[6] Regardless of the legality of the referendum, the use of military force to obtain control of the territory of another state is prohibited under Article 2(4) of the UN Charter and in this instance Russia's unilateral force remains a breach of international law. Condemnation via the Security Council was not possible because of Russia's veto power: as such, an analysis of unilateral force must also hold the impact of a system designed around the maintenance of great power privilege in mind.

The only legal exception to the prohibition on the use of force contained in Article 2(4), in the absence of Security Council authorization, is when force can be justified on the grounds of self-defence.[7] Additional justifications such as humanitarian intervention or the use of force to protect nationals abroad remain subject to dispute as to the nature of their legality. The use of force with the consent of the host state is regarded as a domestic affair of the state inviting intervention, although questions are often raised about the nature of that consent/invitation.

Russian practice in the post-millennium era provides an interesting case study. As Russia's use of military force in Crimea did not constitute self-defence and was not authorized by the Security Council, it remains a breach of international law. Prior to this, in 2008 the Russian state had used military force on the territory of the state of Georgia on the grounds of humanitarian intervention. In this instance the use of force in the Georgian regions of South Ossetia and Abkhazia was declared, by Russia, through claiming a combination of justifications to support separatist groups in the region, including collective self-defence, the protection of nationals abroad, an international authorization (peacekeeping) and humanitarian justifications.[8] This ultimately led

6.   It should be noted that residents in the republic who were not sympathetic to the arrival of Russian forces, where possible, had likely fled to other parts of Ukraine. Furthermore, the boycott from the indigenous Crimean Tatars and the presence of armed Russian forces in Crimea at the time of the referendum raise questions about the legality of the referendum and its outcomes, see further: John Biersack and Shannon O'Lear, 'The Geopolitics of Russia's Annexation of Crimea: Narratives, Identities, Silences, and Energy' (2014) 55 (3) Eurasian Geography and Economics 247, 250–1

7.   Yoram Dinstein, *War, Aggression and Self-defence* (6th edn, Cambridge University Press 2017)

8.   Roy Allison, 'The Russian Case for Military Intervention in Georgia: International Law, Norms and Political Calculation' (2009) 18 (2) European Security 173

to declarations of independence from South Ossetia and Abkhazia. While both areas already functioned as semi-autonomous regions within the Georgian state, the use of force by Russia amounted to a use of unilateral military force prohibited under the UN Charter. The Russian state argued that the use of force was in part to protect nationals abroad.[9]

These instances of force by Russia are indicative of the categories of unilateral force that are subjected to a gender analysis in this chapter: self-defence and humanitarian intervention, as well as the protection of nationals abroad and consent from the host state. Although of questionable legality, each of these Russian military interventions has not engaged the collective security structure and Russian status as a permanent member of the Security Council means that it is unlikely that such acts will gain scrutiny in the future. We return to the examples of unilateral force by the Russian state across this chapter, in part because of the scarcity of research into the gendered nature of Russia's military force in these instances. Throughout the chapter we also highlight the use of military force, outside of the UN Charter regime, by the US, the UK, France and China as permanent members of the Security Council, to support our larger claim about the role of unilateral military force operating to embed inequality and to perpetuate gendered narratives regarding the utility and necessity of military force. As such, this chapter develops the study of law and violence in the previous chapter, to analyse the use of military force outside of the Charter provisions, and thus potentially always as a breach of Article 2(4), to argue for the necessity of feminist approaches that examine the legal conditions that continue to tolerate the reliance on unilateral military force by some states.

As we argued in the previous chapter and in the introduction to this volume, some aspects of the post-millennium developments in collective security, in particular, the creation of the women, peace and security framework, have received considerable attention from scholars working in the field of gender and conflict.[10] This attention stems

---

9. Güven and Ribbelink, above note 5

10. Carol Cohn (ed), *Women and Wars: Contested Histories, Uncertain Futures* (Polity Press 2013); Laura Shepherd, 'The Women, Peace, and Security Agenda at the United Nations' in Anthony Burke and Rita Parker (eds), *Global Insecurity: Futures of Global Chaos and Governance* (Palgrave Macmillan 2017) 139; Sara E Davies and Jacqui True (eds), *The Oxford Handbook of Women, Peace, and Security* (Oxford University Press 2019)

from the post-1325 period,[11] but has its legacy in the earlier writings of key feminist scholars working on international law,[12] international relations[13] and militarism.[14] Through the study of state practice with regard to justifications for unilateral force, this chapter draws out a key tension which we argue is not articulated in contemporary feminist writing on gender and conflict and within the women, peace and security literature. That is, we argue that the call for new types of interventions – legal, political, economic and otherwise – to address women's livelihoods and arrest gendered practices in conflict and post-conflict communities neglects the role of collective security structures in sustaining conflict, sustaining political power in peacetime states and neglects the many instances of force not addressed by the collective security system.

The linking of the authorization and deployment of military force with responses to gendered insecurity ignores the role that

11. Laura Shepherd, *Gender, Violence and Security: Discourse as Practice* (Zed Books 2008); Carol Cohn, Helen Kinsella and Sheri Gibbings, 'Women, Peace and Security Resolution 1325' (2004) 6 (1) International Feminist Journal of Politics 130; Torunn L Tryggestad, 'Trick or Treat? The UN and Implementation of Security Council Resolution 1325 on Women, Peace, and Security' (2009) 15 Global Governance 539

12. Hilary Charlesworth, 'The Sex of the State in International Law' in Ngaire Naffine and Rosemary Owens (eds), *Sexing the Subject of Law* (Law Book Company 1997) 251; Hilary Charlesworth, 'International Law: A Discipline of Crisis' (2002) 65 (3) Modern Law Review 377; Karen Engle, 'International Human Rights and Feminisms: When Discourses Keep Meeting' in Duris Buss and Ambreena Manji (eds), *International Law: Modern Feminist Approaches* (Hart Publishing 2005); Anne Orford, *Reading Humanitarian Intervention: Human Rights and the Use of Force in International Law* (Cambridge University Press 2003)

13. V Spike Peterson (ed), *Gendered States: Feminist (Re)Visions of International Relations Theory* (Lynne Rienner Publishers 1992); J Ann Tickner, *Gender in International Relations: Feminist Perspectives on Achieving Global Security* (Columbia University Press 1992)

14. Carol Cohn, 'Wars, Wimps, and Women: Talking Gender and Thinking War' in Miriam Cooke and Angela Woollacott (eds), *Gendering War Talk* (Princeton University Press 1993); Cynthia Enloe, *Maneuvers: The International Politics of Militarizing Women's Lives* (University of California Press 2000); Cynthia Enloe, *Bananas, Beaches and Bases: Making Feminist Sense of International Politics* (2nd edn, University of California Press 2014)

militarization and militaries play in the perpetuation of insecurity. Ultimately, there is a tension between the call for greater institutional engagement from the Security Council while simultaneously ignoring the many instances of force outside the purview of the Security Council. We argue that the spaces of military force which the Security Council does not actively engage with, or place on its agenda, also regularly fall outside feminist accounts of gender and conflict. This indicates one of the costs of entering the institutional arena where the parameters of which acts of force the international community pays attention to has specific dynamics that are of relevance to the framing of gender and conflict. Even when a specific conflict situation receives attention, for example the ongoing insecurity in the DRC, feminist analysis tends to be constrained by the parameters of the women, peace and security agenda. In the DRC this has led to a hyperfocus on conflict-related sexual violence and insufficient feminist and gender analysis of the ongoing authorizations of military force and measures short of military force.[15]

The reality of global political arrangements, including the permanent member's veto, as well as the role of the Security Council in enacting violence to halt violence, would benefit from further gender analysis. While the women, peace and security framework has attracted a great deal of attention, in this chapter we argue that insufficient feminist scholarship addresses the underlying international legal reality of the use of unilateral force by key states outside of the collective security regime. Consequently, the concerns raised in the previous chapter – with regard to the legitimacy of the Security Council and the use of military means as a solution to gendered harms – become unavoidable in a discussion of unilateral force such that the solutions to the gendered harms and gendered forms of unilateral force are far from self-evident. We argue that a gender analysis that examines the continued justifications for unilateral force via state practice must address the failures of the Security Council to act in these situations while – at the same time – analysing the macro-level political contingencies that permit some states, and not others, to maintain unilateral force as an accepted enforcement mechanism within international relations.

In deploying an intersectional gender approach, the chapter analyses the implicit demand, within scholarship on gender and conflict, that

15. Gina Heathcote, 'Women and Children and Elephants as Justification for Force' (2017) 4 (1) Journal on the Use of Force and International Law 66

there be international-level interventions into women's lives – hoisting new (gender-based) security issues on to the international plane. In contrast to approaches arguing for military interventions to 'save' women or halt gender-based violence, we argue for feminist attention to the consequences of unilateral force (or any military force) within international law – from the expansion of military humanitarianism to new forms of colonial interventions. From Russia's annexation of Crimea, to France's military incursions into its former colonial territories,[16] to the UK and the US military interventions into both Syria and Iraq,[17] as well as Chinese arming of fishers in the South China Sea,[18] and the use of force against claimed Uyghur terrorists,[19] the use of force by the permanent members of the Security Council, and their allies, remains outside of the purview of the Council's business.

Feminist scholarship on unilateral force by states emerges first in Chinkin's 1992 study of self-determination which concludes: '[t]he invisibility of women in any legal justifications for the use of force is striking. When assessing the impact of possible responses to aggression the concerns and needs of women are simply not raised by governments or even by other groups.'[20] Less than ten years later,

16. Isaline Bergamaschi, 'French Military Intervention in Mali: Inevitable, Consensual Yet Insufficient' (2013) 2 (2) Stability: International Journal of Security and Development 20; Dan E Stigall, 'The French Military Intervention in Mali, Counter-Terrorism, and the Law of Armed Conflict' (2015) 223 Military Law Review 1

17. Christine Chinkin, 'Rethinking Legality/Legitimacy after the Iraq War' in Richard Falk, Mark Juergensmeyer and Vesselin Popovski (eds), *Legality and Legitimacy in Global Affairs* (Oxford University Press 2012); Rebecca Barber, 'Uniting for Peace Not Aggression: Responding to Chemical Weapons in Syria without Breaking the Law' (Spring 2019) 24 (1) Journal of Conflict and Security Law 71, 76

18. Conor Kennedy, 'The Struggle for Blue Territory: Chinese Maritime Militia Grey-Zone Operations' (2018) 163 (5) The RUSI Journal 8

19. Chien-peng Chung, 'China's "War on Terror": September 11 and Uighur [*sic*] Separatism' (July–August 2002) 81 (4) Foreign Affairs 8–12; Chien-peng Chung, 'China's Uyghur Problem after the 2009 Urumqi Riot: Repression, Recompense, Readiness, Resistance' (2018) 13 Journal of Policing, Intelligence and Counter Terrorism 185–201

20. Christine Chinkin, 'A Gendered Perspective to the International Use of Force' (1992) 12 Australian Yearbook of International Law 279, 291

of course, the use of gendered violence by states, and the UN, to justify the use of unilateral force in Afghanistan and then by 2003 in Iraq demonstrated an interesting form of international legal acts that parallel the emergence of various feminist 'successes' within international law. That is, as calls for the international community to recognize the gendered violence in Rwanda and the former Yugoslavia were taken up in the development of international criminal law and as the Security Council recognized the specific need to address women, peace and security via resolution 1325, the discourse around the deployment of military force to 'save' or 'protect' women in conflict zones also gained prominence.

Engle's analysis of the tensions between recognizing gendered violence, the gendered effects of armed conflict and the call for military force to protect women was an early signal of the betwixt and fraught consequences of feminist engagements within international law.[21] Engle, through an analysis of changing international discourse on human rights, women's rights and humanitarian intervention, reflects on 'whether it would be a "victory" for feminism if troops were called in on women's behalf'.[22] As such, Engle argues:

> As military intervention increasingly becomes the norm for protecting victims of "serious" human rights violations, those who seek to redress a particular problem are increasingly pressured to couch it in terms of a crisis that only immediate military intervention can resolve. This focus often distorts the nature of the violation or harm and displaces an awareness of the extent to which both military and nonmilitary interventions – such as colonialism, economic and military assistance, and lack of such assistance – have helped produce the crises.[23]

A similar view of the underlying gender politics produced through the unilateral use of force by states is articulated by Otto when she writes: 'there is a paradox involved with appealing to law to censor violence against women when the legal system itself can be characterised as

---

21. Karen Engle, '"Calling in the Troops": the Uneasy Relationship among Women's Rights, Human Rights and Humanitarian Intervention' (2007) 20 Harvard Human Rights Journal 189
22. Engle, ibid., 189
23. Engle, ibid., 190

relying on violence to assert its own authority.'[24] Unilateral justifications for military force under international law function as a further embedding of violence within the legal structure as, despite the existence of the prohibition on military force in Article 2(4) of the UN Charter, the capacity for states to undertake military endeavours outside of the collective security regime remains an accepted component of international law.

In *Boundaries,* Charlesworth and Chinkin dedicate a chapter to the study of the use of force analysing self-determination, self-defence and humanitarian interventions as gendered acts which enshrine a masculine mode of military force as an enforcement mechanism within international law.[25] The work of Charlesworth and Chinkin illustrates the potential of the use of gender analysis to interrogate the structures of international law, or structural bias feminism. Charlesworth also analyses decisions to use force under the guise of humanitarian intervention in 2001, identifying the 'crisis' mode of international law as ignoring an international law of the everyday.[26] Chinkin's contributions to understandings of humanitarian intervention over this period are also significant; although not articulated as specifically deploying a feminist analysis, they examine the unilateral use of force outside of collective security to argue for an international law mindful of power and privilege that underscores acts of unilateral force.[27]

Heathcote's text on the law on the use of force examines unilateral justifications for force to evidence the sexed and gendered dynamics of international law. As an examination of the structural biases in international law, the text critiques the domestic analogy between state and individual justifications for violence to expose the underlying gender of justified violence under law.[28] In subsequent publications, Heathcote examines the possibility of mobilizing force in response

24. Dianne Otto, 'Integrating Questions of Gender into Discussion of the Use of Force in the International Law Curriculum' (1995) 14 Legal Education Review 219, 227

25. Hilary Charlesworth and Christine Chinkin, *The Boundaries of International Law: A Feminist Analysis* (Manchester University Press 2000) ch 8

26. Charlesworth, 'Discipline of Crisis', above note 12

27. Christine Chinkin, 'The State That Acts Alone: Bully, Good Samaritan or Iconoclast?' (2000) 11 European Journal of International Law 31; Christine Chinkin, 'Kosovo: A "Good" or "Bad" War?' (1999) 93 (4) American Journal of International Law 846

28. Heathcote, above note 1, 190

to widespread and systematic sexual violence,[29] the use of force on humanitarian grounds,[30] and the development of protection of civilians mandates as a mechanism for justifying military force in self-defence on peacekeeping mandates.[31] Heathcote argues for increased feminist analysis of the international law on the use of force and, in particular, of unilateral force. This chapter develops her argument to examine the nexus between gender and adjunct power structures to reflect on the consequences of nearly two decades of feminist engagement with the Security Council through the women, peace and security framework. In undertaking this enquiry, we argue for a wider range of feminist accounts of both institutional and state practice in response to unilateral force. That is, we argue against a single feminist account to understand the persistence of the use of unilateral force by states and instead consider how multiple feminist perspectives might add to understandings of insecurity constructed in both peacetime and conflict states.

The chapter draws in important earlier feminist accounts, including Orford's troubling of humanitarian intervention,[32] and various feminist studies of the responsibility to protect doctrine.[33] The latter, articulated by a panel of experts appointed by the Canadian government after NATO's use of military force in Kosovo in 1999, examined the relationship between sovereignty and human rights and concluded that sovereignty must be understood as imposing responsibilities on states that include the three-tiered notion of the responsibility to protect.[34]

---

29. Gina Heathcote, 'Naming and Shaming: Human Rights Accountability in Security Council Resolution 1960 (2010) on Women, Peace and Security' (2012) 4 (1) Journal of Human Rights Practice 82

30. Gina Heathcote, 'Robust Peacekeeping, Gender and the Protection of Civilians' in Jeremy Farrall and Hilary Charlesworth (eds), *Strengthening the Rule of Law through the UN Security Council* (Routledge 2016) 150

31. Heathcote, above note 2, 114

32. Orford, above note 12; Anne Orford, 'Feminism, Imperialism and the Mission of International Law' (2002) 71 Nordic Journal of International Law 275–96

33. Hilary Charlesworth, 'Feminist Reflections on the Responsibility to Protect' (2010) 2 (3) Global Responsibility to Protect 232

34. International Development Research Centre, 'The Responsibility to Protect: Report of the International Commission on Intervention and State Sovereignty' (2001) *ICISS* http://responsibilitytoprotect.org/ICISS%20Report. pdf (accessed December 2019)

The three elements of responsibility to protect are the responsibility to prevent, to react and to rebuild; however, the report emphasizes that sovereignty first imposes the responsibility to protect its citizens onto states and only '[w]here a population is suffering serious harm, as a result of internal war, insurgency, repression or state failure, and the state in question is unwilling or unable to halt or avert it, the principle of non-intervention yields to the international responsibility to protect'.[35] Feminist analysis of responsibility to protect has centred on the gendered silences in the literature and sought to draw responsibility to protect into the women, peace and security framework.[36] For the most part, and following the 2005 General Assembly endorsement of responsibility to protect as a component of collective security, this has hinged on analysis of issues within the collective security framework, including the regulation of conflict-related sexual violence,[37] the role of peacekeepers in the protection of civilians[38] and the responsibility of UN peacekeeping forces to incorporate women, peace and security into mission mandates.[39] Elsewhere, Stamnes argues that 'gender has remained a blind-spot in the central documents and discussions related to R2P' to make a claim for the need to, first, identify women's experiences of mass atrocities and, second, to develop a gender perspective within the contours of the responsibility to protect agenda.[40] Bond and Sherret argue for an explicit linking of the women, peace and security and the responsibility to protect agendas with the

35. ibid., xi

36. Sara E Davies, Zim Nwokora, Eli Stamnes and Sarah Teitt (eds), *Responsibility to Protect and Women, Peace and Security: Aligning the Protection Agendas* (Martinus Nijhoff Publishers 2013)

37. Inger Skjelsbæk, 'Responsibility to Protect or Prevent? Victims and Perpetrators of Sexual Violence Crimes in Armed Conflicts' in Davies et al., ibid., 81–99

38. John Karlsrud and Randi Solhjell, 'Gender-Sensitive Protection and the Responsibility to Prevent: Lessons from Chad' in Davies et al., ibid., 101–20

39. Sahana Dharmapuri 'Implementing UN Security Council Resolution 1325: Putting the Responsibility to Protect into Practice' in Davies et al., ibid., 121–54

40. Eli Stamnes, 'The Responsibility to Protect: Integrating Gender Perspectives into Policies and Practices' (2012) 4 (2) Global Responsibility to Protect 172, 175

goal of developing responsibility to protect 'to afford true protection'.[41] In each of these accounts the risk of sexual violence as an element of mass atrocities is central to the articulation of a claim for a gender-sensitive responsibility to protect. The responsibility to protect agenda has, as is discussed above, not developed to ingrain a unilateral right of states to deploy military force, although it was flagged by the Security Council as part of the reasons behind the authorization of military force in Libya in 2011.[42] Given the use of women's rights as a justification for military force in other contexts and the ongoing attempts by some states to assert a right of unilateral humanitarian force, an agenda for the responsibility to protect that bolsters rather than undoes this is questionable.

In contrast to the feminist analysis of responsibility to protect as a component of collective security that draws parallels with women, peace and security, unilateral humanitarian interventions are challenged as imperialist,[43] and legitimating military solutions[44] while producing a thin analysis of conflict that leads towards crisis mentalities.[45] However, sustained feminist analysis of the modes of unilateral force, whether claimed as humanitarian or defensive, remains limited and has not developed in tandem with contemporary state practice. As such, this chapter calls for further feminist analysis of contemporary accounts of unilateral force to explore the justifications that states use to avoid condemnation for the use of force on the territory of another state, as well as an account of the diversity of feminist knowledge that might be drawn into such a study. We undertake this study in a climate where the vast amount of academic writing and policy initiatives on gender and conflict focus on women, peace and security with little account of the law on the use of force. Given the placement of the women, peace and security agenda within the work of the Security Council, the prior chapter critiqued the Council's complicity in militarism. However, in

41. Jennifer Bond and Laurel Sherret, 'Mapping Gender and the Responsibility to Protect: Seeking Intersections, Finding Parallels' (2012) 4 (2) Global Responsibility to Protect 133, 135

42. Security Council Resolution 1970 (26 February 2011) UN Doc. S/RES/1970; Security Council Resolution 1973 (17 March 2011) UN Doc. S/RES/1973

43. Orford, above note 32

44. Heathcote, above note 1, ch 4

45. Charlesworth, 'Discipline of Crisis', above note 12

this chapter we are concerned with the continued capacity of states to bypass the scrutiny of the Security Council and the continued deployment of unilateral force across a range of situations. Integral to this analysis, we argue, is an account of how power operates to facilitate and perpetuate the use of unilateral force by some actors and not others.

It is important to note the consequences of the limited feminist analysis of unilateral force. First, ongoing military violence, such as Turkish violence against Kurdish communities both on its own territory and in Iraq and Syria, as well as unilateral strikes by the UK and the US against the Syrian state, remains unregulated under international law. We draw attention to this because of the specific development of the radical democracy model in Kurdish enclaves in Syria and through self-governance structures within Turkey, as well as the specific escalations of violence, represented as self-defence, by the Turkish state that were happening as we finished the manuscript.[46] For feminist scholars it is important to note the convergence of the failure of the international community to condemn state military acts with the important role women, and feminist methodologies, play in the articulation of radical democracy from the Kurdish governance structures.[47] Second, unilateral force is often justified through a staging of 'rogue' versus 'good' states, for example, the deployment of force against Syria's chemical weapons by the US and its allies in April 2017 and April 2018. Each of these acts, and undoubtedly more, risk disrupting the security of many more than they save and ultimately embed not only tropes of military masculinity but also hegemonic masculinity as a (civilizing) force for good. A feminist analysis of unilateral force helps to further understand the relationship between law and violence, as well as the gendered underpinnings of the relationship, to incorporate a temporal and geographic account of power, privilege and the entrenched masculinity of force as a solution. Third, the language deployed by states, and some scholars, to justify and explain unilateral force fundamentally undermines the Charter system through the embedding of quasi-legal language that obscures the patriarchal, masculinist modes of decision-making and military mindsets. Transnational histories of feminist activism disrupt the false dichotomy between absolute spaces of war and peace that unilateral

46. Ofra Bengio, 'Game Changers: Kurdish Women in Peace and War' (2016) 70 (1) The Middle East Journal 30, 36–7

47. Abdullah Öcalan, *The Political Thought of Abdullah Öcalan: Kurdistan, Woman's Revolution and Democratic Confederalism* (Pluto Press 2017)

force helps create, and argue for a feminist security structure that holds *peace* and security, defined by the everyday, as a model for international relations and law.

State practice and unilateral force

This section examines state justifications for unilateral force and outlines a range of potential feminist enquiries prompted by both state practice and institutional responses. The first subsection examines self-defence as a justification for force to outline how gendered concepts become embedded in and normalized through law. The following subsection introduces legal accounts of unilateral humanitarian intervention to explore how narratives of protection articulated by states replicate gendered accounts of law that have been critiqued as essentialist. We examine the gendered effects of humanitarian intervention and the value of gender analysis for reorienting the call for a right to unilateral humanitarian interventions by states. Through examining these various justifications for unilateral state force we articulate, on the one hand, a feminist frustration with the continued turn to military force as an enforcement mechanism within international law and, on the other hand, a commitment to moving beyond mainstream US accounts of gender (liberal, radical) that insufficiently examine gender in terms of its investment in other power arrangements and the history of gender deployed as a civilizing tool via legal reform.[48]

Self-defence

Self-defence forms the primary justification for unilateral force used by states. That is, the existence of self-defence is perceived as uncontroversial and universally accepted by states as a justification for force. However, what the right to self-defence includes and excludes remains unclear.[49] Self-defence is established under customary international law and through the UN Charter (Article 51) as an inherent right of states.

---

48. Catherine Powell, 'How Women Could Save the World, if Only We Would Let Them: From Gender Essentialism to Inclusive Security' (2017) 28 Yale Journal of Law & Feminism 271

49. Christine Gray, *International Law and the Use of Force* (4th edn, Oxford University Press 2018) 120

However, the precise contours of the right of states to act in self-defence have always been subject to controversy: from the nature of what constitutes an armed attack for the purposes of self-defence to the possibility of states to use pre-emptive force. Heathcote argues,

> [t]he space for a feminist analysis of the key and accepted components of Article 51 has been made increasingly difficult by the contemporary narrative surrounding preemptive self-defence and the right to use force to combat terrorism.[50]

Heathcote also provides an analysis of the requirements that self-defence be both proportionate and necessary; principles of international law on which there is widespread consensus as applying to the right of self-defence.[51] In this section we present the accepted contours of Article 51, as articulated in the UN Charter, to provide a feminist analysis of the threshold for self-defence.[52] This is followed by an analysis of Russia's account of its use of force as the protection of nationals abroad and the use of self-defence by the Turkish state to justify its attacks on Kurdish communities in northern Syria to illustrate the poverty of the continued acceptance of the existence of a right of states to use military force unilaterally through the self-defence justification.

To advance the substantive (or structural) critique of the right of states to use force in self-defence, a structural bias feminist analysis looks for gendered concepts embedded and normalized by law. Heathcote's earlier account examines the gendered contours of the right which we expand here through an analysis of the armed attack requirement in Article 51. That is, Article 51 states: 'Nothing in the present Charter shall impair the inherent right of individual or collective self-defence if an armed attack occurs'.[53] In the *Nicaragua* case, the US argued that its deployment of support and financing for non-state actors in Nicaragua (the Contras) constituted a form of collective self-defence (on behalf of El Salvador). The ICJ found that under both customary international

50. Heathcote, above note 1, 107
51. Judith Gardam, *Necessity, Proportionality and the Use of Force by States* (Cambridge University Press 2009)
52. *Military and Paramilitary Activities in and against Nicaragua (Nicaragua v United States of America)* (Merits) [1986] ICJ Rep 14; *Oil Platforms (Islamic Republic of Iran v United States of America)* (Merits) [2003] ICJ Rep 161
53. Charter of the United Nations, 26 June 1945

law and the UN Charter, self-defence required an armed attack to have occurred and that the requirements of proportionality and necessity were not met.[54] The Court found:

> Even at a time when the arms flow was at its peak, and again assuming the participation of the Nicaraguan Government, that would not constitute such armed attack.[55]

The Court thus goes on to find that, in the absence of an armed attack from Nicaragua against another state (the US or any perceived ally):

> ... the appraisal of the United States activities in relation to the criteria of necessity and proportionality takes on a different significance. As a result of this conclusion of the Court, even if the United States activities in question had been carried on in strict compliance with the canons of necessity and proportionality, they would not thereby become lawful.[56]

In addition to establishing the requirement that there needs to be an actual armed attack for the right of states to act in self-defence to be triggered under international law, the Court established the effective control test as a means to establish the responsibility of states for the acts of non-state actors.[57]

In the decades after the *Nicaragua* case, important shifts regarding the threshold for the use of force against non-state actors have been made in relation to the use of unilateral military force against terrorist actors. Initially in response to the attacks by Al-Qaida on US soil in September 2001 and articulated by the then US President George Bush as a form of pre-emptive self-defence, subsequent state practice has seen the justification for attacks on the territory of another state argued as existing when the host state is unwilling or unable to control the activities of non-state actors. For Tsagourias these arguments shift international law on self-defence such that '[s]elf-defence then becomes a complementary means of enforcing international law'.[58] State practice

54. *Nicaragua*, above note 52, paragraph 237
55. Ibid., paragraph 230
56. Ibid., paragraph 237
57. Ibid., paragraph 115
58. Nicholas Tsagourias, 'Self-defence against Non-state Actors: The Interaction between Self-defence as a Primary Rule and Self-defence as a Secondary Rule' (2016) 29 (3) Leiden Journal of International Law 801, 812

aligned with this position has been evident in relation to the use of force against ISIS in Syria and Iraq between 2014 and 2019 and the Turkish justifications for the use of force in the Kurdish enclaves in Rojava in northern Syria.[59] The language of unwilling or unable changes the threshold for self-defence and merits further interrogation.

Tsagourias' analysis finds the use of the unwilling or unable test, a significantly lower standard than the Nicaragua effective control test, shifts self-defence away from the armed attack requirement such that:

> … treating self-defence as a means of enforcing international law is not only contrary to the nature of self-defence which is about defence and protection from attacks but also conflates self-defence with the law of state responsibility and in particular with the institution of countermeasures which are decentralized means of enforcing international obligations when a state is unable or unwilling to address or redress wrongfulness.[60]

Tsagourias' solution is to distinguish between the primary right of states to use force in self-defence when activated by an armed attack and 'self-defence as a secondary rule in the law of state responsibility which excuses responsibility for the incidental breach of the territorial state's sovereignty in the course of self-defence' (against a non-state actor).[61] de Wet arrives at a similar conclusion when she argues for 'an exacting standard of necessity' to 'assist in preventing an abusive or pre-textual invocation of the right to self-defence'.[62] The consequence being a significant shifting from the threshold of an armed attack under the *Nicaragua* rule, so that attacks against non-state actors, justified as self-defence, are framed as inevitable and with necessary consequences for the state whose territory the attacks are undertaken on. This largely semantic enquiry undertaken by scholars bypasses, at all stages, the impact of the use of self-defence as an enforcement measure. Whether

59. Ibid., 808; 'Letter dated 9 October 2019 from the Permanent Representative of Turkey to the United Nations addressed to the President of the Security Council' (9 October 2019) UN Doc. S/2019/804

60. Tsagourias, above note 58, 813

61. Tsagourias, ibid., 825

62. Erika de Wet, 'The Invocation of the Right to Self-defence in Response to Armed Attacks Conducted by Armed Groups: Implications for Attribution' (2019) 32 Leiden Journal of International Law 91, 110

against states or against non-state actors, as the imagined military action is articulated as necessary and thus the effects – the deaths and the destruction – are simply regarded as the inevitability of an international legal system that retains, alongside the prohibition on the use of force, the self-defence justification. As such, although the Bush doctrine of pre-emptive self-defence seems to have not received widespread endorsement from states – or scholars – the language of self-defence as justified when states are unable or unwilling to halt the activities of non-state actors on their territory has infiltrated and transformed the landscape of unilateral force. A feminist analysis of pre-emptive or 'pre-textual' self-defence might ask about the manner in which those under attack by this form of military force are feminized, as non-state actors, as rogue groups and as chaotic, disordered threats to the stability of sovereign states. The complicity of powerful states in the mobilization of violent non-state actors, such as ISIS, or the failures of the international community to recognize and protect alternative political framings, such as in Rojava, is thus subsumed by legal language that maintains violence, even when outside the Charter paradigm, as an enforcement mechanism.

States, including Australia, France, the UK and the US, all used military force on the territory of Syria between 2014 and 2019 against ISIS on the grounds that the Syrian state was unable to minimize the threat posed by ISIS.[63] That this threat was predominantly to the Syrian people did not invoke a right to collective self-defence on behalf of Syria; rather, each state argued a version of individual self-defence against global terrorist actors to justify the use of force in Syria because, following the *Nicaragua* case, collective self-defence would require a call for assistance from Syria as the state under attack.[64] This illustrates the distinction Tsagourias makes between self-defence as an enforcement measure and as a secondary rule, as opposed to self-defence in response to an armed attack and as a primary rule. Over the same period, Russia justified military force in Syria as occurring with the consent of the host state and the UK and the US made similar claims with regard to the use of force in Iraq.[65]

63. Monica Hakimi, 'Defensive Force against Non-state Actors: The State of Play' (2015) 91 International Law Studies 1
64. *Nicaragua*, above note 52, paragraph 195. Justifications based on collective self-defence were also put forward, but on behalf of Iraq
65. Tsagourias, above note 58, 808–9

Additional justifications for unilateral force as self-defence have similarly been voiced by Turkey to justify its military incursions into both Syria and Iraq against Kurdish actors over a much longer period of time – using the language of 'unwilling and unable' to address the incursions into the territory of another state despite the absence of actual armed attacks against the Turkish state.[66] In 1997 the Turkish government agreed to compensate Iraq on the grounds that 'violations of Iraq's territory and airspace' had occurred and that 'human suffering [was] inflicted on Iraqi citizens'.[67] As we write this book in 2019, the Turkish state has embarked on a series of deadly attacks on the regions of Syria under Kurdish control and has justified this 'to counter the imminent terrorist threat' and thus as a unilateral use of force, justified as self-defence against terrorist actors.[68] The post-millennium military incursions by Turkey into Iraq and Syria, alongside those by numerous states into Syria on the grounds of self-defence against terrorist actors (ISIS), all remain expansions of the grounds for unilateral force that incur significant consequences for the states on whose territory the attacks are conducted, including the elimination of infrastructure, loss of civilian life and livelihoods, the destruction of cultural property and the displacement of large sections of the population. Turkish attacks on the Syrian territory, although articulated as against ISIS and various Kurdish groups, have been largely confined to the regions controlled by Kurdish actors. The focus of both state and scholarly preoccupations is the legal terms that justify the use of force.

Two important aspects remain hidden in such an approach. First, the limited number of states this expansive form of unilateral force, articulated as self-defence, is available to is symptomatic of global inequalities between states that remain embedded in the language of self-defence and use of military violence. Second, the reality of military force – while achieving the goals of foreign states – as perpetuating insecurity in the state on which the unilateral force is deployed, regardless of whether that force is mobilized against the state or non-state actors operating on the territory of the targeted state. These contemporary developments in the law on self-defence have

66. Tsagourias, above note 58, 824

67. 'Identical Letters Dated 14 June 1997 from the Permanent Representative of Iraq to the United Nations Addressed to the Secretary-General and to the President of the Security Council' (16 June 1997) UN Doc. S/1997/461

68. Turkish letter to Security Council, above note 59

parallels to the development of unilateral humanitarian interventions analysed below. A feminist analysis of self-defence needs to focus on the role of language used to disguise the violence being both enacted and responded to, as well as the perpetuation of unilateral force as an enforcement mechanism open to some states but not all, despite the Charter seemingly definitively prohibiting the use of force on the territory of another state. In the cases under discussion, and many others, earlier anxieties about the form of self-defence (anticipatory, pre-emptive) are displaced by the legal analysis of primary and secondary rules,[69] attribution and necessity under the Articles on the Responsibility of States for Internationally Wrongful Acts,[70] the meaning of unable and unwilling,[71] or whether a non-state actor can be responsible, under international law, for an armed attack within the meaning of Article 51.[72]

All of these understandings of self-defence shift the debates of international lawyers away from recognition of the consequences of military force towards the imagined position where military force can be rationally discussed as a solution to the use of force. Indeed Klabbers argues that 'this is how it should be.'[73] His analysis of the variations of language in relation to the use of unilateral force by states recognizes the necessity of '[p]olitical actors ... to be able to keep wriggle room available for political settlements.'[74] But, is this how it *should* be? Klabbers argues against precision in the classifications of unilateral force on the grounds that 'precise classifications and qualifications' only lead to indeterminacy as states argue whether specific behaviours fall within the precise classification.[75] Interestingly, Klabbers concludes that 'the law on the use of force needs to be able to accommodate

69. Tsagourias, above note 58
70. de Wet, above note 62
71. Ashley Deeks, '"Unwilling or Unable": Toward a Normative Framework for Extraterritorial Self-defense' (2012) 52 Virginia Journal International Law 483
72. Tom Ruys, '*Armed Attack' and Article 51 of the UN Charter: Evolutions in Customary Law and Practice* (Cambridge University Press 2010)
73. Jan Klabbers, 'Intervention, Armed Intervention, Armed Attack, Threat to Peace, Act of Aggression, and Threat or Use of Force: What's the Difference?' in Marc Weller (ed), *The Oxford Handbook of the Use of Force in International Law* (Oxford University Press 2015) 505
74. Klabbers, ibid.
75. Klabbers, ibid., 504

the imperative of peace-making'.[76] Nevertheless, how the law on the use of force, and unilateral force in particular, accommodates peace while tolerating the continued use of military force is not clear. In distinction to legal accounts of unilateral force, feminist approaches on insecurity, militarism and conflict have been centred on everyday security, peace and anti-militarism, including stopping the arms trade, while campaigning for the non-proliferation and prohibition of nuclear weapons.[77] We argue that until the law on the use of force is responsive to accounts of peace it becomes merely a tool to tolerate the perpetual violence of some states.

The use of military force by Turkey against Kurdish communities in both Iraq and Syria is illustrative of the failures of the current legal regime regarding self-defence, the notion of an armed attack and the shifting parameters of what constitutes a breach of international law. While the nature of an armed attack remains controversial, other types of unilateral force also fall under the threshold of Article 51 and would benefit from feminist enquiry and analysis. For example, the use of force by Turkey against Kurdish actors in both Iraq and Syria, as noted above, has been articulated as a form of self-defence. The attacks in 2019 did result in a Security Council debate, although no resolution was adopted. For the Kurdish communities, spread across Turkey, Iraq and Syria, the attacks constitute a sustained cross-generational campaign by the Turkish government to frustrate any forms of Kurdish self-governance from flourishing. Feminist scholarship has highlighted the activism of female military actors, political actors and community organizers in Kurdish communities as well as the gendered power relations that construct and underpin the impunity with which Turkey targets Kurdish communities both on its territory and abroad.[78]

The Russian use of force in Ukraine from 2014, which resulted in the annexation of Crimea and the subsequent Russian assertions of military power in the Black Sea, has led to multiple readings from scholars, insufficient response from other states and ultimately the expansion of

76. Klabbers, ibid., 506

77. Claire Duncanson, 'Anti-militarist Feminist Approaches to Researching Gender and the Military' in Rachel Woodward and Claire Duncanson (eds), *The Palgrave International Handbook of Gender and the Military* (Palgrave 2017)

78. Bengio, above note 46; Lucie Drechselová and Adnan Çelik (eds), *Kurds in Turkey: Ethnographies of Heterogenous Experiences* (Lexington Books 2019); Meral Düzgün, 'Jineology: The Kurdish Women's Movement' (2016) 12 (2) Journal of Middle East Women's Studies 284

Russian control of both land and sea territory. In academic literature there has been a general acceptance of a *de facto* change of control over the territory of Crimea.[79] We challenge feminist scholars to ask what role a gender analysis might play here. Although argued by Russia as a protection of nationals abroad, this example demonstrates the poverty of justifications for unilateral force. This is a deeply gendered justification that imagines force as the ultimate form of diplomacy and raises questions about the maintenance of force at the apex of international enforcement mechanisms. The subsequent control of Crimea by Russia ignores the displacement of civilians that did not regard themselves as aligned with the Russian state and reinforces a gendered divide between military-powerful and militarily vulnerable states.

The study of gender and conflict as a field of research does give some indicators of the types of analysis that might be embarked upon from a feminist perspective. For example, Cohn's study of her 'close encounters with nuclear strategic analysis' in 1984 remains a necessary guide for the feminist scholar seeking to contribute to understand the modes in which language and law embed and normalize military violence.[80] The study of unilateral force and, in particular, the uses of force in self-defence against terrorist actors and to protect nationals abroad are underpinned by a structural bias in international law that genders states and genders military force: such that these perpetrators of military aggression not only remain outside of the collective security structure, but are also for the most part successful in the acquisition of territory and/or the suppression of dissent.

Humanitarian intervention

In April 2017, and again in April 2018, the UK, France and the US conducted joint strikes on the territory of Syria targeting facilities believed to be housing chemical weapons. The attacks involved the deployment of over 50 missiles in 2017 and over 100 were fired in 2018.[81] Unlike earlier attacks on Syrian territory, these attacks were

79. Christian Marxsen, 'The Crimea Crisis – An International Law Perspective' (2014) 74 (2) Heidelberg Journal of International Law 367

80. Carol Cohn, 'Sex and Death in the Rational World of Defense Intellectuals' (1987) 12 (4) Signs: A Journal of Women in Culture and Society 687

81. BBC News Online, 'Syria Air Strikes: US and Allies Attack "Chemical Weapons Sites"' *BBC News* 14 April 2018 https://www.bbc.co.uk/news/world-middle-east-43762251 (accessed December 2019); Barber, above note 17

not against ISIS, were not acknowledged by the Security Council[82] and were not justified by the attacking states on the grounds of self-defence.[83] The April military attacks, in 2017 and again in 2018, targeted chemical weapons facilities in Syria and thus were attacks against Syrian state/military targets on Syrian territory. Under international law, this constitutes a breach of Article 2(4) of the UN Charter. Even where commentators have articulated the possibility that humanitarian intervention might emerge as a customary international law right outside of the UN Charter, they have expressed considerable caution.[84] Nevertheless, Schmitt and Ford use the attacks against Syria to conclude:

> What we may be witnessing, then, is the slow and somewhat painful birth of a nascent right in customary international law allowing States to act forcefully to put an end to the use of particularly repugnant weaponry against a civilian population, or perhaps even one countenancing forceful State responses to other egregious forms of terrorizing and massacring civilian populations in other countries.[85]

Schmitt and Ford argue that while the use of force in Syria in April 2017[86] would not constitute an intervention that can be justified on humanitarian grounds, the right to humanitarian intervention likely exists, such that:

82. Cf Security Council Resolution 2249 (20 November 2015) UN Doc. S/RES/2249

83. Tsagourias, above note 58, 808; Michael N Schmitt and Christopher M Ford, 'Assessing U.S. Justifications for Using Force in Response to Syria's Chemical Attacks: An International Law Perspective' (2017) 9 Journal of National Security Law and Policy 283, 288–90

84. Thomas Franck, 'Humanitarian and Other Interventions' (2005) 43 Columbia Journal of Transnational Law 326

85. Schmitt and Ford, above note 83, 303

86. NB: there was a second period of strikes in April 2018; however, this is not discussed in Schmitt and Ford, above note 83, which was published in 2017; for an analysis of the 2018 strikes, see Andrew Bell, 'Syria, Chemical Weapons, and a Qualitative Threshold for Humanitarian Intervention' *Just Security* 10 April 2018 https://www.justsecurity.org/54665/syria-chemical-weapons-international-law-developing-qualitative-threshold-humanitarian-intervention/ (accessed December 2019); Barber, above note 17

it is becoming increasingly difficult to deny that, if it has not already crystallized as some suggest, a right of humanitarian intervention is emerging. States clearly find it legitimate to intervene in cases of severe humanitarian crisis, even if a corresponding legal right does not definitively exist. Repeated actions based on legitimacy are fertile ground for the growth of new customary norms.[87]

Furthermore, Schmitt and Ford draw out *opinio juris* with regard to humanitarian intervention across a range of contexts, including as argued by the UK in relation to attacks on chemical weapons facilities in Syria, claiming the lawfulness of humanitarian intervention rested on the need 'to alleviate the scale of the overwhelming humanitarian catastrophe in Syria by deterring and disrupting the further use of chemical weapons by the Syrian regime',[88] and statements from the Dutch and Belgian governments to justify the use of force in the former Serbian province of Kosovo in 1999.[89] Nevertheless, Schmitt and Ford conclude that the attacks against Syrian chemical weapons facilities are outside of the right to humanitarian intervention (if it exists) because of the prior small-scale harms inflicted by the Syrian state in its use of chemical weapons, although they do not preclude the development of a right to respond to the type of harm (in this case chemical weapons) as opposed to the scale of harm.[90] Schmitt and Ford argue that the US and allied attacks against Syria simultaneously strengthen the shift towards the crystallization of the right to humanitarian intervention even if these attacks are not themselves undertaken on sufficient grounds to be accepted as within the requirements of such a right. Their argument for the latter position is that the chemical weapons use by Syria had led to the deaths of 83 civilians and 293 injuries which they argue is insufficient to justify a humanitarian intervention outside of the collective security architecture.[91] To make this claim, Schmitt

87. Schmitt and Ford, above note 83, 300
88. Statement, 'Office of the Prime Minister, Chemical Weapon Use by Syrian Regime: UK Government Legal Position' 29 August 2013 http://www.gov.uk/government/publications/chemical-weapon-use-by-syrian-regime-uk-government-legal-position (accessed December 2019)
89. Schmitt and Ford, above note 83, 295
90. Ibid., 303
91. Human Rights Council, 'Report of the Independent International Commission of Inquiry on the Syrian Arab Republic' (8 August 2017) UN Doc. A/HRC/36/55

and Ford ignore the non-intervention into the ongoing Syrian crisis, including the attacks on civilian targets such as health and medical facilities,[92] and ignore the non-interventions into Myanmar, Yemen and other states over the same period.[93] Ultimately, Schmitt and Ford also rely on a limited number of states in their analysis, mostly in the west and largely with powerful militaries, to establish *opinio juris* in favour of humanitarian intervention. Importantly, those states more likely to be the subject of interventions are not given a voice in shaping what is perceived as an emerging customary international law right.

In contrast to Schmitt and Ford's analysis, it is possible to argue that the US and UK strikes are evidence that a right to humanitarian intervention has *not* crystallized into customary international law and remain a breach of the principle of non-intervention and the prohibition on the use of force as they are articulated in the UN Charter. The US and UK strikes in April 2017, and again in April 2018, on the Syrian territory targeting chemical weapons facilities in the name of humanitarianism must be juxtaposed with the push back from states in the global south on the incorporation of a right to unilateral force on humanitarian grounds embedded within responsibility to protect.[94] From a postcolonial feminist perspective, it is important to identify the global temporalities that replay in military interventions, as well as the gendered insecurities, gendered discourses and their intersection with racialized and civilizing histories.[95]

Returning to the women, peace and security agenda, the identification of conflict-related sexual violence as a potential threat to international peace and security continues to haunt feminist approaches and leaves available to powerful states/regional hegemons discourses to use the language of saving women in foreign territories. If histories of international interventions, under the guise of colonialism, trusteeship and mandatory powers, are held in the frame, the production of

---

92. Diana Rayes, Miriam Orcutt, Aula Abbara and Wasim Maziak, 'Systematic Destruction of Healthcare in Eastern Ghouta, Syria' (2018) 360 British Medical Journal 1368

93. Barber, above note 17

94. Pınar Gözen Ercan, 'UN General Assembly Dialogues on the Responsibility to Protect and the Use of Force for Humanitarian Purposes' (2019) 11 (3) Global Responsibility to Protect 313, 330

95. Vasuki Nesiah, 'Resistance in the Age of Empire: Occupied Discourse Pending Investigation' (2006) 27 (5) Third World Quarterly 903

discourses around gender-based violence and the regulation of sexuality can be identified as a technique of exporting assumed civilized modes of regulation. A postcolonial feminist analysis of humanitarian intervention thus identifies and challenges the implicitly gendered narratives of intervention and humanitarianism.

This appears not only in unilateral justifications for humanitarian intervention but equally in the subtle shift away from responsibility to protect towards the protection of civilians within Security Council activity.[96] This is mimicked in other institutional spaces, such as the General Assembly where the account of responsibility to protect shifts to recognize the protection of civilians agenda.[97] Heathcote's analysis emphasizes how the protection of civilians returns to saving women mantras to underpin and reinforce the authorization for military force by the international community. A similar analysis is necessary in the interrogation of powerful state articulations – and practice – with respect to the deployment of unilateral force. The humanitarian concern within state justifications strategically distinguishes between military and humanitarian goals and within the humanitarian concern implicitly addresses all that is not military, including women, children and civilians. The construction of vulnerability elsewhere and internal to states that are otherwise disconnected from the space of international norm making is gendered at multiple levels whilst reproducing the ideologies of empire, power and civilization that inflect the history of international law. This analysis prompts a need for further feminist interrogation in terms of the Security Council's turn to use the language of the protection of civilians rather than the responsibility to protect, alongside the emergent state use of unilateral humanitarian justifications.[98] Importantly, the emphasis on conflict-related sexual violence in the women, peace and security resolutions, which then re-emerges in most protection of civilians mandates, might be returned to as a warning sign of the risks of military intervention, rather than a justification for future military endeavours, unilateral or collective.

---

96. Heathcote, above note 15
97. Ercan, above note 94, 303
98. Haidi Willmot, Ralph Mamiya, Scott Sheeran and Marc Weller (eds), *Protection of Civilians* (Oxford University Press 2016)

Intersectional and structural bias analysis of unilateral force

This chapter is concerned with what a feminist analysis of unilateral force looks like. The gendered effects of military interventions extend from the gender dynamics of military mindsets and military communities to the gendered consequences of military attacks on the communities in the vicinity of the attacks.[99] On the other hand, and for the purposes of this chapter, what is of interest is the relative silence from those working on gender and conflict with regard to international legal debates on the use of unilateral force beyond recognition of the gendered effects of military activity. Feminist analysis has been sparse in its analysis of justifications for unilateral force as self-defence, the use of force with the consent of the host state or via articulation of a right to humanitarian intervention.[100]

In this chapter we have examined how unilateral force often remains unregulated and unexamined under international law while other forms of unilateral force are often justified through a staging of 'rogue' versus 'good' states, perpetuating colonial dynamics. In addition, the language deployed by states, and some scholars, to justify and explain unilateral force fundamentally undermines the Charter system through the embedding of quasi-legal language that obscures the patriarchal, masculinist modes of decision-making and military mindsets. In this final section of the chapter, we introduce feminist methodologies that, we argue, have the potential to arrest and transform the status quo of unilateral force as a mechanism relied upon by states to bypass the collective security regime. We examine intersectionality and structural bias feminisms as means to re-examine and develop a feminist analysis of unilateral force.

Gender as intersectional

Scholarly accounts of, and state justifications for, unilateral force occasionally note gender, or rather women's lives, as a reason for the deployment of unilateral military force. More often, and certainly in each of the examples discussed in this chapter, women's lives are either ignored or implicitly included in the claim as force is deployed to protect

99. Cohn, above note 80; Enloe, above note 14
100. Gina Heathcote, 'Humanitarian Intervention and Gender Dynamics' in Fionnuala Ní Aoláin, Naomi Cahn, Dina Francesca Haynes and Nahla Valji (eds), *The Oxford Handbook of Gender and Conflict* (Oxford University Press 2018)

civilian communities. Our project is to attempt to move beyond an approach that would simply 'add' women's lives to these accounts of why unilateral military force can be justified. Both conflict-related sexual violence and gender-based violence have been articulated, by a range of actors and in a range of contexts, as potential justifications for military force.[101] Not only do these approaches support the continued operations of military force deployed in the 'crisis' moment to save women from other men's violence, these approaches incorporate and understand women's lives as lived uniformly, as always at risk and vulnerable to male violence, including state violence, and ignore the role of mainstream gender politics as entrenched in power relations with other sites of power, including race, class, sexuality and ableism. To arrest a feminist account of unilateral force that potentially collapses back into support of military endeavours to 'save' women, we argue that there is a need for a conscious incorporation of intersectional feminist methodologies.

Feminist intersectionality is a concept that has numerous manifestations and which, at times, has been subject to intense scrutiny via internal feminist debates. Two core sites of development have been in the scholarship of critical race scholars in the US and Black British feminisms in the UK.[102] In international law, important contributions appear in relation to human rights, and the CEDAW in particular, as well as an emergent set of scholarship on women, peace and security.[103] As a

101. Catharine A MacKinnon, 'Women's September 11th: Rethinking the International Law of Conflict' (2006) 47 Harvard International Law Journal 1

102. Jennifer Nash, *Black Feminism Reimagined: After Intersectionality* (Duke University Press 2019); Gail Lewis, 'Questions of Presence' (2017) 117 (1) Feminist Review 1; Avtar Brah, *Cartographies of Diaspora: Contesting Identities* (Routledge 1996) ch 8; Lola Okolosie, 'Beyond "Talking" and "Owning" Intersectionality' (2014) 108 Feminist Review 90

103. Beth Goldblatt, 'Intersectionality in International Anti-discrimination Law: Addressing Poverty in its Complexity' (2015) 21 (1) Australian Journal of Human Rights 47; Meghan Campbell, 'CEDAW and Women's Intersecting Identities: A Pioneering New Approach to Intersectional Discrimination' (2015) 11 (2) Direito GV Law Review 479; Loveday Hodson, 'Women's Rights and the Periphery: CEDAW's Optional Protocol' (2014) 25 (2) European Journal of International Law 561; Nazila Ghanea, 'Intersectionality and the Spectrum of Racist Hate Speech: Proposals to the UN Committee on the Elimination of Racial Discrimination' (2013) 35 (4) Human Rights Quarterly 935; Deborah Stienstra, 'WPS, Gender, and Disabilities' in Davies and True, above note 10

feminist methodology, intersectionality is often plagued with charges of functioning as a form of identity politics where categories of inclusion and exclusion function to solidify rather than undo power relations. Such an approach ignores the core contribution of intersectionality, which is to identify and draw attention to the workings of power at the intersection of categories of social ordering and differentiation rather than to assume the categories as fixed, constant or deterministic. While significant work on intersectionality examines the relationship between race and gender as intertwined power relations, the intersections between gender, sexuality, race, religion, ethnicities, class and ableism are all aspects of feminist methodologies that seek to draw in an intersectional praxis.

The modes of unilateral force discussed in this chapter, self-defence, humanitarian interventions, the protection of nationals abroad, even the consent of host states, as a precursor to unilateral force on the territory of another state, would benefit from an intersectional feminist methodology. That is, rather than an insertion of gender frames that work to include women's harms into the discourse, we argue for feminist approaches that examine how gender frames are *already* co-opted into justifications for unilateral military force and how gender understood in this way embeds further gendered inequalities, including heteronormativity, ableism and economic power, as well as discrimination on the grounds of ethnicity and religion.

Following the analysis in this chapter, it can be seen that Russia's annexation of Crimea, France's use of force in Mali,[104] the UK and the US military attacks on Syrian chemical weapons facilities,[105] Chinese arming of fishers in the South China Sea[106] and the use of force against Uyghur Muslims[107] are all acts of military force, justified in multiple ways and outside the structure of the collective security regime. The use of force by the permanent members of the Security Council reinforces a model of international law, mimicked by some states, such as Turkey, where military force is regarded as a means to effect change and to enforce a specific worldview. The space for gender analysis, of each of these military endeavours and for unilateral force more broadly, should be underpinned by a perception of civilians as feminized in

---

104. Bergamaschi, above note 16, 20; Stigall, above note 16
105. Barber, above note 17
106. Kennedy, above note 18
107. Chung, above note 19

their need for protection and states as masculinized via their capacity to deploy force as a solution. The consequences are not just gendered; rather the consequences, the deaths, the maiming, the legacies of vulnerability are gendered, raced and classed and fused with discourses of heteronormativity and ableism. A feminist analysis of unilateral force, whether in self-defence, in the name of humanitarianism, for the protection of nationals abroad or with the cloak of consent, develops an understanding of international law that at a deep structural level remains biased and which would benefit from intersectional understandings of power and privilege.

To end we wish to return to the *Nicaragua* case, discussed above, which focused on the principle of non-intervention and asserted its importance as a principle of international law. Debates on unilateral force, which often also question the shield of sovereignty and the need for human rights to be protected proactively by the international community, might draw in feminist accounts of the domestic sphere and its gendered formations; yet, the consequence of military interventions on the territory of foreign states is, in a system that preserves the use of force as the ultimate prerogative of states, potentially more interventions and more justifications in contravention of Article 2(4) of the UN Charter. The consequences for international law of attending to and recognizing women's lives and gendered harms within a state (in the current international legal structure) risk lending towards more interventions in the aim of humanitarianism while there remains insufficient analysis of the neocolonial and gender dimensions of force as a solution. This remains a core problem in feminist work which calls for new kinds of feminist interventions that do not consider anti-militarism at the same time.

A focus on feminist anti-militarism thus demands an account of the complicity and impact of the use of force on peacetime states, as equally as on the states where force is deployed, and a focus on the everyday consequences of militarized thinking and solutions. In this chapter we have focused on state justifications for the use of force abroad outside of the collective security structure, identifying the way this inscribes great power politics and privilege into the UN era, fostering a legal system organized around military force as an adequate solution. Ultimately, this circles back to Charlesworth's argument that international law functions as a discipline of crisis – always focusing on whether to intervene or not to intervene, on legality or illegality, justified or unjustified, unilateral or collective – but does not address global and macro international power relations that propel force as a legitimate enforcement measure.

Chapter 3

COUNTERING TERRORISM

International law governing armed conflict has, in recent years, been increasingly shaped by the narrative of the so-called global war on terror. As discussed in the previous chapter, one of the consequences of the post-9/11 response has been the changing threshold for unilateral military force. Over the same period, Security Council resolutions have been adopted which link women, peace and security with strategies for countering terrorism and countering violent extremism. Explicit links were made between these two Security Council agendas in resolution 2122, in resolution 2129, a general resolution on terrorism which identifies a need to incorporate the women, peace and security framework into the work on counter-terrorism, and subsequently in the women, peace and security-focused resolutions 2242 and 2467.[1] This is by no means a new phenomenon, as exemplified by the 2001 deployment of military force in Afghanistan which was justified, in part, in the name of women's rights.[2]

Legal scholarship and global debates on gender and terrorism, including within the women, peace and security frame, largely focus on women as either victims of terrorism, as terrorists or as being useful in helping to counter terrorism. There is less focus, however, on the gendered structures and effects of counter-terrorism strategies. This chapter commences with a review of the debates on women and terrorism in contemporary feminist accounts before drawing on queer perspectives on terrorism, feminist work on everyday violence and postcolonial feminist scholarship to analyse the impact of the global

---

1. Security Council Resolution 2122 (18 October 2013) UN Doc. S/RES/2122; Security Council Resolution 2129 (17 December 2013) UN Doc. S/RES/2129; Security Council Resolution 2242 (13 October 2015) UN Doc. S/RES/2242; Security Council Resolution 2467 (23 April 2019) UN Doc. S/RES/2467

2. Dana L Cloud, '"To Veil the Threat of Terror": Afghan Women and the <Clash of Civilizations> in the imagery of the U.S. War on Terrorism' (2004) 90 (3) Quarterly Journal of Speech 285

shift towards countering terrorism on both international and domestic legal frameworks. We seek, by drawing in these various strands of scholarship, to consciously shift beyond the women and terrorism frame. We focus on the ways in which gender, sexuality, race and Islamophobia, among other factors including class, play out in the biopolitical and necropolitical[3] ordering of life through law in the era of counter-terrorism. The chapter seeks to apply a gender perspective to the erosion of international law, particularly international humanitarian law and human rights law, as well as to the utilization of lawfare, that is, the use of the law to justify military force, in counter-terrorism strategies.[4] At the same time, we use the chapter to examine how counter-terrorism strategies often operate at the margins of legality, increasing targeting and surveying while othering racialized, gendered and classed subjects. The chapter concludes with a discussion of everyday violence in the biopolitical ordering of the domestic sphere in the name of counter-terrorism identifying the intertwined relation between war and peace through a focus on the domestic implementation of counter-terrorism law and policy in the UK and France.

Women and terrorism

Scholarship focusing on terrorism and women can be described as falling into three core strands. The first strand, typified by some paragraphs of Security Council resolutions 2242 and 2467 on women, peace and security, consists of approaches which note the need to protect women

3. The term 'biopolitics' comes from the work of Michel Foucault who defined biopolitics as a form of positive politico-administrative power over life 'to ensure, sustain, and multiply life, to put this life in order ...'. Michel Foucault, *The Will to Knowledge: The History of Sexuality* Volume 1 (1976, trans. Robert Hurley, Penguin 1998) 138. Necropolitics, on the other hand, is a concept coined by Achille Mbembe which notes how the regulation of life and biopolitics has, in recent years, also shifted towards the regulation of death, that is, necropolitics, the power to decide who should live and who should die. See Achille Mbembe, 'Necropolitics' (2003) 15 (1) Public Culture 11
4. Eyal Weizman, 'Legislative Attack' (2010) 27 (6) Theory, Culture and Society 11; David Kennedy, 'Lawfare and Warfare' in James Crawford and Martti Koskenniemi (eds), *The Cambridge Companion to International Law* (Cambridge University Press 2012) 158

and girls from terrorist acts and the need to integrate women's groups into the countering terrorism and violent extremism agenda.[5] The second strand focuses on either the experiences and accounts of women within terrorist organizations or women as participants in counter-terrorism initiatives. Both these strands tend to be underpinned by and uphold essentialist ideas about women who are seen as either the 'wicked purveyors of extremist violence or virtuous saviours of sons, husbands and communities'.[6] The third set of literature, however, seeks to move beyond the study of female actors in relation to terrorism and counter-terrorism discourse to build a feminist or queer analysis of the gendered dynamics of counter-terrorism. In this section we focus on the first two strands before moving on, in the next section, to discuss the third.

While much feminist work has sought to resist racialized and Islamophobic counter-terrorism discourse, some feminist interactions with the law have also worked to re-enforce this narrative.[7] This can be seen, in particular, within the first strand of scholarship on gender and terrorism which focuses on the need to protect women from terrorism and terrorists, as well as the idea that women are a useful tool in countering terrorism and violent extremism. The focus on vulnerable women and 'good' women is something which was adopted by the Security Council in 2015 with resolution 2242. Prior to 2242, the women, peace and security agenda was largely focused on combating sexual violence and women's participation in peace processes and conflict resolution. However, 2242 added a new focus, noting the rise in 'violent extremism'. Civilians are often victims of terrorist activities. These harms are gendered and often women will suffer in different and disproportionate ways at the hands of such groups (as well as at the hands of military and combatant groups). However, the specific focus on women as victims and as needing special protection from terrorist groups, including from sexual violence, can be problematic. Resolution 2242 links the counter-terrorism agenda and the women, peace and security agenda through rendering visible women's victimhood and assumed special

5. S/RES/2242, paragraphs 11–13; S/RES/2467, paragraph 28
6. Fionnuala Ní Aoláin, 'The "War on Terror" and Extremism: Assessing the Relevance of the Women, Peace and Security Agenda' (2016) 92 (2) International Affairs 282
7. Vasuki Nesiah, 'The Ground beneath Her Feet: "Third World" Feminisms' (2003) 4 (3) Journal of International Women's Studies 30

vulnerability. While reaffirming that, under certain circumstances, sexual violence 'may impede the restoration of international peace and security',[8] the resolution calls for greater attention to this violence through protection measures while 'expressing deep concern that acts of sexual and gender-based violence are known to be part of the strategic objectives and ideology of certain terrorist groups'.[9] In 2019, the Security Council reaffirmed the focus on sexual violence as connected to terrorism through resolution 2467.[10] Nevertheless, resolution 2242 is not the first time women were represented as in need of particular protection from terrorist groups, with many authors having highlighted the issue of the special vulnerabilities of women as victims of terrorist attacks.[11]

The narrative described above works to focus on the gendered harms women face at the hands of terrorist groups, yet no attention is paid at this level to defining who these terrorists are. This occurs despite the fact that determining who is a terrorist and who is not is not always self-evident. The designation of which group is to be identified as terrorist is a powerful politico-strategic move which can be used to achieve conflict-related objectives. For instance, during the internal armed conflict in Nepal (1996–2006), the then Royal Nepal Army (RNA) imposed on the Government of Nepal a set of preconditions for its deployment in the conflict. These included the designation of the Communist Party of Nepal-Maoist (CPN-M) as a terrorist organization, the passing of

---

8. The circumstances given are that sexual violence is 'used or commissioned as a method or tactic of war or as a part of a widespread or systematic attack against civilian populations' S/RES/2242, preamble

9. Ibid.

10. S/RES/2467, paragraphs 6, 28, 29

11. Counter Extremism Project, 'ISIS's Persecution of Women' (2017) *Counter Extremism Project* https://www.counterextremism.com/sites/default/files/ISIS%20Persecution%20of%20Women_071117.pdf (accessed December 2019); Nikita Malik, 'Trafficking Terror: How Modern Slavery and Sexual Violence Fund Terrorism' (2017) *Henry Jackson Society* http://henryjacksonsociety.org/wp-content/uploads/2017/10/HJS-Trafficking-Terror-Report-web.pdf (accessed December 2019); Eki Omorogbe, 'The African Union, the Boko Haram Crisis and Violence against Women' (2017) 2 Ragion Pratica 437; International Crisis Group, 'Nigeria: Women and the Boko Haram Insurgency' (5 December 2016) 242 https://d2071andvip0wj.cloudfront.net/242-nigeria-women-and-the-boko-haram%20Insurgency.pdf (accessed December 2019)

anti-terrorist legislation and the declaration of a state of emergency in the areas of its intended deployment.[12] Far from being an exclusively domestic act, the labelling had international aims too. The OHCHR noted how the Government of Nepal attempted 'to link its campaign against the CPN (Maoist) in Nepal with more global concerns about terrorism … to seek international military support'.[13] The strategy paid off when Nepal received military equipment from the US as 'part of its commitment to eliminate terrorism'.[14] Similarly, the UK was reported having 'promised [a] comprehensive package of developmental and military assistance' to support 'the government of Nepal in its struggle against terrorism'.[15] The resources received and the legal measures that were eventually adopted[16] gave ample room for the RNA to manoeuvre. The deployment of the RNA coincided with a dramatic peak in conflict-related deaths.

In addition, for those living under the constant sound of drones and with the constant threat of a drone strike, the US or UK, as drone deploying states, could be seen as undertaking forms of state terror.[17] This is especially the case when one considers the various mental health impacts that have been found to be linked to living under drones.[18] Furthermore, drone strikes, too, have gendered applications

12. Aditya Adhikari, *The Bullet and the Ballot Box: The Story of Nepal's Maoist Revolution* (Verso 2014) 56

13. United Nations, Office of the United Nations High Commissioner for Human Rights, 'Nepal Conflict Report' (October 2012) 44 https://www.ohchr.org/Documents/Countries/NP/OHCHR_Nepal_Conflict_Report2012.pdf (accessed December 2019)

14. United Nations, ibid.

15. Seira Tamang, 'Historicizing State "Fragility" in Nepal' (2012) 17 (2) Studies in Nepali History and Society 267 citing 'UK Meet Pledges to Defeat Maoist Terror' 22 June 2002, *The Rising Nepal*

16. November 2001 Terrorist and Disruptive Activities (Control and Punishment) Ordinance (TADO) which was later successively reaffirmed and extended as Terrorist and Disruptive Activities (Control and Punishment) Act (TADA)

17. Ruth Blakeley, 'Drones, State Terrorism and International Law' (2018) 11 Critical Studies on Terrorism 321

18. Stanford International Human Rights & Conflict Resolution Clinic, 'Living under Drones: Death, Injury, and Trauma to Civilians from US Drone Practices in Pakistan' (2012) 80 https://www-cdn.law.stanford.edu/wp-content/uploads/2015/07/Stanford-NYU-LIVING-UNDER-DRONES.pdf (accessed December 2019)

and impacts.[19] Highlighting these factors does not, of course, excuse terrorist actors but does call for a questioning of how the international debates about these various actors are shaped, challenging the binary narrative of 'good' or 'bad' actors in the global order.[20] It is worth stressing that while the language of terrorist actors and acts of terrorism are regularly used in Security Council resolutions, who and what these actors and actions are, and thus the scope of resolutions such as 2242 and 2467, remain undefined.[21] This definitional ambiguity ultimately ensures that the definitions provided by powerful, dominant states, primarily in the global north, are rendered the norm. Moreover, the specific focus on women as vulnerable to harm from terrorist groups plays into broader narratives in international law in which women are seen inherently as victims and thus rarely as agents. This narrative promotes, once again, the hypervisibility of sexual violence in international law. While the need for eradication of sexual violence is not disputed, we argue that it is also important to continue to stress how a hyperfocus on this subject at the level of international governance does not necessarily help to achieve security for women. Rather, these focal points can work to silence the broader range of women's and gendered experiences of conflict.

Another feminist perspective, bringing together the counter-terrorism agenda with the women, peace and security agenda, can be seen in initiatives that identify women as a useful tool in helping to tackle terrorism and violent extremism. Resolution 2242 epitomizes this, encouraging 'consultations with women and women's organizations' to help inform counter-terrorism work.[22] In addition, the resolution:

> *Urges* Member States and the United Nations system to ensure the participation and leadership of women and women's organizations

19. Cara Daggett, 'Drone Disorientations: How "Unmanned" Weapons Queer the Experience of Killing in War' (2015) 17 (3) International Feminist Journal of Politics 361; Lauren Wilcox, 'Embodying Algorithmic War: Gender, Race, and the Posthuman in Drone Warfare' (2017) 48 (1) Security Dialogue 11
20. Anne Orford, 'Muscular Humanitarianism: Reading Narratives of the New Interventionism' (1999) 10 (4) European Journal of International Law 679
21. Ní Aoláin, above note 6, 283
22. S/RES/2242, paragraph 11 (note this wording is replicated in S/RES/2467)

in developing strategies to counter terrorism and violent extremism which can be conducive to terrorism, including through countering incitement to commit terrorist acts, creating counter narratives and other appropriate interventions.[23]

Khalili, discussing counterinsurgencies, is critical of the 'inclusion' of women in countering terrorism. Counterinsurgencies, notes Khalili, many of which are conducted in the name of the war on terror, change the dynamics of warfare: civilians become central 'as potential objects of military operations' and a core military aim becomes winning 'a largely uncommitted civilian population' over.[24] In this context, resolution 2242, with the aim of using women to 'counterbalanc[e] … male radicalisation',[25] can be seen as a continuation of this common counterinsurgency policy. As Khalili notes, these policies have also been used to justify the increased invasion of the private sphere in the aim of surveying women who are then seen as key to the counter-terrorism agenda.[26] The nexus between women and terrorist organizations might be direct or, more often, is imagined through kinship and sexual relations. As such, female relatives and female partners of suspected terrorists are at once instrumentalized as potential co-conspirators and as potential allies for the purpose of counter-terrorism strategies. Resolution 2242 thus promotes a problematic narrative of 'good' women who can be useful in countering the 'bad' terrorists, whereby women are once again essentialized as natural peacemakers or as influencers of men divest of their own 'politics or ethics'.[27] Women as agential, as political actors and decision-makers, or as important contributors to the development of legal and political strategy, are elided from the discourse and replaced by images and assumptions of women living lives only in relation to men.

The women, peace and security approach to counter-terrorism has worked, in part, to mainstream gender within the counter-terrorism agenda. This can be exemplified by the Counter-Terrorism Committee's development of a new area of focus on 'The Role of Women in Countering Terrorism and Violent Extremism' which was

23. S/RES/2242, paragraph 13
24. Laleh Khalili, 'Gendered Practices of Counterinsurgency' (2011) 37 Review of International Studies 1471, 1472–4
25. Khalili, ibid., 1476
26. Khalili, ibid., 1478–9
27. Khalili, ibid., 1477

inaugurated in 2015 through the Committee's first open briefing on the theme.[28] This open briefing and the subsequent development of this area of focus were developed, in part, in response to the women, peace and security framework.[29] The incorporation of gender policies into counter-terrorism strategies is, however, an example of how international governance institutions absorb feminist critiques while remaining largely unchanged by the inclusion of gender reforms. While, to an extent, the recognition that women may have a role to play in countering terrorism shows a basic recognition of women's power to influence their societies, this move is also dangerous because, as described by Ní Aoláin:

> the terms of inclusion have been set by male-dominated security institutions and states whose interest in a robust dialogue about the definition of terrorism, the causes conducive to the production of terrorism, and the relationship between terrorism and legitimate claims for self-determination by collective groups has been virtually nil.[30]

Similar arguments about the role of 'good' women fighting 'bad' terrorists have been made, for example, in relation to the use of female military personnel by western military forces to prevent and counter terrorism. For example, Female Engagement Teams (FETs) were used

28. Security Council Counter-Terrorism Committee, 'The Role of Women in Countering Terrorism and Violent Extremism' Open Briefing of the Counter-Terrorism Committee 9 September 2015 http://webtv.un.org/meetings-events/watch/the-role-of-women-in-countering-terrorism-and-violent-extremism-open-briefing-of-the-counter-terrorism-committee/4474290840001 (accessed December 2019)

29. The influence of the women, peace and security framework in the Committee's focus on gender is noted on the Counter-Terrorism Committee's website. See Security Council Counter-Terrorism Committee, 'In a first for the Counter-Terrorism Committee, the Security Council body holds open briefing on the role of women in countering terrorism and violent extremism' 9 September 2015 https://www.un.org/sc/ctc/news/2015/09/09/in-a-first-for-the-counter-terrorism-committee-the-security-council-body-holds-open-briefing-on-the-role-of-women-in-countering-terrorism-and-violent-extremism/ (accessed December 2019)

30. Ní Aoláin, above note 6, 276

by NATO and the US as part of the counterinsurgency strategy (COIN) in Afghanistan in the 2000s.[31] FETs were used in the name of enhanced operational effectiveness and intelligence gathering as well as due to their supposed ability to 'gain direct access to women in Afghan communities that is unavailable to their male colleagues'.[32] Gardam and Stephens note the essentializing nature of the debate around FETs which is 'based on the stereotypical and limiting assumption that women are more peace-loving; cooperative; and peace-building by nature than men'.[33] By assuming that all women are the same, not only is the idea that all women inherently feel more comfortable with other women propagated but, simultaneously, the differences between US and Afghan women are erased as is the reality that many Afghan women may not wish to speak to American women any more than they wish to speak to American men. While US/western women are imagined as part of the 'universal sisterhood', Afghan women are imagined in this discourse as helpless family members able to divulge information to assist counterinsurgency actions while benignly waiting in the domestic sphere to welcome foreign soldiers. The complexity of local gender relations, the possibility that women support local terrorist activities, or that complex cultural, social, ethnic and gender relations collide to create the possibilities and terms on which women speak – both as FETs and as women in Afghanistan – is absent from this narrative.

There is a need to question the linking of the women, peace and security agenda to the countering terrorism and violent extremism agenda. This narrative of the good women helping the 'right side' is essentializing, inherently linking women with peace. While we articulate a feminist anti-militarism and peace agenda across these two volumes, the shift from centring women as subject to encountering feminism as method draws out new questions and understandings of gender and conflict. As Ní Aoláin notes, the international security regime around countering terrorism 'is largely closed off to civil society, human rights and gender activism'.[34] The focus on countering terrorism in resolution

31. Judith Gardam and Dale Stephens, 'Concluding Remarks: Establishing Common Ground between Feminism and the Military' in Gina Heathcote and Dianne Otto (eds), *Rethinking Peacekeeping, Gender Equality and Collective Security* (Palgrave 2014) 273–5

32. Gardam and Stephens, ibid., 274

33. Gardam and Stephens, ibid., 275

34. Ní Aoláin, above note 6, 281

2242, she continues, should not be seen as the inclusion of these actors in the regime but, rather, this inclusion 'might prompt critical inquiry into how the international security regime, and the states that support it, can derive legitimizing benefits from co-opting the WPS [women, peace and security] agenda'.[35]

Another strand of scholarship on gender and terrorism focuses on the manner in which mainstream terrorism and security scholarship fails to regard women as participants in violent extremism, either committing violent acts themselves or supporting others to do so.[36] While there has been some research within international law on women as terrorists, and while resolution 2242 requires member states and UN entities 'to conduct and gather gender-sensitive research and data collection on the drivers of radicalization for women',[37] most of the scholarship on this area comes, rather, from outside legal scholarship, being located for the most part in international relations scholarships. When mainstream scholarship does identify women as terrorists, Sjoberg and Gentry argue that this occurs through the articulation of women's acts as dictated by their male counterparts, such that women are characterized as 'mothers, monsters, whores', thus denying 'their capacity to have made an independent, interdependent or even rational

---

35. Ní Aoláin, ibid., 281

36. See, for example, Jamille Bigio and Rachel Vogelstein, 'Women and Terrorism: Hidden Threats, Forgotten Partners' May 2019 *Council on Foreign Relations* https://cdn.cfr.org/sites/default/files/report_pdf/Discussion_Paper_ Bigio_Vogelstein_Terrorism_OR.pdf (accessed December 2019); Megan A O'Branski, '"The Savage Reduction of the Flesh": Violence, Gender and Bodily Weaponisation in the 1981 Irish Republican Hunger Strike Protest' (2014) 7 (1) Critical Studies on Terrorism 97; Maria Holt, 'The Unlikely Terrorist: Women and Islamic Resistance in Lebanon and the Palestinian Territories' (2010) 3 (3) Critical Studies on Terrorism 365; Laura Sjoberg and Caron E Gentry, 'It's Complicated: Looking Closely at Women in Violent Extremism' (2016) 17 (2) Georgetown Journal of International Affairs 23; Swati Parashar, 'Feminist International Relations and Women Militants: Case Studies from Sri Lanka and Kashmir' (2009) 22 (2) Cambridge Review of International Affairs 235; Miranda Alison, *Women and Political Violence: Female Combatants in Ethno-National Conflict* (Routledge 2009); Robin Morgan, *The Demon Lover: The Roots of Terrorism* (2nd edn, Pocket Books 2001)

37. S/RES/2242, paragraph 12

choice to commit violence, even when descriptions of violent men almost always characterise their choices as autonomous.[38] Women, peace and security resolution 2242, as noted, does discuss how women can be and are involved in terrorism and violent extremism. However, the resolution notes that certain 'drivers' cause women to be involved in such extremism.[39] This focus on 'drivers' plays into gendered stereotypes of the need to further explain women's violence with women being seen as inherently peaceful and violent women deemed the exception.[40] The focus on these 'drivers' also works to suggest that there is a need to understand women's violence through their gender, once again working to exceptionalize violent women as inherently different and somehow more unusual or, as domestic criminal legal analysis highlights, more abhorrent than violent men.[41] This narrative occupies the centre of attention allowing for the displacement of a lucid analysis of the political motivations behind terrorist acts.[42]

The narrative of violent women as exceptional and in need of further gendered explanation can also be seen within terrorism studies scholarship. Sjoberg and Gentry note how terrorism studies link

38. Caron E Gentry and Laura Sjoberg, *Beyond Mothers, Monsters, Whores: Thinking about Women's Violence in Global Politics* (Zed Books 2015) 22
39. S/RES/2242, paragraph 12
40. S/RES/2242, ibid.
41. See, for example, Patricia L Easteal, Lorana Bartels, Kate Holland and Noni Nelson, 'How Are Women Who Kill Portrayed in Newspaper Media? Connections with Social Values and the Legal System' (2015) 51 Women's Studies International Forum 31; May-Len Skilbrei, 'Sisters in Crime: Representations of Gender and Class in the Media Coverage and Court Proceedings of the Triple Homicide at Orderud Farm' (2013) 9 (2) Crime Media Culture 136; Marianne S Noh, Matthew T Lee and Kathryn M Feltey, 'Mad, Bad, or Reasonable? Newspaper Portrayals of the Battered Woman Who Kills' (2010) 27 Gender Issues 110; Elisabeth Storrs, '"Our Scapegoat": An Exploration of Media Representations of Myra Hindley and Rosemary West' (2004) 11 (1) Theology & Sexuality 9; Eileen Berrington and Päivi Honkatukia, 'An Evil Monster and a Poor Thing: Female Violence in the Media' (2002) 3 (1) Journal of Scandinavian Studies in Criminology and Crime Prevention 50; Kathryn Ann Farr, 'Defeminizing and Dehumanizing Female Murderers' (2000) 11 (1) Women & Criminal Justice 49
42. Marilyn Friedman, 'Female Terrorists: What Difference Does Gender Make?' (2007) 23 Social Philosophy Today 189

terrorism and women to women's maternal and nurturing characteristics, with women's innate nurturing qualities being seen as so strong that they can lead women into terrorism.[43] Drawing on this analysis, in many ways the gendered narratives of the female terrorist play out in similar ways at both the Security Council level and within terrorism studies. Nevertheless, unlike the gendered assumptions in the Security Council's women, peace and security framework, organizations, including the UN, USAID and the Governance and Social Development Resource Centre, are beginning to realize that women's reasons for participating in violent extremism are similar to men's reasons.[44]

Ultimately, the strand of scholarship which focuses on women as terrorists is key to highlighting a significant gendered failure of political and academic writing in not 'seeing' women as terrorists.[45] However, there remains a gap when it comes to analysing counter-terrorism laws. As Ní Aoláin states, 'the preoccupation with the violent (and as such generally presumed to be aberrational) female is, in itself, the product of an essentialist discourse that requires a critical eye'.[46] In placing terrorist women as the subject to be added into counter-terrorism research, this strand of scholarship highlights the gendered assumptions of mainstream accounts of terrorism which centre around the male as terrorist. However, a feminist analysis of the law requires looking beyond accounts of female acts of terrorism, the use of women in counter-terrorism strategies or of women as victims/vulnerable to terrorism to examine how terrorism discourse and laws are themselves gendered.

43. Laura Sjoberg and Caron E Gentry, *Mothers, Monsters, Whores: Women's Violence in Global Politics* (Zed Books 2007)

44. Sophie Giscard d'Estaing, 'Engaging Women in Countering Violent Extremism: Avoiding Instrumentalism and Furthering Agency' (2017) 25 (1) Gender & Development 103; USAID, 'People, Not Pawns: Women's Participation in Violent Extremism across MENA' September 2015 Research Brief; Becky Carter, 'Women and Violent Extremism' (Governance, Social Development, Humanitarian, Conflict – Applied Knowledge Services, 13 March 2013) http://gsdrc.org/docs/open/hdq898.pdf (accessed December 2019)

45. Laura Sjoberg, Grace D Cooke and Stacey Reiter Neal, 'Introduction' in Laura Sjoberg and Caron E Gentry (eds), *Women, Gender, and Terrorism* (University of Georgia Press 2011)

46. Ní Aoláin, above note 6, 277

The gendered dynamics of counter-terrorism laws

As shown above, most of the literature on gender and terrorism focuses on women and their varying roles within terrorism and counter-terrorism – as victims of terrorists, as being able to help counter-terrorism, as terrorist actors or as supporters of terrorism. However, there is another strand of scholarship on terrorism and counter-terrorism which looks beyond considering women's roles to analyse the gendered and racialized dynamics of counter-terrorism. This scholarship is diverse and can be found in queer perspectives, postcolonial perspectives, critical international relations work and beyond. In this section, we outline some of the scholarship which takes this perspective, using this scholarship to analyse both the impact on the erosion of international legal norms and the impact on domestic legal frameworks.

As Okech notes, in asymmetric conflicts where extremist actors are involved in what have been termed 'new wars',[47] notions of state and human security need to be shifted, with questions needing to be asked around 'security for whom, security based on which values, security from what threats, and security by what means?'.[48] Challenging the state-centred approach to security, Okech calls for a greater focus on socio-economic factors affecting local populations in the name of security, as opposed to using increased military spending as a solution.[49] This shift in focus from state-centred security to the security of the everyday is key. In parallel, critical masculinities studies articulate the othering of non-hegemonic masculinities and the conflation of religious and racialized identities in counter-terrorism law and policy.[50] Khalid writes of 'a benevolent and enlightened USA, protective of women and controlled in its use of violence, [that] is positioned as superior to the backward, barbaric and uncontrolled masculinity of the "Other"'.[51] The production of hegemonic masculinities is created

47. Christine Chinkin and Mary Kaldor, *International Law and New Wars* (Cambridge University Press 2017); Mary Kaldor, *New and Old Wars: Organized Violence in a Global Era* (Polity Press 1999)

48. Awino Okech, 'Asymmetrical Conflict and Human Security: Reflections from Kenya' (2015) 37 (1) Strategic Review for Southern Africa 56

49. Okech, ibid.

50. Maryam Khalid, 'Gender, Orientalism and Representations of the "Other" in the War on Terror' (2011) 23 (1) Global Change, Peace & Security 15

51. Khalid, ibid., 16

in opposition to the figure of the deviant non-western actor. Bringing strands of scholarship such as the work of Khalid and Okech together with wider critical, queer and postcolonial scholarships on terrorism, this section and the rest of the chapter will focus on both the violence of the everyday and the visibility and invisibility of violence as well as the oppositional process of othering and normalizing which permeates dominant accounts of terrorism and counter-terrorism. As such, the term 'queer' in this chapter generally refers to an analysis of the production of the normative and the non-normative, focusing on who is othered and thus who is queer in contemporary counter-terrorism discourse and noting, in particular, the demonization of Muslim communities and individuals. Analysing terrorism from a queer perspective allows for the bringing together of multiple gender methodologies, including the focus on gendered subjects, the need to centre the everyday and intersectional perspectives that approach war and peace as intertwined realities.

While queer theory seeks to avoid definition, it can, in some ways, be understood through that which it seeks to resist. As Jagose notes, '[t]hese days it almost goes without saying that queer is conventionally understood to mean "antinormative".'[52] However, Jagose continues, queer theory has not always situated itself as antinormative *per se*, although it has clearly always articulated a 'strong sense of resistance to social forces characterized as dominant or hegemonic'.[53] This has included, for example, a space through which to think about sex in alternative and non-hegemonic ways,[54] as well as a strong need to problematize overly simplistic politics of identity[55] and seek alternative forms of kinship.[56] Jagose challenges scholars to problematize the antinormative as 'not a homogenous thing'.[57] As such, there is a need to question the very lines drawn between the normative and the antinormative. In our understanding, queering is a continuous process,

---

52. Annamarie Jagose, 'The Trouble with Antinormativity' (2015) 26 (1) Differences 26

53. Jagose, ibid., 31

54. Jagose, ibid., 33

55. Jagose, ibid., 32

56. See Dianne Otto, 'Resisting the Heteronormative Imaginary of the Nation-state: Rethinking Kinship and Border Protection' in Dianne Otto (ed), *Queering International Law: Possibilities, Alliances, Complicities, Risks* (Routledge 2018) 236

57. Jagose, above note 52, 44

a conversation as opposed to a blueprint.[58] This conversation inevitably includes the debate over what queering exactly is and can be. Queer theory is therefore difficult to define through some universalizing phrase. However, there are a few key commonalities between many of the queer perspectives on international politics and law, and these commonalities are even easier to locate when looking at the literature specifically on queer theory and terrorism.

One clear frame of reference for those queering global politics is the tension between liberal LGBT rights projects and queer accounts of liberation. While a lesbian and gay or LGBT rights perspective broadly calls for equality at law, a queer perspective challenges this frame, asking: *equal to what?* One example can be seen when considering gay marriage. While a lesbian or gay perspective may be pro-marriage, seeing this as a fundamental equality issue, a queer perspective may seek to challenge the entire framework of marriage, noting, for example, marriage's colonial and racist framing, both historically and in the present day, with marriage acting as a tool for immigration enforcement, often leaving people, for example, stuck in abusive relationships in order to maintain their visa status.[59] As Kapur notes, the liberal focus on LGBT equality and rights works to limit dominant accounts of freedom to these liberal values alone, with queer/more radical ideas of freedom beyond the 'liberal fishbowl' thus being sidelined and silenced.[60]

58. Emily Jones, 'Review of Dianne Otto (ed), Queering International Law: Possibilities, Alliances, Complicities, Risks' (2019) 27(1) Feminist Legal Studies 115; Jack Halberstam, *The Queer Art of Failure* (Duke University Press 2011); Nikki Sullivan, *A Critical Introduction to Queer Theory* (New York University Press 2003)

59. Dean Spade and Craig Willse, 'Marriage Will Never Set Us Free' *Organising Upgrade* 6 September 2013 http://archive.organizingupgrade.com/index.php/modules-menu/beyond-capitalism/item/1002-marriage-will-never-set-us-free (accessed December 2019); Ryan Conrad (ed), *Against Equality: Queer Critiques of Gay Marriage* (AK Press 2010)

60. Ratna Kapur, *Gender, Alterity and Human Rights: Freedom in a Fishbowl* (Edward Elgar 2018) 60–75; Ratna Kapur, 'The (Im)possibility of Queering International Human Rights Law' in Dianne Otto (ed), *Queering International Law: Possibilities, Alliances, Complicities, Risks* (Routledge 2018) 131; Ratna Kapur, 'On Gender, Alterity and Human Rights: Freedom in a Fishbowl' (2019) 122 Feminist Review 167

While queer scholarship within many other disciplines has long been flourishing, queer approaches to international law are a relatively new area of scholarship, but one in which there are already multiple conversations, perspectives and debates.[61] The recently released edited volume, *Queering International Law: Possibilities, Alliances, Complicities, Risks*, which brings several voices to bear on a wide array of topics, exemplifies this diversity well.[62] From chapters which focus on the inclusion of queer subjects in the (international) legal order,[63] to those which note the links between race, colonialism and sexuality,[64] to those which challenge the possibility of queering liberal international legal frameworks such as that of human rights,[65] or state borders,[66] to work

61. See Dianne Otto (ed), *Queering International Law: Possibilities, Alliances, Complicities, Risks* (Routledge 2018); Dianne Otto, 'Queering Gender [Identity] in International Law' (2015) 33 (4) Nordic Journal of Human Rights 299; Dianne Otto, 'Transnational Homo-Assemblages: Reading "Gender" in Counter-Terrorism Discourses' (2013) 4 (2) Jindal Global Law Review 79; Doris E Buss, 'Queering International Legal Authority' (2007) 101 Proceedings of the Annual Meeting of the American Society of International Law 122; Aeyal Gross, 'Queer Theory and International Human Rights Law: Does Each Person Have a Sexual Orientation?' Proceedings of the Annual Meeting of the American Society of International Law 129; Dianne Otto, '"Taking a Break" from "Normal": Thinking Queer in the Context of International Law' (2007) Proceedings of the Annual Meeting of the American Society of International Law 119; Doris E Buss, 'Queering International Legal Authority' (2007) 101 Proceedings of the Annual Meeting of the American Society of International Law 122; Amr Shalakany, 'On a Certain Queer Discomfort with *Orientalism*' (2007) 101 Proceedings of the Annual Meeting of the American Society of International Law 125

62. Otto, *Queering International Law*, ibid.

63. Monika Zalnieriute, 'The Anatomy of Neoliberal Internet Governance: A Queer Critical Political Economy Perspective' in Dianne Otto (ed), *Queering International Law: Possibilities, Alliances, Complicities, Risks* (Routledge 2018)

64. Doris Buss and Blair Rutherford, '"Dangerous Desires": Illegality, Sexuality and the Global Governance of Artisanal Mining' in Dianne Otto (ed), *Queering International Law: Possibilities, Alliances, Complicities, Risks* (Routledge 2018) 35; Rahul Rao, 'A Tale of Two Atonements' in Dianne Otto (ed), *Queering International Law: Possibilities, Alliances, Complicities, Risks* (Routledge 2018) 15

65. Kapur, 'The (Im)possibility ...', above note 60

66. Bina Fernandez, 'Queer Border Crossers: Pragmatic Complicities, Indiscretions and Subversions' in Dianne Otto (ed), *Queering International Law: Possibilities, Alliances, Complicities, Risks* (Routledge 2018) 193; Otto, above note 56

which questions the possibility of ever being able to use law for queer analysis given law's inherent violence,[67] the book serves to highlight both the diversity of queer scholarship and many of its tensions.[68] A core tension clearly present in this scholarship is between focusing on queer subjects and on queering structures, debates and discourses. It is the latter approach which this chapter calls into focus. While terrorism clearly impacts on LGBTQIA subjects, and while these subjects may participate in terrorism, we seek to analyse, drawing on the multiple strands of scholarship on gender and race as outlined above, the various normative underpinnings of terrorism discourse. This includes both a focus on the multiple intersecting assemblages which structure terrorism discourse, including narratives of sexuality, race and colonialism, as well as a focus on the everyday, contrasting the vast focus on security within terrorism discourse with the lack of focus on the insecurity of everyday life for many.[69] In part, we are interested in the relevance and importance of queer approaches to feminist anti-militarism, at once articulated as an adjunct project that practises and identifies the nexus between race, sexuality, colonialism and gender while simultaneously incorporating a challenge to mainstream feminist accounts of conflict that tend to consider sexuality as primarily understood through female vulnerabilities.

Puar develops an account on homonationalism that links counter-terrorism discourses in western states with accounts of violations and repressive laws in non-western states via the representation of queer subjects. Homonationalism describes the ways in which the 'acceptance' or 'tolerance' of queer lives has 'become a barometer by which the right to and capacity for national sovereignty is evaluated'.[70] While homonationalism is not the core focus of this chapter which seeks, rather, to understand the impact of counter-terrorism on the law and the

---

67. Vanja Hamzić, 'International Law as Violence: Competing Absences of the Other' in Dianne Otto (ed), *Queering International Law: Possibilities, Alliances, Complicities, Risks* (Routledge 2018) 77

68. Jones, above note 58

69. Jasbir K Puar and Amit S Rai, 'Monster, Terrorist, Fag: The War on Terrorism and the Production of Docile Patriots' (2002) 20 (3(72)) Social Text 117

70. Jasbir K Puar, 'Rethinking Homonationalism' (2013) 45 International Journal of Middle East Studies 336. See also, Jasbir K Puar, *Terrorist Assemblages: Homonationalism in Queer Times* (Duke University Press 2007)

subsequent lived experiences of the law, homonationalism does make up one component of the civilizing discourse of 'us' against the terrorist 'others'. This is highlighted by Puar who notes that the 'invocation of the terrorist as a queer, nonnational, perversely racialized other has become part of the normative script of the US war on terror'.[71] Thus, homonationalism looks at how patriotism works to include queers at home at the expense of othering peoples elsewhere, a process which essentially marks some lives, as Otto highlights, as ungrievable.[72] This chapter draws on these debates to focus on the others both 'elsewhere' and 'here', noting the ways in which terrorism, while visualized as being about countries in conflict, has also reconfigured domestic and international legal spaces, working to other and then police, in particular, Muslim communities. We analyse the racist and colonial dimensions of domestic terrorism laws and policies and interpretations of international law, noting how the figure of the terrorist is scripted in as, what Puar and Rai describe as, the monstrous, queer, other.[73] We highlight how law, in the era of counter-terrorism, can seemingly – and without controversy – delimit a domestic and international space of enforcement through security discourses that target particular bodies and communities in a regressive manner while simultaneously producing narratives that tell of the structural march towards progress through the drawing in of the good LGBT citizen into law's remit.

Analysing terrorism studies scholarship alongside debates on terrorism in the popular media, Puar and Rai, drawing on Foucault, outline how the monster has a long history in western thought: representing the human or partially human other in need of correction. Often an assumed sexual deviant, the power of the monster figure is to be found within its 'dispersal in techniques of normalization and discipline'.[74] For feminist theorists this figure has always included violent women, who are often imagined outside of the bounds of humanness rather than political (or angry, or self-defending) agents. Drawing on Foucault and showing the historical link between monstrosity and sexuality, Puar and Rai note the 'relays, reinvestments, and resistances between

71. Puar, *Terrorist Assemblages,* ibid., 37

72. Dianne Otto, 'Transnational Homo-Assemblages', above note 61. Here, Otto draws on the work of Judith Butler in her analysis; Judith Butler, *Frames of War: When Is Life Grievable?* (Verso 2010)

73. Puar and Rai, above note 69, 119

74. Puar and Rai, ibid.

the monstrous terrorist and the discourse of heteronormativity.[75] One example of the way monstrosity, sexuality and the terrorist are linked together can be seen in the focus in mainstream western narratives on the terrorist's motives, often told through the imagery of the 'sexually frustrated Muslim men' who are 'promised the heavenly reward of ... sometimes even seventy virgins if they are martyred in jihad.'[76] Such a narrative promotes the idea that terrorism is also a form of 'failed heterosexuality'.[77] However, as AbuKhalil has argued,

> ... [i]n reality, political – not sexual – frustration constitutes the most important factor in motivating young men, or women, to engage in suicidal violence. The tendency to dwell on the sexual motives of the suicide bombers belittles these socio-political causes.[78]

The focus on sexuality here works, not only to sideline the political motives of terrorists but to diminish them, pushing political motivations aside as irrelevant, the 'real aim' being the virgins in *jannah*. However, the links between monstrosity, sexuality and terrorism are not the only interlinking factors in terrorism narratives. Other factors, such as culture and race, also play a key role.[79] The 'terrorist-monster' for Puar and Rai becomes not-'us-in-the-west', this other, in contemporary neo-colonial form, is seen as inferior due to their lack of democracy/ freedom/humanity/rights.[80] Thus, the terrorist-monster 'has become both a monster to be quarantined and an individual to be corrected';[81] the uncivilized other in need of the powers of the global north to save them and bring them democracy and rights. Such narratives not only work to continue international law's colonial legacy, these narratives also justify interventionist policies. An example of this can be seen in the war in Afghanistan, which, as noted above, was partially justified based on the need to save the Afghan people, and especially women, from the Taliban. Such a narrative, promoting the global north as the

75. Puar and Rai, ibid.
76. Puar and Rai, ibid., 124
77. Puar and Rai, ibid.
78. As'ad AbuKhalil, 'Sex and the Suicide Bomber' *Salon.com* 13 November 2001 https://www.salon.com/2001/11/07/islam_2/ (accessed December 2019); as quoted in Puar and Rai, ibid.
79. Puar and Rai, ibid., 119
80. Puar and Rai, ibid., 120–1
81. Puar and Rai, ibid.

standard of civilization despite clear issues existing on women's rights and human rights generally across all countries, when implemented through the use of force, resulted in the killing of many civilians in a conflict that is still ongoing.[82]

Feminist scholarship outside of the law, in particular, has long sought to focus on conflict and the violence of the everyday.[83] Writing on counterinsurgencies, Khalili notes how gender, 'masculinities and femininities, especially in imperial contexts, are already always "cross-hatched" with racial and class designations'.[84] Khalili notes, much in the same vein as the queer scholarship outlined above does, how the racialized and colonized subject is sexualized and gendered as inferior, highlighting the ways in which sexuality is transformed into a technology of coercion, this possibly being most famously depicted in the abuse committed by US military personnel in Abu Ghraib prison in Iraq in the early 2000s.[85] Noting how counterinsurgencies are by no means a new phenomenon, having been used to colonize populations and as a means to enforce colonial expansion and systems of colonialism,[86] Khalili draws parallels between counterinsurgencies then and now in the name of the war on terror.[87] Colonial and racial violence against othered populations and the construction of the queer inhuman who terrorizes the stable democratic order are a core element of the war on terror. Despite this, however, such gendered violence is outside the narrow focus of the women, peace and security agenda and, in addition, with most of the scholarship on everyday violence coming from disciplines outside the law. There is a need to question what the law and legal scholarship encompasses and what it does not. For

---

82. In the first half of 2019 more civilian deaths were caused by Afghan and US forces than by the insurgents; Thomas Gregory, 'Potential Lives, Impossible Deaths: Afghanistan, Civilian Casualties and the Politics of Intelligibility' (2012) 14 (3) International Feminist Journal of Politics 327, 328

83. See, for example, Cynthia Enloe, *Bananas, Beaches and Bases: Making Feminist Sense of International Politics* (2nd edn, University of California Press 2014); Cynthia Enloe, *Nimo's War, Emma's War: Making Feminist Sense of the Iraq War* (University of California Press 2010)

84. Khalili, above note 24, 1473, referring to Anne McClintock, *Imperial Leather: Race, Gender and Sexuality in the Colonial Contest* (Routledge 1995)

85. Khalili, ibid., 1474; Jasbir K Puar, 'Abu Ghraib and U.S. Sexual Exceptionalism' (2011) 29 (57/58) Works and Days 115

86. Khalili, ibid., 1471–2

87. Khalili, ibid., 1474

example, as Khalili notes, counterinsurgencies create a whole host of gendered everyday experiences. While women in conflict are generally seen as 'womenandchildren' (civilians) in need of protection, in counterinsurgency operations, these women are transformed into either actors deemed to be 'complicit with the combatants' or into 'hostages and literal or symbolic message-bearers for the work of counterinsurgency.'[88]

Khalili draws on the example of 2003 Iraq to highlight this point, noting how, while international humanitarian law clearly establishes that civilians are not legitimate targets, civilian spaces in counterinsurgency operations were transformed through military goals. These goals resulted in the 'constant monitoring' of the private sphere and of women, in particular, who became the 'direct targets of violence' through '[h]ouse invasions' as well as, for example, through being 'taken as hostages to compel the men to surrender' with the aim being to 'send a message' to the opposing side.[89] Further to this, Khalili also notes the high prevalence of violence against men outside of combat violence, with male populations being heavily monitored based on the idea that any man could be the enemy.[90] Such everyday violence included the undressing of men at checkpoints 'and the use of language which is intended to dishonour men'; the aim being also to effeminize these men,[91] drawing on 'orientalist gender stereotypes' about Muslim and Arab men.[92] The destabilization of identities also plays a role here, with US women from disadvantaged backgrounds being suddenly elevated in the social hierarchy over local males, 'their bodies and their sexuality' thus being 'deployed as technologies of power' as a means through which to humiliate local men.[93] These examples show, once again, the erosion of the law (here, international humanitarian law and the protection of civilians), in the name of counter-terrorism. Despite this gendered violence during conflict, these examples fall to the wayside when looking at the women, peace and security agenda and in mainstream accounts of gender and conflict where the focus is primarily on either inclusion of women or on tackling sexual violence in conflict. This focusing in and out on certain issues is based on gender essentialisms, power dynamics, race and colonial narratives and is another example

88. Khalili, ibid., 1479
89. Khalili, ibid.
90. Khalili, ibid.
91. Khalili, ibid., 1480
92. Khalili, ibid., 1481
93. Khalili, ibid.

of the ways in which gender, race, class and other intersections are 'cross-hatched'. Legal scholars can and must draw on more complex intersectional feminist accounts of counter-terrorism, as exemplified by the work of scholars such as Khalili and Puar, as a mechanism to draw the analysis away from a simplistic account of gender to think through the investment of gender narratives (for instance, on rescuing women) in colonial and racialized ideas of who needs saving and whose life is of less value or is even ungrievable.

From drones to domestic law in the global war on terror

Anti-terror laws often operate at the margins of legality through the deployment of emergency laws and the infringement of human rights laws in the name of security. Ní Aoláin argues that the use of words such as 'global' when referring to the war on terror works both to encourage actors globally to join in this war via the implication that 'we' are all affected, and to create legal ambiguities around the application of existing legal regimes such as international humanitarian law and international human rights law. The suspension of the law to create a response to the threat of terrorism deploys shadowy legal arguments 'designed to undercut the traditional armed conflict rules' and the application of human rights law.[94]

Drone warfare is one example of states operating at the margins of legality in order to sustain support for counter-terrorism. Drone strikes have increased in use over the past few decades in the name of targeting terrorist actors. As Wilcox states, 'drone warfare is premised upon the identification of individuals in space as killable enemies', creating some bodies which matter and some which are out of place, are discounted as monstrous, queer or inhuman.[95] Thus, some bodies are constructed as targetable despite the lack of consistency with the established parameters of international humanitarian law. The use of targeted strikes by drones has been propped up by counter-terrorism discourse and the idea that enemies in this 'new form' of warfare could be anywhere, are scattered, hiding in plain sight.[96] While drones were

94. Ní Aoláin, above note 6, 280
95. Lauren Wilcox, 'Drone Warfare and the Making of Bodies Out of Place' (2015) 3 (1) Critical Studies on Security 127, 128
96. Wilcox, ibid., 127

originally used to target known Al-Qaida suspects in the northwest of Pakistan, the scope of drone missions has been vastly broadened, with drones now being used to target subjects whose movements or 'pattern of life', as determined by data collection, are deemed to look like that of someone who *could be* conducting military operations in the key regions associated with terrorist activity.[97] The 2013 leaked US Department of Justice White Paper stated that killing US citizens abroad (and, as Wilcox notes, presumably anyone else) is legal if they pose an 'imminent threat' to the US and capture is not feasible.[98] For someone to be targeted via drone warfare they need not be part of any plot or known plan to strike first.[99] Following this, as Calhoun notes, 'today, the summary execution without trial of suspects in lands far away is carried out overtly and unselfconsciously and has come to be regarded by US military and political elites as a standard operating procedure'.[100]

In drone warfare, technology is used to create and support shadowy legal arguments made in the context of drone strikes, with the data collected on potential terrorists being posed as infallible despite the multiple errors which have been made in targeting decisions made through drawing upon such data.[101] Conducted via intelligence networks, those who order the strikes appoint themselves as 'police, the judge, the jurors and the executioners' all in one.[102] This has a clear impact on the rule of law, these actors often being 'accountable to no one'.[103] This is despite the fact that things have and do go wrong when it

97. Joseph Pugliese, *State Violence and the Execution of Law: Biopolitical Caesurae of Torture, Black Sites, Drones* (Routledge 2013) 193–4; Derek Gregory, 'Drone Geographies' (2014) 183 Radical Philosophy 7, 13; Grégoire Chamayou, *A Theory of the Drone* (trans. Janet Lloyd, The New Press 2015) 49; Wilcox, above note 19, 6

98. US Department of Justice, 'Lawfulness of a Lethal Operation Directed against a US Citizen Who Is a Senior Operational Leader of Al-Qa'ida or an Associated Force', https://fas.org/irp/eprint/doj-lethal.pdf (accessed December 2019); Wilcox, above note 95, 128

99. Wilcox, ibid.

100. Laurie Calhoun, *We Kill Because We Can: From Soldiering to Assassination in the Drone Age* (Zed Books 2016) 3

101. Gregory D Johnsen, *The Last Refuge: Yemen, Al-Qaeda, and the Battle for Arabia* (Oneworld 2013) 251–2; Calhoun, ibid., 22; Chamayou, above note 97

102. Calhoun, ibid., 18

103. Calhoun, ibid.

comes to intelligence and decision-making. An example of this can be seen in a cruise missile attack conducted in Yemen in 2009, where, after only an hour's overview of the intelligence by Pentagon top lawyer Jeh Johnson, a Bedouin camp was struck, having been mistaken for an Al-Qaida training camp. The missiles ended up killing fifty-eight people.[104]

Kebriaei notes the global war against terror in the post-9/11 climate in the US domestically legalized US strikes against Al-Qaida and its associates elsewhere. This domestic authorization has left a grey space in terms of the compatibility of international law with the domestic authority of the US to target a range of states and territories.[105] The application of international humanitarian law and the law of armed conflict to drone strikes relies on the recognition of an existing armed conflict. When the conflict shifts to new terrain the continued application of the law of armed conflict can be questioned, with Kebriaei arguing that:

> it is far from clear that the groups at issue are sufficiently organized and "associated" with al Qaeda to render them cobelligerents under international law. To the extent these groups are untethered to the armed conflict between the United States and al Qaeda, the laws of war do not apply. Domestic and international human rights law is the correct framework.[106]

Furthermore, targeting in drone warfare is based not only on data and intelligence collection, but also upon human judgement and analysis of that data. Human analysis of whether a target 'effectively resembles' an enemy or not is key; decisions thus being based on what is *felt*, with emotions such as fear and hatred inevitably leading to inaccuracy, bias and, sometimes, the killing of civilians.[107] Not surprisingly, assumptions with regard to gender, race and status of the individuals are also applied. The term 'military aged man' as a former category used by US military personnel akin to a synonym for a targetable body is an example of this necropolitical turn embodied by drone

104. Johnsen, above note 101, 251–2; Calhoun, ibid., 22

105. Pardiss Kebriaei, 'The Distance between Principle and Practice in the Obama Administration's Targeted Killing Program: A Response to Jeh Johnson' (2012) 31 Yale Law and Policy Review 151, 153

106. Kebriaei, ibid., 158

107. Wilcox, above note 19, 12

strikes in the war on terror, marking some lives more or less targetable than others.[108] The 'military aged man' is also understood through and upholds gendered assumptions about women and children who are generally identified as non-targets, this reinforcing the ideas that 'military aged men' are inherently legitimate targets.[109] This need to gender the subject has led, at times, to confusion over the gender of the possible targets and thus confusion, in the eyes of the drone pilots, as to whether the subject is a target or not based on their inability to clearly read their gender.[110] While the term 'military aged man' is no longer used by the US military, the understanding behind this term and the culture exemplified through it cannot be erased by taking the term out of use. Other examples of the marking of some lives as more or less targetable than others can be seen in the use of praying and preparing to pray as evidence of an intent to do something 'nefarious'.[111] This can be likened to the way Sikh men were targeted as enemies in the US post-9/11, being inaccurately religiously profiled as Muslims and therefore as terrorists.[112] As Puar notes in relation to this example, '[w]hat is being pre-empted is not the danger of the known subject but the danger of not-knowing'.[113]

Drone warfare in the global war against terror has been used to erode human rights globally. For example, while capital punishment is illegal in the UK, drones have been used by the British military to kill British citizens abroad. Reyaad Khan, a British citizen and known ISIS supporter who was targeted by a drone strike conducted by the UK in Syria in 2015, was one such person killed. While the UK government argued that his killing was an act of self-defence, preventing him from committing terrorist acts in the UK in the future,[114] as Calhoun points out, 'the assertion by the government of the right to kill citizens neither indicted

---

108. Ibid.

109. Ibid., 14

110. Ibid.

111. Ibid., 10

112. Jasbir K Puar, '"The Turban Is Not a Hat": Queer Diaspora and Practises of Profiling' in Jasbir K Puar (ed), *Terrorist Assemblages: Homonationalism in Queer Time* (Duke University Press 2007) 166

113. Puar, ibid., 185

114. Intelligence and Security Committee of Parliament, 'UK Lethal Drone Strikes in Syria' April 2017 http://isc.independent.gov.uk/news-archive/ 26april2017 (accessed December 2019)

nor tried for crimes … [is] a radical expansion of executive power'.[115] Calhoun continues, this use of power 'was accepted by many people for the simple reason that it happened so far away'.[116] The phenomenon of drone warfare and killing from afar, as well as the emergence of the figure of the Islamic terrorist, raises issues around which lives are grievable and which are not, as well as questions around the expansion of the powers of the executive and the erosion of human rights.[117] Heathcote notes, '[t]argeted strikes against terrorist actors have not been explicitly addressed by the Security Council although the Council has an extensive regime of targeted sanctions that member states, particularly the US, rely on to justify targeted strikes'.[118] Thus, Heathcote continues, it is important as feminist scholars to note the silence of the Security Council on targeted strikes despite its loud proclamations on counter-terrorism, noting the ways in which this shift between silence and proclamation works to prop-up targeted strikes and the legally shadowy or illegal, gendered and racialized necropolitical dimensions of countering terrorism.[119] State justifications for unilateral force have been stretched beyond familiar accounts to encompass targeted strikes on a range of territories. International law has then been further stretched to change the parameters with respect to human rights laws domestically in the name of security and countering terrorism.

As Otto highlights, while counter-terrorism gains much mainstream international attention, the 'daily terror' of the everyday, including 'of those in communities marked by non-normative practices of gender and sexuality … completely escapes the attention of mainstream international efforts'.[120] Security is used to justify the increased militarization of everyday life through surveillance and profiling that travels from the battlefield to peacetime state. Thus, moving away from the impact of terrorism on the everyday for subjects living in states that are the direct target of the global war on terror, another strand of gender

---

115. Calhoun, above note 100, viii

116. Calhoun, ibid.

117. Butler, above note 72; Fionnuala Ní Aoláin and Oren Gross, 'A Skeptical View of Deference to the Executive in Times of Crisis' (2008) 41 Israel Law Review 545

118. Gina Heathcote, *Feminist Dialogues on International Law: Successes, Tensions, Futures* (Oxford University Press 2019) 232

119. Heathcote, ibid.

120. Otto, above note 72, 95

scholarship on terrorism and the everyday focuses on the everyday terror of counter-terror measures in 'peacetime' states.[121]

As noted above, the UN Security Council, through resolutions such as 1373 (2001) and 1624 (2005), has been clear in highlighting state-level domestic duties to counter terrorism.[122] Resolution 1373 epitomizes this turn: setting out counter-terrorism as a global priority and calling on all states to act to counter terrorism. The development of targeted sanctions against named terrorist actors, as a measure under Article 41 of the UN Charter, imposes obligations on states that must be mobilized via domestic legal provisions. In addition, resolution 1373 established the Counter-Terrorism Committee which seeks to create policies around countering terrorism and support states in their efforts in this arena.[123]

Anti-terror laws have vastly shaped domestic legal frameworks in the twenty-first century. Domestic implementations of the countering terrorism and violent extremism agenda are often racialized, working to uphold and strengthen the biopolitical, hierarchical ordering of citizens which has always permeated the law. For example, classed, raced and gendered violence is produced via the regulation of foreign spouses in the UK where, under current regulations, the British spouse has to earn a certain amount of money in order for a spousal visa to a non-EEA national to be granted.[124] Innes and Steele note the long 'tradition of the (post)colonial governance of family life and intimacy' in which such visa laws are implicated, noting the reinforcement, through

---

121. Caron E Gentry, 'Epistemological Failures: Everyday Terrorism in the West' (2015) 8 (3) Critical Studies on Terrorism 362; Akanksha Mehta, 'The Aesthetics of "everyday" Violence: Narratives of Violence and Hindu Right-wing Women' (2015) 8 (3) Critical Studies on Terrorism 416; Laura Sjoberg, 'The Terror of Everyday Counterterrorism' (2015) 8 (3) Critical Studies on Terrorism 383

122. Security Council Resolution 1373 (28 September 2001) UN Doc. S/RES/1373; Security Council Resolution 1624 (14 September 2005) UN Doc. S/RES/1624

123. S/RES/1373 and S/RES/1624

124. Home Office (UK), 'Immigration Directorate Instruction Family Migration: Appendix FM Section 1.7, Appendix Armed Forces, Financial Requirement' August 2017 https://assets.publishing.service.gov.uk/government/uploads/system/uploads/attachment_data/file/826340/Appendix-FM-1-7-Financial-Requirement-ext_1.pdf (accessed December 2019)

salary requirements, of the heteronormative family ideal where the male spouse earns the money for his wife, as well as the racialized and classed elements which exclude people based on education, income, sexual identity, nationality, etc.[125] Furthermore, such laws foster and create fear around being separated from one's family, as well as around having to prove oneself constantly. Innes and Steele highlight the links between such regimes and the global war on terror which, they note, has permitted the increased power and violence of such regimes through creating a political environment in which the hyper-categorization of the wanted and unwanted is deemed acceptable.[126]

Immigration controls have vastly increased under the political arrangements of the global war on terror, with migrants and visitors from perceived higher-risk regions being subject to increasing checks and rejections, usually after the payment of often high-cost visa application fees.[127] At the same time, the use of biometrics and surveillance at airports have helped to increase border controls.[128] Legal and political changes such as these mark the increase in the biopolitical ordering of life, under which some lives become more or less valued than others. While all citizens might be subject to the imposition of border regimes and biometric surveillance, this has a very different meaning for those who are racialized and thus seen as 'potential terrorists', those who do not have extensive financial means and gendered and sexed bodies that might be deemed incompatible with dominant discourses of heteronormativity.

Another key legal change linked to the global war against terror but operationalized domestically is the increasing use of emergency laws and the erosion of human rights in the name of security. As Ní Aoláin argues, terrorism in the context of the post-9/11 world has 'enabled democratic states to make use of emergency powers by invoking human rights regimes, and to do so with less justification or excuse than would previously have been deemed necessary'.[129] Such uses of the law in the

---

125. Alexandria J Innes and Brent J Steele, 'Spousal Visa Law and Structural Violence: Fear, Anxiety and Terror of the Everyday' (2015) 8 (3) Critical Studies on Terrorism 401, 401–2

126. Innes and Steele, ibid., 401

127. Nazli Avdan, *Visas and Walls: Border Security in the Age of Terrorism* (University of Pennsylvania Press 2019)

128. Innes and Steele, above note 125, 404

129. Ní Aoláin, above note 6, 281; Sophia Dingli and Navtej Purewal (eds), 'Special Issue: Gendering (In)Security' (2018) 3 (2) Third World Thematics

name of security, however, blur the lines between peace and conflict, suggesting that peacetime states are somehow internally in conflict and thus the law must reflect this through the erosion of human rights. An example of the use of security derogations from human rights law in the name of counter-terrorism can be seen through the UK's detention without charge policies. For example, under S.23 of the Anti-Terrorism, Crime and Security Act 2001 (ATCSA), the UK legislated that foreign suspected terrorists who cannot be deported 'may be detained … whether temporarily or indefinitely' at the order of the Home Secretary.[130] This provision was passed in response to the attacks in the US in September 2001 despite the clear human rights concerns posed by such a provision. However, under S.3 of the Human Rights Act 1998 (HRA), courts are required – '[s]o far as it is possible to do so' – to interpret both primary and subordinate legislation in accordance with the provisions under the European Convention on Human Rights (ECHR), with S.4 of the HRA allowing the courts to declare legislation 'incompatible' with a Convention right where judicial interpretation to make the law compatible with the ECHR would entail encroaching on the Parliament's legislative role.[131] While detaining anyone temporarily or indefinitely without charge seems to clearly sit in violation of Article 5 of the ECHR, the right to liberty and security (this provision detailing that people should not be arbitrarily detained without lawful arrest and/ or trial),[132] the UK government at the time claimed that the ATCSA remained compatible with human rights.[133] The UK stated that they were still acting within the remit of the ECHR by arguing that they had derogated from Article 5 as per Article 15 of the ECHR, which states that the provisions of the convention may be derogated in times of a 'public emergency threatening the life of the nation'.[134] The consequent national legislation was eventually deemed incompatible with the ECHR, first by the House of Lords, drawing on the HRA,[135] this then

---

130. Anti-Terrorism, Crime and Security Act 2001 (ATCSA), S.23(1)
131. Human Rights Act 1998, S.3 and S.4
132. Convention for the Protection of Human Rights and Fundamental Freedoms (European Convention on Human Rights, as amended) (hereafter ECHR), Article 5
133. *A and Others v the United Kingdom* ECHR (Application no. 3455/05) 19 February 2009
134. ECHR, Article 15
135. *A and Others v Secretary of State for the Home Department* [2004] UKHL 56 (Belmarsh Case)

being upheld by the European Court of Human Rights (ECtHR) in *A and Others v the United Kingdom*.[136] The UK did eventually amend the ATCSA; nevertheless, many people were detained arbitrarily and indefinitely while these legal debates were ongoing, including the nine men who brought the case to the ECtHR. The fact that the UK government thought that indefinite detention would be permissible is itself symbolic of the ways in which the global war against terror has shaped the UK legal framework, with the impacts of laws such as these being, as noted above, gendered and racialized.

The UK is not the only state which has responded to the perceived need for greater security through a derogation from human rights standards. Other examples can be seen in the French state of emergency which began in November 2015 (following the Paris attacks) and ended in November 2017.[137] As noted above, international human rights law does allow for certain rights to be temporarily suspended during emergencies which threaten 'the life of the nation'.[138] Derogations are allowed from some rights as long as they do not breach international law and, following the International Covenant on Civil and Political Rights (ICCPR), 'involve discrimination solely on the ground of race, colour, sex, language, religion or social origin'. Furthermore, emergency measures must be proportionate, in that they need to be limited 'to the extent strictly required by the exigencies of the situation'.[139] As stated by the Human Rights Committee, the requirement of proportionality 'relates to the duration, geographical coverage and material scope of the state of emergency and any measures of derogation resorted to because of the emergency'.[140] However, the extent of the powers granted under the state of emergency and related laws on surveillance of electronic

136. *A and Others v the United Kingdom*, above note 133

137. See Décret n° 2015–1475 du 14 novembre 2015 portant application de la loi n° 55–385 du 3 avril 1955 https://www.legifrance.gouv.fr/eli/decret/2015/11/14/INTD1527633D/jo/texte (accessed December 2019)

138. International Covenant on Civil and Political Rights (adopted 16 December 1966, entered into force 23 March 1976) 999 UNTS 171 (hereafter ICCPR), Article 4(1); ECHR, Article 15

139. ICCPR, Article 4(1)

140. UN Human Rights Committee, CCPR General Comment no. 29: Article 4: Derogations during a State of Emergency (31 August 2001) CCPR/C/21/Rev.1/Add.11, adopted at the 1950th meeting on 24 July 2001, paragraph 4

communications in France were questionable from a human rights perspective, with several UN Special Rapporteurs expressing concern about these laws imposing 'excessive and disproportionate restrictions on fundamental freedoms'.[141]

The power to declare a state of emergency (*état d'urgence*) was established through a 1955 law.[142] The law establishing the *état d'urgence* was created in the context of the Algerian War of Independence from French colonization (1954–1962). The continuities that the emergency law, although subsequently modified to erase the references to Algeria, bears with colonial and racial frames cannot be ignored.[143] While the *état d'urgence* was intended to be a distinct measure to the pre-existing *état de siège* (state of siege), the link between the two *états* is clear, with many measures being imported from the second (meant to deal with conflict) to the first (meant to deal with – albeit exceptional – peacetime).

An *état d'urgence* in France was declared on 14 November 2015 and the 1955 *état d'urgence* provisions were thus put in place with some modifications.[144] Under Article 11 of the law regarding the *état d'urgence*, searches could be ordered, both physical and digital, without the need for judicial authorization, these searches falling below the threshold set by French criminal law in non-emergency circumstances.[145] According to state statistics, 3,242 searches were conducted between

141. Office of the United Nations High Commissioner for Human Rights, 'UN rights experts urge France to protect fundamental freedoms while countering terrorism' 19 January 2016 http://www.ohchr.org/EN/NewsEvents/Pages/DisplayNews.aspx?NewsID=16966&LangID=E (accessed December 2019)

142. Loi n° 55–385 du 3 avril 1955 instituant un état d'urgence et en déclarant l'application en Algérie, Journal Officiel de la Republique Française https://www.legifrance.gouv.fr/jo_pdf.do?id=JORFTEXT000000695350&page Courante=03479 (accessed December 2019)

143. Loi n° 2011–525 du 17 mai 2011 de simplification et d'amélioration de la qualité du droit https://www.legifrance.gouv.fr/eli/loi/2011/5/17/BCRX0929142L/jo/article_176 (accessed December 2019), Article 176

144. Décret n° 2015–1475, above note 137

145. Loi n° 55–385 relative à l'état d'urgence, version consolidée au 20 mars 2019 https://www.legifrance.gouv.fr/affichTexte.do;jsessionid=EABAFB8124A2E64C3DB6BF0423ECD2A0.tplgfr28s_3?cidTexte=JORFTEXT000000695350&dateTexte=20190320 (accessed December 2019), Article 11

14 November 2015 and 29 January 2016.[146] In addition, Article 8 of the same provision permitted the temporary closure of public places and gatherings.[147] This provision was further modified following the attack in Nice in 2016 to include places of worship where statements are made which provoke hatred or violence or provoke the commission of acts of terrorism. The 2016 modification also added that demonstrations and gatherings of people on the public road '*voie publique*' may also be prohibited.[148] The 2016 law additionally modified the law on national security (*Code de la sécurité intérieure*), allowing for all French nationals to be potentially suspended from being allowed to leave the country if it was believed they may be making trips abroad to participate in terrorist activities or to plan terrorist acts which may potentially be conducted upon return to France; the decision to prevent someone from being able to leave the country being made by the Minister of Interior and could now be renewed without limitation.[149] While there was a process of appeal included in the legal framework,[150] the person to whom this was ordered against had to give over their national identity card and passport as soon as they were notified of such a decision;[151] these being documents needed to travel but also essential documents to take part

146. Amnesty International, 'Upturned Lives: The Disproportionate Impact of France's State of Emergency' 2016 https://www.amnesty.org/download/ Documents/EUR2133642016ENGLISH.pdf (accessed December 2019) Data of the Ministry of Interior published by the National Assembly as reported by Amnesty International 10

147. Loi n° 55–385, above note 145, Article 8

148. Loi n° 2016–987 du 21 juillet 2016 prorogeant l'application de la loi n° 55–385 du 3 avril 1955 relative à l'état d'urgence et portant mesures de renforcement de la lutte antiterroriste (Article 3) https://www.legifrance.gouv. fr/affichTexteArticle.do;jsessionid=EABAFB8124A2E64C3DB6BF0423ECD 2A0.tplgfr28s_3?idArticle=JORFARTI000032921929&cidTexte=JORFTEXT 000032921910&dateTexte=20160722&categorieLien=id (accessed December 2019)

149. Code de la sécurité intérieure, Article L224-1, Modifié par LOI n° 2016-987 du 21 juillet 2016, Article 11 https://www.legifrance.gouv.fr/ affichCodeArticle.do;jsessionid=174991DEC30B43BBF84E49CA0F92DBBB. tplgfr28s_3?cidTexte=LEGITEXT000025503132&idArticle=LEGIARTI00003 2925346&dateTexte=20190401&categorieLien=id#LEGIARTI000032925346 (accessed December 2019)

150. Code de la sécurité intérieure, Article L224-1, ibid.

151. Code de la sécurité intérieure, Article L224-1, ibid.

in public life, for example, to open a bank account. The documents were to be invalidated, and a receipt (*récépissé*) was issued in lieu as a form of valid identification document. This receipt was not valid for travel abroad. In addition, the 2016 law modified the French Penal Procedure Code (*Code de procédure pénale*), modifying, for example, the time children as young as sixteen can be held in pre-trial detention for certain offences, increasing this time period from two to three years under Article 12.[152] These Penal Code changes remained in French law even after the *état d'urgence* was declared over, leading Human Rights Watch to state that '[t]he decision to introduce permanent changes to French criminal law without allowing time for adequate parliamentary scrutiny and debate is highly problematic'.[153] This change was not abrogated until September 2019.[154]

A 2016 Amnesty International report documented some of the ways in which people in France were affected by the *état d'urgence*, noting that people's 'daily lives and human rights had been severely impacted'.[155] The report, which interviewed several people affected, noted that many interviewees did not understand why measures were taken against them, with many seeing their treatment as a form of punishment.[156] Many interviewees clearly felt that this was occurring because they were Muslim.[157] The Amnesty International report notes that 'these measures have been applied in an overly-broad manner and, in some instances, arbitrarily'.[158] Examples given in the report include Amar, who was subjected to a house search on 16 November 2015. Amar is recorded in the report as saying:

152. Code de procédure pénale, Article 706–24-4, Créé par Loi n° 2016–987 du 21 juillet 2016, Article 12 et Abrogé par Ordonnance n° 2019–950 du 11 septembre 2019, Article 4 https://www.legifrance.gouv.fr/affichCodeArticle.do ;jsessionid=174991DEC30B43BBF84E49CA0F92DBBB.tplgfr28s_3?cidTexte= LEGITEXT000006071154&idArticle=LEGIARTI000032923638&dateTexte= 20190401&categorieLien=id#LEGIARTI000032923638 (accessed December 2019). See also Human Rights Watch, 'France: Prolonged Emergency State Threatens Rights' 22 July 2016 https://www.hrw.org/news/2016/07/22/france-prolonged-emergency-state-threatens-rights (accessed December 2019).
153. Human Rights Watch, ibid.
154. Code de procédure pénale, Article 706–24-4, above note 152
155. Amnesty International, above note 146, 6
156. Amnesty International, ibid.
157. Amnesty International, ibid.
158. Amnesty International, ibid., 7

It feels like if you display your religion, if you are bearded or wear a religious symbol or dress or if you pray in a particular mosque you can be considered to be "radical" and thus targeted. If you try not to display your religion too much, then they think you are concealing something. We don't know any more who they want us to be, we don't know how we're supposed to behave.[159]

The Amnesty report also notes that force was used, with another interviewee stating:

I thought that was it. They said they were police, but I did not believe them. My wife and my son were panicking. Then, as soon as I opened the bathroom's door, they punched me in the face and handcuffed both me and my wife.[160]

It is evident that these legal changes, read alongside these testimonies, raise serious human rights concerns, with the ability to shut down public gatherings potentially violating freedom of assembly rights, serious issues being raised around police brutality and with increased search powers having impacts on privacy and surveillance. At the same time, as Amnesty notes, these measures are discriminatory,[161] increasing the biopolitical surveillance and policing of Muslim communities in particular within France and arguably violating Article 4 of the ICCPR which, as noted above, states that human rights derogations – through, for example, the declaration of an *état d'urgence* – must not 'involve discrimination solely on the ground of race, colour, sex, language, religion or social origin'.[162] These changes also have clear implications in relation to due process and movement as well as having repercussions around the ability for people to participate fully in society.

There is a nexus between the use of emergency legislation in states such as France and the UK and the decision by states globally to use military force abroad in the name of the global war on terror. Eroding human rights and international humanitarian law abroad via drone strikes, these states define the conditions for increased unilateral strikes while simultaneously denouncing terrorist activities through the work of the Security Council and Counter-Terrorism Committee. The war

159. Amnesty International, ibid.
160. Amnesty International, ibid., 11
161. Amnesty International, ibid., 7
162. ICCPR, Article 4(1)

on terror, however, has also been used to justify the implementation of emergency laws in the domestic space that erode human rights in the name of terrorist threats while contributing to narratives of the threat of Muslim terrorists. The rise of right-wing populism and its violence has, however, remained unnamed and unregulated in these narratives. The linkage between the use of force abroad – also legitimated by the Security Council after the Paris attacks[163] – and the tightening of domestic laws helps produce the conditions in which the terrorist is understood as the monstrous other. Domestic law then works to shift the discourse of othering from the foreign terrorist to local racialized communities. The suspension of human rights laws, although potentially applicable to all citizens, is justified through the articulation of a racialized threat that simultaneously demonizes certain religious populations. The gender dimensions of this can be understood through the lens of queer accounts which demonstrate the biopolitics at the heart of the law and the perpetuation of this system through the 'state of exception',[164] highlighting the racialized and gendered impacts of such laws. Implicit in these acts is the colonial narrative of the denial of Muslim populations of belonging.

Conclusion

This chapter has demonstrated that while the majority of feminist work on terrorism focuses on women as victims of terrorists, as potential allies to counter-terrorism strategies or as actors within terrorist networks, there is much to be learnt from considering the broader gendered nature of the global war against terrorism. Noting, however, how much of the literature on the gendered dynamics of terrorism comes from outside of the legal discipline, this chapter has brought literature together from queer scholarship and international relations to apply it to the law. We have highlighted how counter-terrorism has been used to justify the erosion of both international and domestic legal frameworks. One impact of these erosions has been the racialized and gendered biopolitical and necropolitical ordering of life through the law. Examples given include the erosion of international humanitarian

---

163. Security Council Resolution 2249 (20 November 2015) S/RES/2249
164. Giorgio Agamben, *State of Exception* (trans. Kevin Attell, University of Chicago Press 2005)

law and human rights protections through drone warfare and targeted strikes in the global war on terror. In addition, the increased erosion of human rights in the global north in states such as France and the UK in the name of the war on terror has been exemplified, with provisions particularly targeting and thus discriminating against racialized populations. In this way this chapter highlights some of the ways in which conflict infiltrates the legal effects within peacetime states and how the continuum of gendered and racialized effects can be understood.

While the parameters of terrorism are deemed as understood without ever having been defined, as though terrorism is known even in the absence of clear definitions, this chapter has worked to disrupt this narrative, noting the violence and terror created in the everyday and justified in the name of counter-terrorism, highlighting the gendered, raced and homophobic elements to these measures. The reach of the international as found, for example, in the framing of legal responses against ISIS after the Paris attacks, is seen as intimately connected to the increased regulation of Muslim lives in western states. This works to create lives which are deemed to have more or less value than others, the racialized, occupied, colonized subject becoming the queer and the inhuman to other, to monitor, be fearful of, humiliate and even kill if deemed to be a threat in the necropolitical order of the global war against terror.

Chapter 4

INTERNATIONAL HUMANITARIAN LAW OF ARMED CONFLICT

The law of armed conflict is an inherently pragmatic discipline that accepts that war is a recurring feature of human existence. Rather than outlawing war, it merely offers balanced solutions that take account of both military necessity and humanitarian sentiments. It seeks to limit human suffering to the greatest extent possible without negating the rights of the warring parties to pursue their military objectives.[1]

This is the female norm that is considered worth protecting, to some extent, by the law of armed conflict. She is perceived only in terms of her body as a sexual object ...[2]

The Henriksen quote, above, summarizes the mainstream legal understanding of the international humanitarian law of armed conflict in its uncritical representation as pragmatic and 'of vital importance for the maintenance of peaceful and well-organized relations among states'.[3] The second quote, from Gardam, identifies the fraught imaginary of the international humanitarian law of armed conflict, the assumed genderless nature of its key actors (combatants) and the constructed gender of civilians, as well as the gendered narratives of protection.[4] In this chapter we analyse the laws of war, or *jus in bello*, to demonstrate the contours of existing feminist analysis on international humanitarian law and to further develop feminist approaches to the

---

1. Anders Henriksen, *International Law* (2nd edn, Oxford University Press 2019) 280
2. Judith Gardam, 'An Alien's Encounter with the Law of Armed Conflict' in Ngaire Naffine and Rosemary Owens (eds), *Sexing the Subject of Law* (Law Book Company 1997) 250
3. Henriksen, above note 1, 279
4. Gardam, above note 2

laws of armed conflict. Building on the queer analysis of the previous chapter, we also analyse the constructed subjects of the international humanitarian law of armed conflict, noting who is seen and who is not seen when the law is understood as a gendered and racialized regime.[5]

The international humanitarian law of armed conflict, or the law of war, regulates the conduct of war. The Hague Conventions, agreed in 1899 and 1907, govern both the methods and means, and the respective peace conferences were initially convened to find ways to limit the increase of armaments and to prevent conflict. These are joined by customary law and a body of additional treaties on the conduct of hostilities. While the actors and tactics of war have changed over time, due to technological advances and the increased participation of non-state groups, one thing that has remained constant is the vulnerability of civilian populations during armed conflicts. Indeed, across the twentieth century the number of civilian casualties in armed conflict has increased dramatically. The 1949 Geneva Conventions and their Additional Protocols were drafted to humanize conflict and curtail the amount of violence experienced by those most vulnerable during conflict. However, in practice, the concepts of proportionality and military necessity have provided militaries with sufficient leeway to pursue harmful tactics, as well as distorting understandings of proportionality to ultimately protect powerful militaries via the deployment of new types of weaponry, such as drones.

As Henriksen records above, the core of international humanitarian law is the acceptance that loss of life is inevitable and that certain types of killing are legally condoned. These accepted parameters of the international humanitarian law of armed conflict have frustrated feminists who have sought to analyse these laws in order to develop a greater understanding of the gendered harms of armed conflict and the long-term insecurity that follows war which are more often understood as unremarkable effects of armed conflict. In this chapter, we draw in the contours of international humanitarian law and the law of armed conflict alongside existing feminist engagements with both regimes to consider the tensions between two persistent binaries in

---

5. See further Gina Heathcote, 'LAWs, UFOs and UAVs: Feminist Encounters with the Law of Armed Conflict' in Dale Stephens and Paul Babie (eds), *Imagining Law: Essays in Conversation with Judith Gardam* (University of Adelaide Press 2016)

feminist analysis. The first tension is presented as between resistance and compliance, the second between victims and agents.[6] We use this chapter to explore a feminist methodology that avoids the simplicity of either/or and avoids binary structures when critiquing the law via a disruptive gender model.[7]

Gardam's scholarship provides the key feminist analysis on international humanitarian law. Her work develops feminist approaches on the laws of armed conflict by linking international humanitarian law with international human rights law generally and with CEDAW specifically.[8] Gardam has critiqued the concepts of proportionality and military necessity that have tended to prioritize masculine understandings of armed conflict.[9] Analysis of the silence on women's suffering within armed conflict and the lack of attention to women's experiences during armed conflict has been a predominant feature of feminist engagements with international humanitarian law. While there have been positive gains as a result of feminist interventions into international humanitarian law, for example via international criminal legal prosecutions, feminist work on international humanitarian law has generally not been successful in transforming the legal status quo. In addition, feminist accounts have developed understandings and analyses which often function within binary understandings of male/ female experiences reinforcing rather than disrupting essentializing narratives. In a sense, this is the risk of compliance: where the radical potential of feminist discourse is subsumed by the existing boundaries for engagement. Through not expanding the understanding of women's

6. Sari Kouvo and Zoe Pearson (eds), *Feminist Perspectives on Contemporary International Law: Between Resistance and Compliance?* (Hart Publishing 2011)

7. Dianne Otto 'A Sign of "Weakness"? Disrupting Gender Certainties in the Implementation of Security Council Resolution 1325' (2006) 13 Michigan Journal of Gender & Law 113, 158

8. Judith Gardam, 'Women, Human Rights and International Humanitarian Law' (1998) 38 (324) International Review of the Red Cross 421. See also Judith Gardam and Michelle Jarvis, 'Women and Armed Conflict: the International Response to the Beijing Platform for Action' (2000) 32 Columbia Human Rights Law Review 1

9. Judith Gardam, 'Proportionality as a Restraint on the Use of Force' (1999) 20 Australian Yearbook of International Law 9; Judith Gardam, 'A Role for Proportionality in the War on Terror' (2005) 74 (1) Nordic Journal of International Law 3

roles and realities during armed conflict, the binaries of war and peace, men and women, security and insecurity remain steadfast. Gardam identifies these limitations and highlights the 'endless focus on sexual violence' that has dominated feminist scholarship in the area, curtailing understandings of gendered harms in armed conflict that do not affirm traditional, essentializing and heteronormative understandings of civilian-combatant relations.[10] The gendered contours of the law remain largely unremarked upon when women are identified as vulnerable and as civilians, reinforcing war as men's business.[11] This epitomizes the need for identifying, recognizing and naming women's experiences of armed conflict that then become used to reify gender norms rather than disrupt them.

To examine the tension between resistance and compliance in feminist approaches, this chapter first details the international humanitarian law of armed conflict, summarizing the Hague and Geneva Conventions as well as the Additional Protocols.[12] We then analyse the inclusion of women within international humanitarian laws, focusing particularly on narratives that have asserted women

10. Judith Gardam, 'War, Law, Terror, Nothing New for Women' (2010) 32 Australian Feminist Law Journal 61

11. Helen Kinsella, 'Gendering Grotius: Sex and Sex Difference in the Laws of War' (2006) 34 (2) Political Theory 161

12. See Final Act of the International Peace Conference (29 July 1899) https://ihl-databases.icrc.org/ihl/INTRO/145 (accessed December 2019); Final Act of the Second Peace Conference (18 October 1907) https://ihl-databases. icrc.org/applic/ihl/ihl.nsf/INTRO/185 (accessed December 2019); Geneva Convention for the Amelioration of the Condition of the Wounded and Sick in Armed Forces in the Field (12 August 1949) 75 UNTS 31 (hereafter GC I); Geneva Convention for the Amelioration of the Condition of the Wounded, Sick and Shipwrecked Members of Armed Forces at Sea (12 August 1949) 75 UNTS 85 (hereafter GC II); Geneva Convention Relative to the Treatment of Prisoners of War (12 August 1949) 75 UNTS 135 (hereafter GC III); Geneva Convention Relative to the Protection of Civilian Persons in Time of War (12 August 1949) 75 UNTS 287 (hereafter GC IV); Protocol Additional to the Geneva Conventions of 12 August 1949, and Relating to the Protection of Victims of International Armed Conflicts (Protocol I) (8 June 1977) 1125 UNTS 3 (hereafter AP I); Protocol Additional to the Geneva Conventions of 12 August 1949, and relating to the Protection of Victims of Non-International Armed Conflicts (Protocol II) (8 June 1977) 1125 UNTS 609 (hereafter AP II)

as in need of protection and the sexed nature of their constructed subjectivity. This section also discusses international humanitarian law in relation to discourses of victimization and the ways in which laws create binaries as though they are inevitable narratives of armed conflict. Understandings of 'protection' are analysed using the Geneva Conventions as an example of law prioritizing the combatant body and the state in times of war. Drawing on Kinsella and Otto, we argue for a more complex version of subjectivities that moves beyond the heteronormativity found in law and that incorporates plural subjectivities that address the complexity of security.[13] The final section of the chapter explores the wider structure of international law which also readily positions women as the victims of conflict, and men and states as their violators and saviours. This section problematizes the framework of the international humanitarian law of armed conflict as inherently at odds with feminist aims, drawing attention to dialogues on the tensions between resistance and compliance within feminist projects. This section also signals some possibilities for the future of feminist engagement on international humanitarian law and the law of armed conflict via feminist posthumanism and an analysis of the use of contemporary technologies in conflict, a topic we take up at length in Volume Two. In engaging feminist posthumanism we shift towards a space where the tension between resistance and compliance within feminist legal projects can be re-thought as a mechanism for the critique of legal arrangements to commence rather than conclude.

The structure of international humanitarian law

Any engagement with international humanitarian law is seemingly at odds with feminist scholarship that seeks to understand gendered insecurity in peacetime as well as war, which challenges the persistence of military masculinities and interrogates international law from structural bias, intersectional, queer or postcolonial framings. Working within the boundaries of the international humanitarian law of armed conflict signals acceptance of that framework, which ultimately condones killing and, moreover, seeks to regulate killing in a 'humane' manner. In the words of Kouvo, it means 'adapting to what is *possible*

---

13. Kinsella, above note 11; Otto, above note 7

rather than to what is *necessary*'.[14] Some feminist projects might accept the importance of recognizing and working within military structures, as a strategy to lessen the impact of armed conflict on women in efforts to 'protect' women via law. Nevertheless, we argue that the law and violence relationship must be examined, noting the persistent tension between feminist approaches and the principles that inform both the law of armed conflict and international humanitarian law. In addition, recognizing the limits of law opens the possibility for structural reimagining of core concepts, such as how subjectivity is conceived of and understood.

Feminist scholarship has sought to expose international humanitarian law as a framework that is particularly ill-equipped to address gendered insecurity. Nevertheless, the next steps for feminist critique have remained somewhat unclear, with resisting the law versus using it, and ultimately complying with it, emerging as an either/ or scenario that is in the end unhelpful. Furthermore, while feminist scholarship has been debating the spaces of potential inclusion for recognition of gendered livelihoods, the laws of war have moved on to consider new forms of warfare and military behaviour, from drones to superior airpower, asymmetrical warfare, new forms of surveillance and threats of cyberattacks. Feminist scholarship thus not only encounters its own tensions, between resistance and compliance and between the production of gendered bodies and a need for structural bias analysis, but must also move beyond the engagement with law as it was in order to critique and challenge the changing modes of warfare and the regulation of new sites of militarized technology and knowledge. For example, although we give an account of the Hague and Geneva Conventions in this section of the book, we challenge the reader to reflect and consider Wilcox's account of the metaphor of the swarm for new military technologies:

> Contemporary developments in artificial intelligence and warfare suggest that the future of warfare will not be 'robots' as technological, individualised substitutions for idealised (masculine) warfighters, but warfighters understood as *swarms:* insect metaphors

14. Sari Kouvo, 'Feminism, Gender and International (Criminal) Law: From Asking the "Woman Question" in Law to Moving beyond Law' (2014) 16 (4) International Feminist Journal of Politics 666 (emphasis in the original)

for non-centrally organised, self-organising problem-solving. The swarm is not 'merely' a metaphor, but the organisational basis for military tactics.[15]

Wilcox's analysis not only points to the archaic modes of the laws of armed conflict imagined in response to a vastly different battlefield but also configures an alternative set of feminist approaches that draw in technology, human/non-human relations and alternative accounts of subjectivity. We come back to this scholarship in the following section of this chapter as a means to think beyond the binaries of international humanitarian law towards alternative feminist imaginaries.

International humanitarian law regulates the conduct of armed conflicts once hostilities have commenced and reflects the contours of warfare, largely between states rather than within states, at the time the key legal tools were drafted. In addition, international humanitarian law, as the *jus in bello*, is unconcerned with questions regarding the legality of the inception of conflict which falls under the *jus ad bellum*.[16] International humanitarian law and the law of armed conflict apply to all the parties involved in the conflict. Furthermore, the *jus in bello* traditionally marked the classification between the laws of peace and the laws of war, reifying the idea of neatly separating between war and peace and the laws which govern each. The twentieth century saw this rigid distinction collapse, as the declaration of a formal status of an armed conflict could no longer be used by states to avoid international obligations.[17] In this chapter, we are interested in how the legacy of this distinction – where the law of war casts privileges onto belligerent states to avoid responsibilities, and peace is understood as the absence of war – influences contemporary legal arrangements. The former legal binary between the law of war and the law of peace not only informs the book's title but also, we argue, infuses international law with a specific gendered reality that holds a range of power structures at the core of international legal

15. Lauren Wilcox, 'Drones, Swarms and Becoming-Insect: Feminist Utopias and Posthuman Politics' (2017) 116 Feminist Review 25, 26 (emphasis in the original)

16. See discussion in the introduction of this volume

17. Christopher Greenwood, 'The Concept of War in Modern International Law' (1987) 36 International and Comparative Law Quarterly 283, 304

obligations. While the strict legal distinction between the law of war and the law of peace is no longer operative, conflicts continue to be defined as either internal or external, with differing rules applying.[18] In addition, the gendered distinction between war, as an enforcement mechanism that calls for 'hard' security decisions, and peace, which hides and maintains gendered harms and insecurities of the everyday, is one of our key concerns.

The international humanitarian law of armed conflict is generally understood as being composed of two bodies of law, one focused on the regulation and limitation of military violence (conventionally referred to as 'the law of the Hague') and the other concerned with the protection of particular categories of individuals involved in armed conflict ('the law of Geneva'). These neat divisions have come under scrutiny as reflected in debates over the convergence of the Hague and Geneva Laws following the adoption of the 1977 Additional Protocols, particularly the First Additional Protocol, to the Geneva Conventions. A further layer of complexity has also been added by debates around the continued applicability of international human rights law during conflict.[19] Gardam notes, however:

> Whether or not a particular rule is part of the law of warfare or restricted to the traditional definition of humanitarian law assumes importance when it comes to discussing changes to the rules. States are less willing to countenance changes to "combat rules" to protect civilians, such as noncombatant immunity, than to rules which operate outside that area.[20]

18. For instance, the key treaty law applicable to internal armed conflicts is that contained in Article 3 common to the four 1949 Geneva Conventions and in AP II. See, above note 12

19. Compare *Legality of the Threat or Use of Nuclear Weapons* (Advisory Opinion) [1996] ICJ Rep 226 paragraph 25 and *Legal Consequences of the Construction of a Wall in the Occupied Palestinian Territory* (Advisory Opinion) [2004] ICJ Rep 136 paragraph 106 with Human Rights Committee, General Comment 31 (2004) UN Doc. CCPR/C/21/Rev.1/Add.13 paragraph 11. See, Ilias Bantekas and Lutz Oette, *International Human Rights Law and Practice* (2nd edn, Cambridge University Press 2016) 657–62

20. Judith Gardam, 'Gender and Non-combatant Immunity' (1993) 3 Transnational Law & Contemporary Problems 352

In fact, the negotiations of the First Additional Protocol, which includes rules concerning the conduct of hostilities, proved comparatively more difficult than the negotiations of the four Geneva Conventions. The methods and means of warfare, notwithstanding the development of the Additional Protocols, remain governed by provisions in the Hague Conventions that are still relevant, customary law and additional specific treaty agreements. These are given meaning through military manuals, or Rules of Engagement, and domestic courts which direct and govern the activities of armed forces, thus also developing through state practice.

At the commencement of the twentieth century, armed conflicts were initiated with a declaration of war and concluded with a peace treaty; however, neither convention is in common usage any longer.[21] The twentieth century thus shifted towards regarding the existence of an armed conflict as a factual question and the definition usually adopted in these situations was provided by the International Criminal Tribunal for the former Yugoslavia in the *Tadić* case: 'whenever there is a resort to armed force between States or protracted armed violence between governmental authorities and organized armed groups or between such groups within a State'.[22] This is a factual rather than a legal test and its broad nature has contributed to both the widening of the scope of what constitutes an armed conflict and the failure to recognize other conflicts as within the purview of international law. For example, when the consequences are largely humanitarian rather than military.

Another key twentieth-century development has been the recognition under international law of international *and* internal armed conflicts as potentially impacting on the maintenance of international peace and security. For the laws of war, the increased recognition of the international dimensions of internal armed conflict creates a potential

21. Henriksen, above note 1, 283. On peace agreements, see discussion in Christine Bell, *On the Law of Peace: Peace Agreements and the Lex Pacificatoria* (Oxford University Press 2008) 79–104. See also Sara Bertotti, Gina Heathcote, Emily Jones and Sheri Labenski, *The Law of War and Peace: A Gender Analysis Volume Two* (Zed Books, forthcoming)

22. ICTY Appeals Chamber, *Prosecutor v Tadić*, Decision on the Defence Motion for Interlocutory Appeal on Jurisdiction, Case IT-94-1, 2 October 1995, paragraph 70

vacuum in the law, as both the Hague Conventions and the Geneva Conventions primarily govern the behaviours of states. Common Article 3 of the Geneva Conventions provides reach into non-international armed conflicts through the creation of a baseline protection for those not participating in hostilities. Although directed at states, common Article 3 applies to all parties to non-international armed conflicts and sets a minimum standard of protection for persons not taking part in the hostilities.

The Hague conferences, first held in 1899 and again in 1907, were both organized with the aim of discussing and setting out new rules for warfare. Multiple agreements were reached at both conferences, with the 1899 conference adopting the Convention for the Pacific Settlement of International Disputes, creating the Permanent Court of Arbitration,[23] and the 1907 conference leading to several conventions including the affirmation and expansion of the Convention for the Pacific Settlement of International Disputes as well as creating conventions on: the laying of automatic submarine contact mines;[24] the status of enemy merchant ships;[25] and the Convention Respecting the Rights and Duties of Neutral Powers and Persons in case of War on Land,[26] among others.[27] While the Hague Conventions were an important step, as were the later Geneva Conventions, they are also limited. One limitation of the legal regime can be seen when focusing on arms control. Many of the proposed limitations to armaments, in both the 1899 and 1907 conferences, failed to be passed. Limited declarations were made in 1899 on the prohibition of the use of dumdum bullets (expanding bullets), the use of asphyxiating gases, and the discharge of projectiles and explosives from balloons, with the 1907 conference affirming the prohibition on the

23. Convention for the Pacific Settlement of International Disputes (29 July 1899) 1 Bevans 230
24. Convention Relative to the Laying of Automatic Submarine Contact Mines (18 October 1907) 1 Bevans 669
25. Convention Relating to the Status of Enemy Merchant Ships at the Outbreak of Hostilities (18 October 1907) in Carnegie Endowment for International Peace, Pamphlet No 14 (The Endowment 1915)
26. Convention Respecting the Rights and Duties of Neutral Powers and Persons in case of War on Land (18 October 1907) 1 Bevans 654
27. Final Act of the Second Peace Conference, above note 12

discharge of projectiles and explosives from balloons.[28] Symptomatic of the ways in which states and state sovereignty shape the laws of war, sovereign states must agree to legal developments due to the centrality of state consent and the pursuit of consensus, leading to less radical adoptions of prohibitive measures. Contemporary examples of these limitations are rendered visible in international debates on the use of autonomous weapons, where states have largely referred back to the existing law rather than drafting new rules.[29]

Despite the primary focus on weapons and military decision-making (the law of the Hague) and protections for the sick, wounded and prisoners of war (the law of Geneva), both sets of conventions do include some form of what is known as the Martens Clause, a clause declaring that even when conduct is not specifically regulated by law, it should not go against the principles of 'humanity' and 'public conscience'.[30] While this provision is little applied and vague, it has become a useful tool for those working in both disarmament and weapons regulation, with disarmament and regulation being, after all, one of the core aims of the Hague 1899 and 1907 conferences. For example, in working towards the prohibition of nuclear weapons, the clause is cited in and

28. See Declaration Concerning Asphyxiating Gases (29 July 1899) 187 CTS 453; and Declaration Concerning Expanding Bullets (29 July 1899) 187 CTS 459; Declaration to Prohibit for the Term of Five Years the Launching of Projectiles and Explosives from Balloons, and Other Methods of a Similar Nature (29 July 1899) 1 Bevans 270; Declaration Prohibiting the Discharge of Projectiles and Explosives from Balloons (18 October 1907) 1 Bevans 739. Also note the reaffirmation of the prohibition on employing poison or poisoned weapons and to employ arms, projectiles, or material calculated to cause unnecessary suffering in the 1907 Convention Respecting the Laws and Customs of War on Land (18 October 1907) 1 Bevans 631

29. Report of the 2016 Informal Meeting of Experts on Lethal Autonomous Weapons Systems (LAWS), Geneva (12–16 December 2016) UN Doc. CCW/ CONF.V/2

30. See Convention with Respect to the Laws and Customs of War on Land (29 July 1899) 1 Bevans 247, 248 preamble; Convention Respecting the Laws and Customs of War on Land (18 October 1907) 1 Bevans 631, 633 preamble; the clause was inserted in the provisions on the denunciation in each of the four Geneva Conventions, above note 12; in AP I, Art 1(2), above note 12; and AP II, preamble. See also *Nuclear Weapons* (Advisory Opinion), above note 19, paragraph 84

clearly inspired, in part, the creation of the Convention on Certain Conventional Weapons which allows for certain weapons to be banned if so agreed.[31] Despite the successful creation of the Convention on Certain Conventional Weapons, with some weapons, such as blinding lasers being banned as a result, many weapons which arguably are against 'public conscience' are still used and are still legal.[32] Ultimately, as the slow progress towards ratification of the prohibition on nuclear weapons alongside the lack of new law to regulate autonomous weapons demonstrates, states prioritize self-interest over global change when it comes to regulating weapons and their use.

The 1949 Geneva Conventions represent the key legal instruments of post-Second World War international humanitarian law. They followed the previous Geneva Conventions and enjoy universal ratification.[33] The first 1949 Geneva Convention deals with the Wounded and Sick in Armed Forces in the Field.[34] The second 1949 Geneva Convention covers the Wounded, Sick and Shipwrecked Members of Armed Forces at Sea.[35] The third 1949 Geneva Convention deals with the Treatment of Prisoners of War while the fourth Convention concerns the Protection of Civilian Persons in Time of War.[36] The four Geneva Conventions

31. Convention on Prohibitions or Restrictions on the Use of Certain Conventional Weapons which may be deemed to be Excessively Injurious or to have Indiscriminate Effects (10 October 1980) 1342 UNTS 137, preamble

32. See Additional Protocol to the Convention on Prohibitions or Restrictions on the Use of Certain Conventional Weapons which may be deemed to be Excessively Injurious or to have Indiscriminate Effects (Protocol IV, entitled Protocol on Blinding Laser Weapons) (13 October 1995) 2024 UNTS 163; Convention on Cluster Munitions (30 May 2008) 2688 UNTS 39. See also Article 36, 'Science, Technology and Weaponization: Preliminary Observations' November 2017, *Article 36* http://www.article36.org/wp-content/uploads/2017/11/Science-tech-and-weaponisation-preliminary-observations-FINAL-Nov17.pdf (accessed December 2019); Article 36, 'Effects of Explosive Weapons: Working Paper on Explosive Weapons in Populated Areas' December 2019, *Article 36* http://www.article36.org/wp-content/uploads/2019/12/Working-paper-Article-36.pdf (accessed December 2019)

33. The 1949 Geneva Conventions have 196 states parties (data: ICRC 27 November 2019) available on the ICRC website at https://ihl-databases.icrc.org/ihl (accessed December 2019)

34. GC I, above note 12

35. GC II, above note 12

36. GC III and GC IV, above note 12

apply to international armed conflict as well as 'to all cases of partial or total occupation.'[37] As indicated above, Article 3 common to the four Conventions applies to 'armed conflict not of an international character' and codifies a core of minimum protections to be applied by all parties to a non-international armed conflict.[38]

The First 1977 Additional Protocol to the 1949 Geneva Conventions relates to the Protection of Victims of International Armed Conflicts, while the Second 1977 Additional Protocol covers the Protection of Victims of Non-International Armed Conflicts.[39] Different from the 1949 Geneva Conventions, the two 1977 Additional Protocols do not enjoy the same number of state parties and their status as customary international law remains less clear-cut.[40] The First Additional Protocol applies to situations of international armed conflict as well as to conflicts between states and non-state actors in which 'peoples are fighting against colonial domination and alien occupation and against racist régimes in the exercise of their right of self-determination.'[41] The First Additional Protocol contains some provisions dealing with the conduct of hostilities, which were previously regulated under the Hague Conventions.[42] The Second Additional Protocol applies to conflicts 'in the territory of a High Contracting Party between its armed forces and dissident armed forces or other organized armed groups which, under responsible command, exercise such control over a part of its territory as to enable them to carry out sustained and concerted military operations and to implement this Protocol.'[43] While Article 27(2) of the Fourth Geneva Convention and Article 76(1) of the First Additional

---

37. Article 2 common to the four 1949 Geneva Conventions, above note 12
38. Article 3 common to the four 1949 Geneva Conventions, above note 12
39. AP I and AP II, above note 12
40. AP I has 174 states parties, AP II has 169 (data: ICRC 27 November 2019) above note 33. According to Sassòli, '[m]ost, but not all, rules of Protocols I and II correspond to customary international law.' Marco Sassòli, *International Humanitarian Law: Rules, Controversies, and Solutions to Problems Arising in Warfare* (Edward Elgar 2019) 38
41. AP I, above note 12, Art 1(4)
42. See, for instance, ibid., Art 35 AP I. AP II also contains some basic rules protecting civilians against the effects of conflict
43. AP II, above note 12, Art 1(1), but see also Art 1(2)

Protocol state that women shall be 'protected' against rape, rape has been specifically prohibited in Article 4(2)(e) of the Second Additional Protocol.[44]

The law of armed conflict is characterized by a number of principles that both derive from and inform the application of its rules. The principle of distinction establishes that it is forbidden to employ methods or means of warfare that are indiscriminate; the parties to a conflict must distinguish between civilians and combatants, as well as civilian objects and military objectives.[45] In international conflicts and conflicts covered by the First Additional Protocol, provided they comply with the relevant requirements under international humanitarian law, combatants enjoy prisoner of war status and combatant immunity, but can otherwise legally be targeted with lethal violence.[46] Civilians cannot be legally targeted unless they take up arms, while combatants have an obligation to distinguish themselves from civilians. However, in practice the distinction between civilians and combatants is not quite as clear as it would appear from these principles.[47] Following Arendt, Kinsella provides an analysis of the application and discursive history of the principle of distinction by showing how the 'invocation of women, children, and elderly men' comes to give meaning to this key principle in practice:

> … it would be in error to accept it is as only a descriptive claim, for it accomplishes more than that. This invocation of women, children, and elderly men also identifies and rationalizes the difference of combatant and civilian that, in turn, marks the distinction of permissible and impermissible acts of war.[48]

44. GC IV, above note 12, Art 27(2); AP I, above note 12, Art 76(1); AP II, above note 12, Art 4(2)(e). See also: Art 3 common to the four 1949 Geneva Conventions; GC I, above note 12, Art 12; GC II, above note 12, Art 12; GC III, above note 12, Arts 14, 25, 29, 88, 97, 108; GC IV, above note 12, Arts 38(5), 76, 85, 97, 124, 132; AP I, above note 12, Arts 75, 76; AP II, above note 12, Arts 5(2)(a), 6(4)

45. See AP I, above note 12, Arts 48, 51(2), 52(2). See also *Nuclear Weapons* (Advisory Opinion), above note 19, paragraph 78

46. GC III, above note 12, Art 4; AP I, above note 12, Art 44. See discussion in Sassòli, above note 40, 250-6, 259

47. Kinsella, above note 11, 162, 163

48. Kinsella, ibid., 163

Kinsella goes on to argue that 'it is discourses of gender that *produce* the distinction of combatant and civilian upon which the laws of war depend. The explicit regulation of the difference of combatant and civilian is enabled by, and occurs through, the regulation of sex and sex difference.'[49] Kinsella draws on the work of Butler to demonstrate how sex is not a natural category, but rather given meaning by the discourses it is drawn into.[50] Butler's analysis of the discursive construction of sex difference as a category of meaning is useful to revisit:

> ... gender is not to culture as sex is to nature, gender is also the discursive/cultural means by which 'sexed nature' or 'a natural sex' is produced and established as prediscursive ... a *politically neutral surface* on which culture acts.[51]

Sex difference is the characteristic through which women are construed as the quintessential civilian; as, different from children or the wounded, their 'condition' is understood to be natural or permanent and not the 'result of unfortunate circumstances and transient conditions'.[52] This has been emphasized in the global war on terror where the identification of the assumed sex of those being watched by drone operators has been a reason to target and in cases where sex is unclear this might still provide a reason to target.[53] The laws of war and the principle of distinction, however, require ambiguity to be read in favour of civilians, and thus restraint.[54]

---

49. Kinsella, ibid. (emphasis in the original)
50. Kinsella, ibid., 177
51. Judith Butler, *Gender Trouble: Feminism and the Subversion of Identity* (Routledge 1990) 7 cited in Kinsella, ibid., 166 (emphasis in the original)
52. Kinsella, above note 11, 183
53. Lauren Wilcox, 'Embodying Algorithmic War: Gender, Race, and the Posthuman in Drone Warfare' (2017) 48 (1) Security Dialogue 11
54. AP I, above note 12, Art 50(1). While some states included this rule in their military manuals, others expressed reservations. Nevertheless, the ICRC study on customary international humanitarian law concludes that 'when there is a situation of doubt, a careful assessment has to be made under the conditions and restraints governing a particular situation as to whether there are sufficient indications to warrant an attack.' Jean-Marie Henckaerts and Louise Doswald-Beck (eds), *Customary International Humanitarian Law: Volume I: Rules* (International Committee of the Red Cross 2005) 24

Analysis of the principle of distinction has, ultimately, produced an underlying tension within feminist accounts of international humanitarian law and exposes a range of additional concerns. Feminist scholarship has endeavoured to identify and expose how civilians are both a gendered category and exposed the gendered harms experienced within civilian spaces.[55] The latter has been influential in the framing of international criminal law and the promotion of carceral approaches to post-conflict justice, as we discuss in the following chapter, but less so in international humanitarian law or the law of armed conflict. The assumption of civilians as gendered female (or sexed, to use Kinsella's approach) perpetuates the denial of women's agency, as well as the potentially harmful narratives around gendered protection and sexual vulnerability. The articulation of women and children as dominating civilian communities (and elderly men, as Kinsella suggests, above) further perpetuates the ideas that women are not full citizens but are, rather, childlike and best protected rather than consulted on security matters while simultaneously denying the insecurity experienced by male civilians.[56] However, in identifying and emphasizing these gendered effects of armed conflict, feminist scholars risk reproducing the same gendered tropes that they seek to dismantle. The assumption that rape and sexual violence are perpetrated by (assumed male) combatants against civilian groups (assumed to be predominantly female) further situates a specifically feminized vulnerability within the combatant/civilian binary. Ultimately, this returns us to the opening reflections where we highlighted the fraught space of engaging international humanitarian law of armed conflict via feminist analysis which presupposes an acceptance of the necessity of armed conflict within international relations.

Additional principles within international humanitarian law include the principle of humanity, to avoid unnecessary suffering, the principles of military necessity and proportionality. The prohibition of unnecessary suffering forbids the use of means and methods of warfare that cause unnecessary suffering and superfluous injury. This principle is directed at military attacks against military targets given that, as noted, targeting the civilian population is prohibited. The principle of humanity is

55. Catherine O'Rourke, *Gender Politics in Transitional Justice* (Routledge 2013)

56. R Charli Carpenter, '*Innocent Women and Children*': *Gender, Norms and the Protection of Civilians* (Routledge 2006) 25

encapsulated by the above-mentioned Martens Clause.[57] The concept of humanity in war can be traced back to Christian notions and the writing of Grotius and other scholars, combining an understanding of the actions of 'civilized' militaries within the evolving laws of war.[58] Arguably rape and sexual violence committed in armed conflict violate the principle of humanity. This understanding does not presuppose that the act is committed against civilians alone, allowing for the fact that sexual violence is perpetrated against civilian and combatant communities. Recognition of this fact in law, however, would require unhooking the origins of the crime of rape in war from understandings of male honour and the gendered binary of war.[59] However, the principle of humanity and the prohibition of unnecessary suffering have been more often used to develop provisions against the use of specific types of weapons and/or the deployment of nuclear weapons in particular, than as a means to target and challenge sexual violence in armed conflict.[60]

The principle of military necessity requires that only the measures *necessary* to achieve a legitimate military objective can be legally carried out. In practice, however, military necessity gives military commanders a means to justify a great range of acts, as the principle requires an assessment of what the decision-maker understood at the time of making the decision, regardless of the actual later consequences of that decision (for instance, on civilian communities). As such, during the authorized use of military force against the Iraqi military in the early 1990s the bombing of the Iraqi electrical grid was perceived as within military necessity, given the impact this had on breaking down the capabilities of the Iraqi forces to communicate. The long-term civilian consequences of the destruction to an essential utility were not regarded as relevant to

57. See above note 30
58. Kinsella, above note 11, 172; Robert Kolb, 'The Main Epochs of Modern International Humanitarian Law Since 1864 and Their related Dominant Legal Constructions' in Kjetil Mujezinović Larsen, Camilla Guldahl Cooper and Gro Nystuen (eds), *Searching for a 'Principle of Humanity' in International Humanitarian Law* (Cambridge University Press 2012) 35
59. Kinsella, above note 11, 175, 178; Gardam, above note 2, 248, 249; Judith Gardam and Michelle Jarvis, *Women, Armed Conflict and International Law* (Kluwer Law International 2001) 108, 111
60. *Nuclear Weapons* (Advisory Opinion), above note 19, paragraph 78

that decision.[61] For Gardam this requires a micro and macro analysis of international humanitarian law:

> Military necessity is part of the broader framework of the relationship between militarism, sexism, and patriarchy, and most significantly in this context, the demands of national security. National security – the defense of the State – determines to a large extent the content of the rules of armed conflict and what limitations States are prepared to tolerate on their freedom of action during war. Military necessity is used to achieve the preeminence of national security over other factors.[62]

Gardam's analysis demonstrates how military necessity embeds a privileging of combatants within the laws of war and a prioritizing of the law of the Hague, the methods and means of armed conflict, as opposed to the humanitarian protections offered by the law of Geneva.[63] Gardam demonstrates how the aerial bombing of Iraq in the 1990s was justified on the grounds of military necessity, essentially prioritizing the lives of combatants in the attacking force over those of civilians on the ground.[64] A simple gender analysis potentially then conflates the former with men and the latter with women and children, gendering the law of armed conflict. However, an intersectional gender analysis asks further which larger, macro power dynamics, as well as historical assumptions regarding the civilizing nature of the laws of war, also play out in military decision-making.

The principle of necessity and the principle of proportionality, discussed below, have some philosophical basis in the doctrine of double effect which, when applied to armed conflict, addresses the unintentional killing of those not taking part in the hostilities. Gardam writes of the doctrine as having 'little or no meaning for many feminists who see no gains for women in such convoluted analyses'.[65] Gardam's description of the doctrine is as follows:

---

61. Gina Heathcote, *The Law on the Use of Force: A Feminist Analysis* (Routledge 2012) 106

62. Gardam, above note 20, 345, 349

63. Gardam, ibid., 353

64. Gardam, ibid., 355

65. Gardam, ibid., 357; see also Laura Sjoberg, 'Gendered Realities of the Immunity Principle: Why Gender Analysis Needs Feminism' (2006) 50 (4) International Studies Quarterly 889

This rule is concerned with circumstances involving the indirect killing of the innocent. Under the principle of double effect the indirect evil effect of an act not wrongful in itself is accepted as legitimate as long as it is directed towards a 'just' end.[66]

Double effect may thus provide a justification for military decision-makers to not 'see' the potential 'collateral' civilian consequences. The gendered effects of military means and methods are generally understood through their potential effect on the male civilians even if women 'experience warfare in many ways differently from men'.[67] As such, although the status of civilian is feminized, the lived experience of civilians is assumed from a male standard.

The laws of armed conflict are also governed by the principle of proportionality which requires that all military measures undertaken by the parties to a conflict must be proportionate. This requires that 'incidental' injury or damage to civilians and/or civilian objects must not be 'excessive' when weighed against the 'concrete and direct military advantage anticipated' as a result of an attack.[68] Therefore, international humanitarian law of armed conflict 'accepts that at least *some* civilian casualties and/or *some* damage to civilian objects will be inevitable in most military operations'.[69] Article 51 paragraph 5(b) of the First Additional Protocol identifies attacks 'which may be expected to cause incidental loss of civilian life, injury to civilians, damage to civilian objects, or a combination thereof, which would be excessive in relation to the concrete and direct military advantage anticipated' as indiscriminate and thus a violation of international humanitarian law.[70] However, these requirements have been interpreted to address the immediate effects of a military strike such that long-term consequences for the civilian community via loss of infrastructure or the impact of displacement are not part of the proportionality equation.[71] Charlesworth and

---

66. Gardam, above note 20, 357
67. Gardam, ibid.
68. AP I, above note 12, Art 57
69. David Turns, 'The Law of Armed Conflict (International Humanitarian Law)' in Malcom D Evans (ed), *International Law* (5th edn, Oxford University Press 2018) 857 (emphasis in the original)
70. AP I, Article 51(5)(b)
71. Judith Gardam and Hilary Charlesworth, 'Protection of Women in Armed Conflict' (2000) 22 Human Rights Quarterly 148, 161

Gardam conclude that international humanitarian law is 'an ancient, conservative, and relatively inflexible area of international law'.[72]

Feminist engagements with international humanitarian law have demonstrated the failure of the law to attend to the gendered manifestations of harm during armed conflict. Nevertheless, these engagements reproduce a persistent bind for feminist theorists, as each critique potentially legitimizes and reinforces the value of a series of laws that underpin and sustain military behaviours. Alternative projects that focus on challenging military masculinities and dismantling the production of a gendered status quo, however, are easily ignored by those actors committed to military endeavours and solutions. This captures the feminist tension between resistance and compliance. Reviewing the work of scholars, such as Gardam or Kinsella, and the international humanitarian law of armed conflict as they have critiqued it should, however, encourage a more complex account of gender analysis where insider accounts are as valid and as important as spaces of resistance. Consequently, feminist mechanisms for structural change emerge through the accounts of the law as it is and an understanding of spaces of resistance and the construction of alternative world views; we demonstrate this further in the analysis of victims/agents in the following section.

Beyond victims/agents and resistance/compliance

... this series of binary oppositions is accepted as given, and their prior existence presumed, they become points of origin for these analyses rather than their subject.[73]

This section explores the wider structure of international law and the temptation to articulate women as the (eternal) victims of armed conflict, while placing men, states and militaries as always potential violators or as saviours. This section also considers how the framework of the international humanitarian law of armed conflict is at odds with feminist aims that examine the insecurity of the everyday, in conflict and peacetime, and the gendering of militarism. Through drawing out

72. Gardam and Charlesworth, ibid., 166
73. Kinsella, above note 11, 166

our own dialogues on the tensions between resistance and compliance within feminist projects, we signal some possibilities for the future of feminist engagement on international humanitarian law of armed conflict: inside and outside the existing legal regimes and with a turn towards posthuman feminisms that articulated structural reimagining of law and life.

One consequence of the women, peace and security resolutions has been the rise of the role of gender experts, including in militaries, to facilitate the implementation of National Action Plans on women, peace and security.[74] The presence of gender experts within international law, while increasingly seen as an important component of international legal institutions and military forces, also exposes those taking up the role of gender expert to the structural gender inequalities present and perpetuated by international legal institutions themselves.[75] Ferguson argues that two dilemmas exist for gender experts. First, gender is framed as an 'add on' issue, never challenging beliefs or behaviour and never recognizing the larger structural issues that underpin existing gendered frames.[76] Second, having a gender analysis as a part of an institution lends the institution (or military) a degree of credibility. However, this can be a form of 'lip service' that does not actually change embedded issues.[77] Ferguson's arguments exemplify the dangers of 'adding women' and hoping that institutions, which might be more obviously wedded to neoliberal and militaristic aims, will be fundamentally 'bettered' by 'feminism'. Importantly, adding women does not automatically facilitate the development of inclusive practices within institutions. Likewise, discussing women's relationship with the law does not automatically provide a more nuanced perspective on the legal system, international or domestic. Gardam recognizes this difficulty and at the same time acknowledges that international humanitarian law is often the only applicable body of law during conflict and therefore has the potential to lessen the effects of war.[78] The tension, thus, is that to resist means

---

74. Laura J Shepherd, 'Making War Safe for Women? National Action Plans and the Militarisation of the Women, Peace and Security Agenda' (2016) 37 (3) International Political Science Review 324

75. Lucy Ferguson, '"This Is Our Gender Person": The Messy Business of Working as a Gender Expert in International Development' (2015) 17 International Feminist Journal of Politics 380

76. Ferguson, ibid., 392

77. Ferguson, ibid., 393

78. Gardam, above note 10, 62

to fail to enter or be included in important conversations, and yet to seek inclusion is to risk co-optation of the frames that are perceived as important within feminist knowledge. An alternative rendering might be that only through inclusion can the structural dynamics of an organization or institution be brought to light although this requires a maintenance of outside strategies to facilitate and underpin the internal work of the gender expert or advisor within the institution.

Feminist scholarship has detailed how the international humanitarian law of armed conflict has developed in ways that reinforce masculine understandings of military action and perpetuate further violence, which simultaneously silence women's suffering.[79] Women experience a range of gendered harms during armed conflict, including personal instances of sexual violence, as well as the consequences of broader harms like environmental degradation and agricultural losses, which are not captured as violations of international humanitarian law.[80] Yet, as Gardam and Charlesworth acknowledge, and in line with our larger argument across the book:

> [o]ne of the assumptions that frequently underlies initiatives designed to include women in public roles is that women are intrinsically more peaceful and cooperative than men. This assumption is problematic because it reinforces stereotypes of women that limit their options and fail to take account of their diverse potentials.[81]

Through building on the drawing in of queer theory in the prior chapter, we wish to analyse the constructed subjects of the international humanitarian law of armed conflict that might be reimagined as encompassing multiple genders and gender fluidity, as a means to challenge narratives of female victimhood and passivity and women as peace-bringers.[82] This is a conscious drawing in of Otto's contention that, '[w]ithout active contestation of gender dualities and hierarchies, the "mindset" will never change and the purportedly social understanding of gender will blur with the biological certainties that have legitimated militarism and women's inequality'.[83] However, the shift from a binary

---

79. Gardam and Charlesworth, above note 71, 160
80. See Karen Hulme, *War Torn Environment: Interpreting the Legal Threshold* (Brill 2004)
81. Gardam and Charlesworth, above note 71, 165
82. See Heathcote, above note 5
83. Otto, above note 7, 167

production of gendered subjects to gender fluidity as a strategy for gender reform is not always self-evident in terms of how to achieve this goal. In addition, we regard feminist peace activism, its histories and methods, of importance, noting the idea of 'peaceful women' which underpins many such initiatives – such as the 1915 Women's Peace Congress – and wishing to distance ourselves from such gender essentialism while retaining peace activism and anti-militarism as a core feminist value. Otto's recognition that the women at the 1915 conference were identified as troublemakers and yet simultaneously gendered and feminized for their attempts to respond to the ongoing armed conflict demonstrates how the 'peace' label becomes feminized even when peace-work might not fit the traditional gender stereotype of western femininity.[84]

Different feminist methods have dominated analysis of the law of armed conflict. For example, asking 'the woman question' has been a legal tool used by feminists in order to expose the gender biases in supposed neutral laws. Often, asking 'the woman question' has been a way to recognize how legal rules have failed to consider the experiences of women and how current rules actively disadvantaged women. Within domestic legal spaces asking 'the woman question' has tended to focus on issues of reproductive rights, maternity and family life, workplace inequalities and sexual violence. International legal spaces have focused on empowering women through human rights law, as well as encouraging prosecutions of sexual violence during armed conflict. Both CEDAW and the Security Council women, peace and security agenda have created a space for conversations around women's access to rights and their unique experiences during peacetime as well as armed conflict. Nevertheless, Charlesworth points out that despite the sustained feminist critiques of international law, '[i]t is very hard to find any response from the mainstream to feminist questions and critiques'.[85] If this is so for projects that work to address and acknowledge women's experience of the law, a commitment to dismantling the gender binary risks pushing feminist analysis even further from mainstream analysis of international law.

Furthermore, and as we have noted, gender analysis of the international humanitarian law of armed conflict has often focused

84. Otto, ibid.
85. Hilary Charlesworth, 'The Women Question in International Law' (2011) 1 (1) Asian Journal of International Law 33, 35

on women as victims of sexual violence. While this work has proven essential, it has also proven problematic. Limiting gender analysis to women misses the ways in which conflict impacts men, non-binary, trans and queer people who might also experience specifically gendered harms. For example, when discussing reproductive health in armed conflict spaces it is often assumed that women are the only subjects at risk, ignoring that men also experience forced sterilization and losses to their reproductive capacity as a result of warfare. Employing a gender analysis should address the breadth of gendered experiences and not solely focus on women's experiences of sexual violence in conflict. Ultimately, asking 'the woman question', as important as it is to help surface gendered harms, has the potential to reinforce the binary between men and women, excluding those whose experience or identity does not sit neatly within this binary. Below, we draw on Otto's articulation of a need for appreciation of the diverse gendered lives that traverse conflict and peacetime alongside posthuman feminist scholarship which argues for further feminist engagements with new forms of military technology so as to ask 'who or what the "human" of international *human*itarian law is, and can be, in the posthuman condition'.[86]

Rather than centring concerns on women's experience under international humanitarian law, this chapter encourages further research to develop feminist questions on the gendered assumptions embedded in existing legal relations. As such, this provides space to recognize gendered harms while not assuming the legal structures, as they exist, as offering a means to address or respond to those harms without an additional critique of the structural biases of the law. This re-positioning broadens the scope of enquiry allowing for feminist analyses that move beyond a focus on women as victims of sexual violence in armed conflict or analyses that focus solely on 'adding women' into predetermined debates and institutional forms. However, a shift from women's experience towards the development of feminist questions/methods does not automatically absolve feminist projects from the issues that have been highlighted as a result of narrowly focusing on women. Many feminist projects have been equally complicit

---

86. Matilda   Arvidsson,   'Targeting,   Gender,   and   International *Posthuman*itarian Law and Practice: Framing the Question of the Human in International Humanitarian Law' (2018) 44 (1) Australian Feminist Law Journal 9, 11 (emphasis in the original); Otto, above note 7

in excluding different feminist voices, posing the question of who the gatekeepers are and which academic interventions are privileged.[87] Our choices across this book have been to shift between a range of voices, intersectional, structural bias, postcolonial, posthuman and queer to resist settling on a meta- or overarching narrative of feminist prescriptions. We expand this enterprise further here, via the analysis of international humanitarian law of armed conflict, with attention to both gender fluidity and feminist posthumanism and via analyses of contemporary developments within the conduct of hostilities. Feminist posthumanisms question the subject of knowledge and scholarship, in particular, the assumption of humanness as distinct and disconnected from non-human animals, the environment and matter, such that an interconnected and non-elevated understanding of the human condition is articulated. We consider the possibility of this approach as a means to draw in a recognition of gender fluid lives, of human and non-human encounters with recognition of the interdependency between environmental and human survival.

Prior to the drawing in of feminist posthumanisms we articulate three further (potential) spaces for feminist engagement with the international humanitarian law of armed conflict, each with specific relevance to our reflections on seeing gender-fluid lives and understanding the complexity of subjectivity beyond the gender binary. The first discussion focuses on female violence and highlights the failures of the gendered assumptions with respect to who the perpetrators and instigators of the most extreme violations of international humanitarian law of armed conflict might be. This theme is taken up further in the next chapter. The second discussion argues that state and high-level officials are also imagined as male, such that men are the un-acknowledged perpetrators, law-makers and decision-makers within military frames. An underdiscussed consequence of the hypervisibility of conflict-related sexual violence is the assumption of male actors in armed conflict as predominantly placed outside of private spaces (the local, the home, the civilian community) and therefore controlling and framing discourses within public spaces. This renders female actors who are also decision-makers, authorizing military strikes and propping up nationalisms, absent from feminist, and mainstream, analysis. The gendered tensions between victims and agents, we argue, map onto gendered perceptions

---

87. See Gina Heathcote, *Feminist Dialogues on International Law: Successes, Tensions, Futures* (Oxford University Press 2019)

of combatants and civilians and benefit from projects for dismantling their dominance in military, legal and political discourses. The third discussion draws in contemporary accounts of new wars, as argued by Chinkin and Kaldor, as the dominant, contemporary frame of the battlefield, consequently rendering many of the assumptions of the international humanitarian law of armed conflict archaic.[88]

When the prisoner abuse scandal at Abu Ghraib broke in 2003 and female US soldiers were found to have participated in the abuse, along with others, feminists condemned the actions of the US military, as well as the female soldiers themselves.[89] While female soldiers were found guilty of committing abuse and later court martialled, there were also male soldiers involved and subsequently tried before US military courts. However, much of the focus of the outrage expressed – in the media – remained centred on the women and very little attention was paid to the Iraqi men who suffered the abuse or the male US soldiers in the images.[90] For Enloe, within the condemnation against the female soldiers existed thinly veiled gendered assumptions about what effect the inclusion of women should have had on predominantly masculine spaces like the military. That is, the gendered idea that women – by their own presence and nature – should make things 'better'. This perspective is also present within the resolutions on women, peace and security which prioritize the inclusion of female peacekeepers in UN missions. For instance, resolution 1820 encourages troop and police contributing countries to:

> ... consider steps they could take to heighten awareness and the responsiveness of their personnel participating in UN peacekeeping operations to protect civilians, including women and children, and prevent sexual violence against women and girls in conflict and post-conflict situations, including wherever possible the deployment of a higher percentage of women peacekeepers or police.[91]

88. Christine Chinkin and Mary Kaldor, *International Law and New Wars* (Cambridge University Press 2017); Mary Kaldor, *New and Old Wars: Organized Violence in a Global Era* (Polity Press 1999)

89. Cynthia Enloe, 'Wielding Masculinity inside Abu Ghraib: Making Feminist Sense of an American Military Scandal' (2004) 10 (3) Asian Journal of Women's Studies 89

90. Enloe, ibid., 91

91. Security Council Resolution 1820 (19 June 2008) UN Doc. S/RES/1820 paragraph 8

The underlying assumption is that women can infiltrate masculine spaces and then work towards better outcomes, including a reduction in crimes of sexual violence. Reflecting on this, Melone questioned the premise of equality projects if the outcome is female violence that mimics male atrocities.[92] Melone's frustration is one shared by many: feminists have strived for equality, allowing them the opportunity to have careers of their own choosing, and yet, as exemplified by Abu Ghraib, when women have entered into these spaces, violence has continued as usual with its racialized, sexualized and abhorrent reality. In fact, in Abu Ghraib, women did not 'make things better' but rather played an active part of making things worse. The promotion of the idea that women are somehow 'good' ultimately, we argue, ignores the persistence of power structures, including of patriarchy, racial and religious hatreds and sexualized discourses of power and privilege. Indeed, patriarchal systems – like those which permeate the military – are not dissolved simply by adding women; indeed thin equality projects that add women without attention to the means through which gender regimes interlock with broader power structures will not only comply with the status quo but often reinforce existing power relations. Some women benefit from patriarchy and with the inclusion of more women into traditionally male spaces, women have become indispensable to maintaining gendered state structures.

Puar argues that the abuse at Abu Ghraib must be recognized as unexceptional.[93] Puar's analysis recognizes that the larger discourse presented to the US public and beyond functioned not only to represent gender but was deeply racialized, homophobic and Islamophobic:

> This Orientalist discourse has resurfaced in relation to the violence at Abu Ghraib, as both conservatives and progressives claim that the illegal status of homosexual acts in Islamic law demarcates sexual torture as especially humiliating and therefore very effective from a military security perspective.[94]

92. Mary Jo Melone, 'You've Come a Long Way Baby; Was It for This?' 7 May 2004, *St. Petersburg Times*, on file with authors
93. Jasbir K Puar, 'Abu Ghraib: Arguing against Exceptionalism' (2004) 30 (2) Feminist Studies 522
94. Puar, ibid., 526

Puar notes the irony of the US emerging from the abuse scandal as the more tolerant, indeed civilized, society to be juxtaposed against the 'repressed, modest, nudity-shy "Middle East"'.[95] Puar's reading of the Abu Ghraib abuses notes the cultural reception of these events within the US. Puar thus argues for the crimes committed at Abu Ghraib to be used as a mirror to understand US institutions, such as the military, noting that 'rather than being cast as exceptional, [these events need] to be contextualized within a range of other practices and discourses, perhaps less obvious than the Iraqi prisoner abuse, that pivotally lasso sexuality in the deployment of U.S. nationalism, patriotism, and increasingly, empire'.[96] The crimes and abuses committed by US troops in military prisons in Iraq thus frame the complex sexualized, gendered and racialized power of militaries and ultimately highlight the fact that the contours of international humanitarian law of armed conflict are weak tools in comparison to entrenched power relations. When campaigns for 'seeing' the sexual violence of militaries and recognizing women as gendered victims of war are read beside the violence of Abu Ghraib, it becomes apparent that an understanding of gendered power must be developed in conjunction with an analysis of power more generally. Furthermore, the potential for gender fluidity must be theorized as a direct challenge to the maintenance of the status quo which deploys the gender binary to reinforce and underpin the relation between law and violence.

Likewise, the principles of proportionality and military necessity have historically tended to obscure the gendered effects of armed conflict through a focus on both the inevitability of violence and the accepted reality of destructive military procedures. Even though there has been greater awareness of women's lived experiences within the international legal framework, the international humanitarian law of armed conflict has continued to favour military tactics and authorized violence. Scholars have used the phrase 'lawfare' in order to exemplify the use of legal arguments and interpretations to justify killing.[97]

---

95. Puar, ibid., 527

96. Puar, ibid., 533

97. David Kennedy, *Of War and Law* (Princeton University Press 2006) 12, 125; David Kennedy, 'Lawfare and Warfare' in James Crawford and Martti Koskenniemi (eds), *The Cambridge Companion to International Law* (Cambridge University Press 2012); Eyal Weizman, 'Legislative Attack' (2010) 27 (6) Theory, Culture and Society 11

Kennedy states that law has allowed 'us' to lose our 'moral compass', as the claimed legality of an act can obscure the lives lost or affected by the military act.[98] Similarly, international humanitarian law's ability to accept violent and destructive tactics as an inevitable component of armed conflict disguises the gendered structures embedded in the law as well as the intersectional realities of war's by-products. The lawfare thesis neglects to analyse the assumed gender of the actors who are able to enter the 'game' of lawfare and thus at once acknowledges the law and violence nexus but ignores the manner in which interlocking structural assumptions perpetuate lawfare and warfare in gendered and racialized ways that reproduce global power dynamics.

The lawfare thesis acknowledges the malleability of principles such as proportionality and necessity to give a wide range of acts the cloak of legality. Reminiscent of Charlesworth's critique of mainstream scholarship which fails to acknowledge the feminist engagement with the law of armed conflict, critical scholars debating and articulating lawfare, although likely familiar with key feminist texts, have not acknowledged the gendered contours of lawfare. A feminist analysis might examine how decision-making processes, from the state to military commanders, deploy gendered framings of authority and governance, where assertiveness and unemotive capacity to make 'hard decisions' are assumed characteristics. That increasingly women have entered the 'war room' and held key positions within command structures of powerful states has been given little, if any, analysis. The equal capacity of women to authorize military strikes, to use the principles of proportionality and necessity to justify new forms of warfare, to in effect use the assumed objectivity of law to achieve other, questionable goals, for example under the global war on terror, challenges the myth of a gender binary and requires a more complicated understanding of gender to inform analysis. That is, gender as an intersectional power dynamic and the potential for gender to be understood as a fluid and diverse power structure asks new questions of lawfare and complicates the theorization of the relationship between law and military behaviours. If female co-optation into gendered, sexualized and racialized violence informs our first space of analysis, the role of women as agents and actors within lawfare further complicates the simple gendered binaries of male agents and female victims.

98. Kennedy, 'Lawfare and Warfare', ibid., 181

Furthermore, the concept of 'new wars' recognizes that the wars of today are fought by a variety of actors that do not necessarily have state affiliations, these wars are fought in the name of identity and their methods do not follow the typical ideas of 'battle' or acquisition of territory.[99] In new wars, violence is directed at civilians as a method to control territory, and small-scale local conflicts are knitted into large spaces of insecurity.[100] Kaldor argues that 'this insistence on viewing conflicts in Old War terms is a huge obstacle to solving many of the world's deep-rooted problems and indeed may exacerbate them'.[101] It is only through acknowledging that the wars of today have changed that law can begin to adapt in order to better understand ways to both prevent and respond to conflict. Kaldor warns against applying the concepts of insecurity found in 'old wars' to 'new wars'.[102] Similarly, the ever-growing gendered effects of armed conflict, which can extend to food shortages, water scarcity, lack of educational prospects, increased instance of domestic abuse, and a varying degree of quality healthcare were not necessarily understood as a consequence of 'old wars'. Yet, these effects, many of which have long-term implications, must be included in the remit of new wars, as these by-products have in many cases the potential to worsen gender inequalities and create greater insecurity for individuals in post-conflict communities. Ignorance to these factors also has the potential to hinder peace processes, which is why they not only need to be incorporated in post-conflict conceptions of justice but also in understanding the framework of international humanitarian law of armed conflict so as to remain visible within the law during and after the conflict.

States remain positioned as central in international law. State consent remains the underlying basis of all international law with other international legal subjects gaining their authority through state delegations of power.[103] Nevertheless, while states are deemed to be

---

99. Chinkin and Kaldor, above note 88; Kaldor, above note 88

100. Chinkin and Kaldor, ibid.

101. Mary Kaldor, 'Old Wars, Cold Wars, New Wars, and the War on Terror' (2005) 42 International Politics 491

102. Ibid., 498

103. *Reparation for Injuries Suffered in the Service of the United Nations* (Advisory Opinion) [1949] ICJ Rep 174

equal in international law, it is evident that, in terms of power, they are not and never have been.[104] In addition, as feminists have shown, the way the sovereign state is conceived comes from a particular, masculinist, liberal ideology which needs to be challenged and critiqued.[105] These critiques prove problematic for international humanitarian law of armed conflict in that these laws which make some violence permissible and some not are drafted and agreed by states with a vested interest, the most powerful states having more of an influence than others.

Sovereign equality is a legal fiction. States differ in strength, size and power. While sovereign equality is an important legal fiction in some ways – formal equality being better than no equality at all – this legal fiction works to conceal the fact that international law is based upon, and has always been based upon, inequality and exclusion.[106] Some states historically were seen as too 'uncivilized' to join the international community of states; similar colonial power dynamics continue to the present day with some states' voices being heard more strongly than others despite proclamations of sovereign equality.[107] Algerian diplomat and jurist, Bedjaoui, for example, described sovereign equality as working to conceal real inequalities that have 'favoured the seizure of the wealth and possessions of weaker peoples'.[108] The phenomenon

104. See Matthew Craven, 'What Happened to Unequal Treaties? The Continuities of Informal Empire' (2005) 74 Nordic Journal of International Law 335

105. Hilary Charlesworth, 'The Sex of the State in International Law' in Ngaire Naffine and Rosemary Owens (eds), *Sexing the Subject of Law* (Law Book Company 1997); Yoriko Otomo, 'Of Mimicry and Madness: Speculations on the State' (2008) 28 Australian Feminist Law Journal 53

106. Gerry Simpson, *Great Powers and Outlaw States: Unequal Sovereigns in the International Legal Order* (Cambridge University Press 2004) xii

107. See Antony Anghie, *Imperialism, Sovereignty and the Making of International Law* (Cambridge University Press 2007); Antony Anghie, 'Finding the Peripheries: Sovereignty and Colonialism in Nineteenth-Century International Law' (1999) 40 (1) Harvard International Law Journal 1. Note that the same patterns of inclusion and exclusion can also be seen through state recognition practices whereby it tends to be entities with powerful allies who are given recognition. See Rose Parfitt, 'Theorizing Recognition and International Personality' in Anne Orford and Florian Hoffmann (eds), *The Oxford Handbook of the Theory of International Law* (Oxford University Press 2016)

108. Mohammed Bedjaoui, *Towards a New International Economic Order* (Holmes & Meier 1979) 49

of drone warfare has allowed powerful states to intervene in a range of conflicts while proclaiming that they are not *really* involved. Via drone warfare and the loose application of the laws of armed conflict, the laws determining who is a 'legitimate target' and what amount of 'collateral damage' are deployed to restrict violence while working to reinforce the violence which is not deemed illegal, thus legitimizing it.[109] This works to uphold a false notion of, to draw on the Martens Clause, 'humanity' and 'public conscience'. In that, some lives are, under this model, deemed to be less grievable, and more targetable than others; these lines tend to be drawn on gendered and racialized boundaries.[110]

The international humanitarian law of armed conflict, although focused on the methods and means of armed conflict and the development of humanitarian restraints on the conduct of hostilities, is underpinned by much larger gender framings that require further structural bias feminist analysis. This structural bias feminist analysis, as we have begun to provide in this chapter, might challenge the structures of military laws and behaviour via a wider and deeper understanding of subjectivity and global power structures, that draws in intersectional feminist accounts as well as queer accounts of the diversity of the lived experiences of gender.

Conclusion

Therefore, as we seek to understand and to respond to the current configurations of war – in which distinctions of civilization and definitions of 'humanity' abound, and the liberation of women in blue burkas designates a putative U.S. triumph while demarcating the difference of combatant and civilian – it is to this inheritance that we must turn if we are to think what we are doing.[111]

It is with these words that Kinsella concludes her analysis of the gendered nature of international humanitarian law, prefiguring Arvidsson and

109. Judith Gardam, 'A Role for Proportionality in the War on Terror', above note 9

110. See Judith Butler, *Frames of War: When Is Life Grievable?* (Verso 2009); Laleh Khalili, 'Gendered Practices of Counterinsurgency' (2011) 37 Review of International Studies 1471; Wilcox, above note 53

111. Kinsella, above note 11, 185

Jones' later concerns with who the 'human' in humanitarianism is.[112] The study of who the 'players' in armed conflict are reminds us that violence does not have a gender, although its effects may be gendered. As such, we draw on Otto's approach to the tension between resistance and compliance in identifying the risk of essentialism through inclusion and the enduring militarism of international institutions as a barrier to inside strategies. Otto thus argues for the recognition of the 'footholds' created by feminist actors in institutions while maintaining, investing and strengthening feminist activism that is outside of those same institutions, thus proposing that resistance and compliance feminisms are seen and held together.[113] In doing so Otto also calls for a feminist activism that is 'multi-gendered' and attentive to 'gender disruptions'.[114]

To Otto's gender disruptions, we add contemporary work that imagines the posthuman, and posthuman feminist approaches, to think differently about subjectivity, militarism and the use of technology for military ends. Posthuman feminism interrogates distinctions made between humans and non-humans. As Jones writes:

> Feminist posthumanism uses technology (alongside the nonhuman animal and matter) to question what it means to be human, deconstructing the very notion of what the human is, noting that the concept of the human in dominant Western accounts of subjectivity creates hierarchies between humans as well as between the human and other living beings.[115]

Posthuman feminism thus re-thinks dominant narratives of military technologies, such as drones, where the human is imagined as the decision-maker and the machine is imagined as the other-object acting on human orders. Challenging this narrative, posthuman feminism notes the connections between the human and the machine. Jones, for example, challenges this construction of the drone and, in fact, all military technologies as machine-object-other. She does this, for example, through noting ways in which data collection, as collected by drones and other forms of technology, is collated together in drone

---

112. Arvidsson, above note 86; Emily Jones, 'A Posthuman-Xenofeminist Analysis of the Discourse on Autonomous Weapons Systems and Other Killing Machines' (2018) 44 (1) Australian Feminist Law Journal 93
113. Otto, above note 7, 117
114. Otto, ibid.
115. Jones, above note 112, 95

warfare to create a file that, in the words of Chamayou, 'once it becomes thick enough, will constitute a death warrant'.[116] As Chamayou's words and as posthuman feminist analyses highlight, the idea of the human being as the one making the decision in this narrative must be questioned. While it is, indeed, the human making the 'ultimate' decision to target, fly the drone and use weaponry, the scope for decision-making which is left after the machines have provided such a mass of data is to be questioned.

While noting the importance of understanding machine-human connections, however, Jones also works to centre feminist anti-militarism when analysing and understanding the larger military apparatus, defining anti-militarism as aiming to challenge gendered and colonial power dynamics as well as the 'the industrial, technologically crafted, capitalist-driven military complex'.[117] This view on anti-militarism, drawing in the complicity of militarism in larger structures and the maintenance of power, the flow of capital and imposition of a specific worldview from dominant knowledge forms is illustrative of how gender framings that add women's or gendered lives to existing legal arrangements will not shift the underlying structures which rely on gender, and the gender binary, for their continued dominance.

In this chapter we have used a feminist analysis of the international humanitarian law of armed conflict and the risks of compliance and essentialism as a means to bridge towards alternative conceptions of and engagements with law. This has required an analysis and acceptance of the value of feminist accounts of the international humanitarian law of armed conflict, its various treaties and principles, to develop an understanding of how discourses of victimhood and vulnerability are entrenched within accounts of military masculinities and function to reproduce intersectional power structures/inequalities. The chapter provides an account of the international humanitarian law of armed conflict as it has been critiqued by feminist scholarship while also problematizing the acceptance of the *jus in bello*, both in terms of the acceptance of the assumed inevitability of armed conflict and the assumed distinction between war and peace. In raising an account of the gendered construction of subjectivity, feminist analysis shifts towards a deeper account of violence in peacetime and conflict states as co-opted

116. Grégoire Chamayou, *A Theory of the Drone* (trans. Janet Lloyd, The New Press 2015) 49

117. Jones, above note 112, 116

and produced through larger vectors of power and their intersections. Importantly, a study of female violence and spaces where women are the agents of military violence leads to an interrogation beyond the attachment to a stable gender binary to question the potential for fluid and diverse accounts of gender. This structural account then questions the very conceptualization of the subject of law, asking about the nature of the human imagined within humanitarian law and considering human and non-human encounters as a space for future feminist encounters with law, violence, war and peace.

Chapter 5

INTERNATIONAL CRIMINAL LAW

A criminal trial institutionalizes a legal sensibility and ritualizes grief and the feeling of loss.[1]

... a hallmark of enlightened nations is to exercise restraint and moderation, to practice judgment and reason; accordingly, transparent displays of sheer physicality, prurient excitement, and poor judgment indicate barbarity. Thus, better nations conclude, 'rape should not go unpunished in war'.[2]

We close Volume One with a gender analysis of the contemporary landscape of international criminal law. Specifically, we interrogate existing feminist interventions into international criminal law, alongside the contours of the discipline, in order to contrast the hypervisibility of sexual violence with the lack of visibility given to women who perpetrate international criminal offences. We argue that exploring this aspect of international criminal law leads to a better understanding of gender within legal accounts of armed conflict. The chapter analyses and contrasts essentialized understandings of gender and conflict via developments in international criminal law. We examine the consequences of primarily identifying women in war as victims of sexual violence to conclude with a critique of carceral feminist assumptions and, in particular, of the idea that justice should and can be provided primarily through criminalization and incarceration.

Similar to domestic law, international criminal law functions through, and therefore perpetuates, the existence of binaries: guilty/ not-guilty, victim/violator, legal/illegal, domestic/international, public/

1. Maria Elander, 'The Victim's Address: Expressivism and the Victim at the Extraordinary Chambers in the Courts of Cambodia' (2013) 7 The International Journal of Transitional Justice 95, 96

2. Helen Kinsella, *The Image before the Weapon: A Critical History of the Distinction between Combatant and Civilian* (Cornell University Press 2011) 73

private. Feminist legal scholars have long shown 'the gendered coding' of these binaries.[3] While the criminal trial requires the use of these categories, it also reinforces gendered knowledge paradigms that potentially displace alternative accounts and mechanisms for justice. This is evident in the construction of narratives around the roles of women in war. We argue for an understanding of peace and conflict that is not only a continuum, but also entertains a fluid and complex relationship, which can help in challenging reductive meta-conflict narratives and essentializing accounts of gender.[4] This approach provides a useful preface for the following volume and the study of the persistence of militarism in post-conflict states, the role of protection narratives in peacekeeping missions and the continued return to an approach of 'adding women' in both peace agreements and transitional justice mechanisms in a manner that reinforces, rather than undoes, dominant conflict narratives.

Although feminists in the 1990s were successful in making important interventions within international criminal law, pursuing the inclusion of crimes of sexual violence within the definition of international crimes and thus ensuring some key early prosecutions were undertaken,[5] a range of other gendered consequences resulted from these interventions. Such consequences included the limited analysis of indirect and other forms of violence and their gendered effects, the challenges and consequences of sexual violence perpetrated against men, and the production of women's sexuality as the central pivot through which women's experiences of armed conflict were understood.

While there has been some, albeit limited, recognition of gendered outcomes of the hyperfocus on sexual violence, such as the recognition

3. Hilary Charlesworth and Christine Chinkin, *The Boundaries of International Law: a Feminist Analysis* (Manchester University Press 2000) 49, referring to Carol Cohn, 'Wars, Wimps, and Women: Talking Gender and Thinking War' in Miriam Cooke and Angela Woollacott (eds), *Gendering War Talk* (Princeton University Press 1993)

4. Dianne Otto, *Rethinking Peace from a Queer Feminist Perspective*, 26 September 2019, Public Lecture at LSE Centre for Women, Peace and Security, London

5. See Janet Halley, 'Rape at Rome: Feminist Interventions in the Criminalisation of Sex-Related Violence in Positive International Criminal Law' (2008) 30 (1) Michigan Journal of International Law 1; ICTR Trial Chamber I, *Prosecutor v Akayesu*, Judgment, Case ICTR-96-4-T, 2 September 1998

that sexual violence also occurs against men,[6] female perpetrators, defendants and accused remain on the peripheries of both international criminal law and scholarly enquiry. This exemplifies the narrow understanding of women's roles in law and armed conflict,[7] and is representative of a deeper structural bias within international criminal law: that is, the placing of individuals as well as harms into specific gendered categories. Thus, we use feminism to search for paths beyond the gendered binaries created in dominant narratives of international criminal law to examine how feminist knowledge travels horizontally as well as how it illuminates the discourses of race, sexuality and gender that inflect international criminal law spaces and, in particular, the victim/perpetrator binary. This chapter builds on the work of Labenski's analysis of the binary of victim/defendant evident in international criminal law as well as a product of, primarily, western radical feminist intervention into international criminal law.[8] Our goal is not to dismiss the importance of the integration of women's issues into international law since the 1990s. Women are often disproportionately victims of insecurity and work must still be carried out to interrogate the reasons behind the gendered violence that occurs in armed conflict; nevertheless, we regard the shift away from a hyperfocus on women as victims and women's sexuality as an important component of such an approach.

An analysis of female perpetrators in international criminal justice therefore becomes important when juxtaposed to predominant essentialist narratives of victimhood and peacefulness of women. This analysis is not carried out with the intent of demonstrating women as

6. ICTY Trial Chamber II, *Prosecutor v Tadić*, Opinion and Judgement, Case IT-94-1-T, 7 May 1997; ICTY Trial Chamber I, *Prosecutor v Mucić et al*, Judgement, Case IT-96-21-T, 16 November 1998; ICTY Appeals Chamber, *Prosecutor v Tadić*, Judgement in Sentencing Appeals, Case IT-94-1-A, 26 January 2000; ICTY Trial Chamber I, *Prosecutor v Todorović*, Sentencing Judgement, Case IT-95-9/1-S, 31 July 2001; ICTY Trial Chamber II, *Prosecutor v Simić*, Sentencing Judgement, Case IT-95-9/2-S, 17 October 2002; ICTY Trial Chamber I, *Prosecutor v Češić*, Sentencing Judgement, Case IT-95-10/1-S, 11 March 2004; see Leila Ullrich, "'But What about Men?'": Gender Disquiet in International Criminal Justice', Theoretical Criminology, published online 28 November 2019 https://doi.org/10.1177/1362480619887164 (accessed December 2019)

7. Sheri Labenski, *Female Defendants in International Criminal Law: Feminist Dialogues* (Routledge 2021, forthcoming)

8. Labenski, ibid.

evil too, rather to promote reflection on how narrative absences are indicative and perpetuating of gender stereotypes. Feminist authors have already provided a substantive contribution on the experiences of women in active combat roles and more widely in resistance movements.[9] This work has been crucial in contrasting dominant gendered understandings of who can be seen as a combatant and which behaviours count as resistance during armed conflict.[10] Importantly, these contributions should be distinguished from collections of female biographies or romanticized narrations of, for instance, women supporting a fascist regime, as these were not written with the intent to contribute to a gender analysis.[11]

We offer a reflection on the functioning of law that is cognisant of law's multifaceted effects: its capacity to deliver forms of justice and protection as well as its more violent dimension through analyses of women's active roles in participating or supporting armed violence.[12] An account of criminal trials where experiences of conflict must be termed in the categories available in law (victim/perpetrator) in order to receive legal attention presupposes the design and structure of law within a very specific knowledge history. Therefore, it could be argued that feminist interventions aimed at providing further visibility for women's experiences of harm in conflict are constrained through the available language of law in the articulation of their demands and of the range of legal perceptions perceived as available. While in the context of a criminal trial dominant legal categories can be useful to receive redress for the harm experienced, when entire narratives of gender in conflict are articulated duplicating the same categories they risk delivering essentialist pictures of seemingly unavoidable female victimhood and male violence.

9. Dyan Mazurana, 'Women, Girls, and Non-State Armed Opposition Groups' in Carol Cohn (ed), *Women and Wars: Contested Histories, Uncertain Futures* (Polity Press 2013); Miranda Alison, 'Women as Agents of Political Violence: Gendering Security' (2004) 35 (4) Security Dialogue 447; Caroline Moser and Fiona Clark (eds), *Victims, Perpetrators or Actors? Gender, Armed Conflict and Political Violence* (Zed Books 2001)

10. Anna Maria Bruzzone and Rachele Farina, *La Resistenza Taciuta: Dodici Vite di Partigiane Piemontesi* (2nd edn, Bollati Boringhieri 2016)

11. RJB Bosworth, *Claretta: Mussolini's Last Lover* (Yale University Press 2017)

12. See our discussion in Chapter 1

Carceral feminist projects have supported the increasing conflation of justice and peace with imprisonment. Scholars such as Halley, Engle and Grady have interrogated carceral feminisms, that is, feminist approaches which centre incarceration as a dominant mode of providing justice in international criminal law.[13] We argue, using a feminist analysis, that criminalization should not be the primary focus when supporting the move from armed conflict to peace. We define international criminal law and transitional justice projects as always partial rather than as a moment of closure. This approach moves towards the focus of Volume Two, where we develop an analysis of what peace processes can achieve when analysed via a feminist methodology, as well as through the knowledge and understanding of transnational feminisms.

In the following section of this chapter, we briefly introduce the Nuremberg and Tokyo Tribunals to demonstrate the foundational, yet limited, understandings that inform the contours of international criminal law today. This section highlights the larger aims and objectives of international criminal law as well as their gendered understandings. We also provide examples of female perpetrators, defendants and accused who have not entered into mainstream understandings of the Second World War, further evidence of

13. See, for a focus on the link with international human rights law: Karen Engle, 'Feminist Governance and International Law: From Liberal to Carceral Feminism' in Janet Halley, Prabha Kotiswaran, Rachel Rebouché and Hila Shamir (eds), *Governance Feminism: Notes from the Field* (University of Minnesota Press 2019); Halley, above note 5; Janet Halley, 'Rape in Berlin: Reconsidering the Criminalisation of Rape in the International Law of Armed Conflict' (2008) 9 (1) Melbourne Journal of International Law 78; Kate Grady, 'Towards a Carceral Geography of International Law' in Sundhya Pahuja and Shane Chalmers (eds), *The Routledge Handbook of International Law and the Humanities* (Routledge 2020); on carceral feminism in anti-trafficking debates, see Elizabeth Bernstein 'The Politics of Sex, Rights, and Freedom in Contemporary Anti-trafficking Campaigns' in Janet Halley, Prabha Kotiswaran, Rachel Rebouché and Hila Shamir (eds), *Governance Feminism: Notes from the Field* (University of Minnesota Press 2019); Elizabeth Bernstein 'Militarized Humanitarianism Meets Carceral Feminism: The Politics of Sex, Rights, and Freedom in Contemporary Antitrafficking Campaigns' (2010) 36 (1) Signs: Journal of Women in Culture and Society 45

international criminal law's gendered scope. We argue that even with the gender law reforms that are apparent from the 1990s, these foundations constrain the possibilities of achieving justice through international criminal law.

The third section introduces the International Criminal Tribunal for the former Yugoslavia (ICTY) and the International Criminal Tribunal for Rwanda (ICTR), to discuss the hypervisibility of sexual violence against women before juxtaposing this with the first example of female perpetrators prosecuted in international criminal tribunals. Section four then draws out an analysis of the various hybrid courts to further complicate the possibilities and limitations of international criminal law and considers local justice histories as potentially holding the lynchpin to the transition to peace after war. In the final section we draw on each of the claims articulated through the range of international criminal institutions introduced, so as to situate the development of the International Criminal Court's (ICC) practice, while examining the future of international criminal law and its potential to undo the gendered legacies of the current structures. The gendered legacies include the failure of international criminal law to address indirect violence, the simplistic binary of 'female victims' and 'male perpetrators', and the reducing of local justice mechanisms to adjuncts for transitional justice modes. The interplay of accounts of feminist and international criminal legal histories allows for a theoretical framework within this chapter that is at once grounded in and a response to existing legal knowledge, yet simultaneously open to explore alternative legal futures.

By way of conclusion we argue against carceral modes of feminist engagement and in favour of a shift away from a focus on criminalization towards new knowledge projects that are directed by local, diverse and creative voices. While we do not explore these alternatives in this book, this sets the frame for Volume Two, where we centre the relationship between law, war and gender through the lens of post-conflict processes – peace agreements, peacekeeping, peacebuilding – while also addressing the tensions between powerful *state* investment in the technologies of war and feminist anti-militarism.

International criminal law: Gendered origins and aims

In 1945 the International Military Tribunal (IMT) was established in Nuremberg, Germany, to try the most senior war criminals of the

Second World War.[14] The Nuremberg Tribunal was the first international institution to carry out international criminal prosecutions. In 1946 the Allied Powers established the International Military Tribunal for the Far East (IMTFE),[15] also known as the Tokyo Tribunal. The creation of these tribunals was a landmark achievement, establishing the principle of international individual responsibility for crimes against peace, war crimes and crimes against humanity, and reversing the principle whereby state officials could only be judged by their respective domestic courts.

The Tribunals created the foundations for present-day international criminal law, even if this was underscored by the dismissal of the atrocities committed by the Allied Powers and the primacy given to the international criminal justice trials over domestic courts. Henry argues that through the work of the two Tribunals international criminal justice was enshrined as a source of legal certainty, capable of both providing an accurate history of past events and also as a way to suitably account for the 'inhumanity' of armed conflict.[16] Both Tribunals only prosecuted individuals from the defeated parties and obscured the breadth of harm that had occurred in the conflict, which interlocks with a crisis approach to international law.[17] Today, there is a distinction within the women, peace and security framework between the focus on conflict-related sexual violence (mostly assumed to be perpetrated by non-state actors), and sexual exploitation and abuse (the key category of gender-based violence attributable to UN actors). This perpetuates a similar set of assumptions about where in the world significant violence is believed to occur, which acts the international community sees as desirable to bring to global attention, and who is held accountable.[18]

14. Charter of the International Military Tribunal – Annex to the Agreement for the Prosecution and Punishment of the Major War Criminals of the European Axis (8 August 1945) [hereafter London Agreement]

15. Special Proclamation – Establishment of an International Military Tribunal for the Far East and Charter of the International Military Tribunal for the Far East (19 January 1946)

16. Nicola Henry, 'Memory of an Injustice: The "Comfort Women" and the Legacy of the Tokyo Trial' (2013) 37 (3) Asian Studies Review 362, 363

17. Hilary Charlesworth, 'International Law: A Discipline of Crisis' (2002) 65 (3) Modern Law Review 377

18. Gina Heathcote, 'Robust Peacekeeping, Gender, and the Protection of Civilians' in Jeremy Farrall and Hilary Charlesworth (eds), *Strengthening the Rule of Law through the UN Security Council* (Routledge 2016)

Present-day international criminal law constructs the means for holding individuals (primarily political and military leaders) accountable for the commission of serious violations of international humanitarian law (i.e. war crimes), the crime of genocide, and crimes against humanity during international and non-international armed conflicts.[19] The crime of genocide and crimes against humanity exist in 'peacetime' as well as during armed conflict.[20] The categories of crimes within international criminal law also include the crime of aggression, although this is yet to be operationalized within contemporary court structures.[21] One of the aims of international criminal law is to address the impunity of leaders and deter future atrocities through prosecution, punishment and the public condemnation of brutal and destructive acts. Additional goals include providing justice to victims, aiding in community reconciliation and recording an accurate historical account of the armed conflict. However, these latter aims are not necessarily

19. Despite the work of Lemkin to articulate the crime of genocide in 1943, and the subsequent creation of the Convention on the Prevention and Punishment of the Crime of Genocide, adopted by the UN General Assembly in 1948, genocide was not a crime under the jurisdiction of the Tribunals; International Law Commission, 'The Charter and Judgement of the Nürnberg Tribunal: History and Analysis' Appendix II (1949) UN Doc. A/CN.4/5; London Agreement, above note 14; Convention on the Prevention and Punishment of the Crime of Genocide, 78 UNTS 277 (adopted 9 December 1948, entered into force 12 January 1951) [hereafter Genocide Convention]

20. See, for an introduction, Antonio Cassese and Paola Gaeta, *Cassese's International Criminal Law* (Oxford University Press 2013); see, for a feminist account of developments within international criminal law, Louise Chappell and Andrea Durbach (eds), 'The International Criminal Court – a Site of Gender Justice' (2014) Special Issue of International Feminist Journal of Politics; Louise Chappell, *The Politics of Gender Justice at the International Criminal Court: Legacies and Legitimacy* (Oxford University Press 2016). While the ICTY Statute retained the need for a nexus between armed conflict and crimes against humanity, this was discarded as a substantive element in ICTY Appeals Chamber, *Prosecutor v Tadić*, Decision on the Defence Motion for Interlocutory Appeal on Jurisdiction, Case IT-94-1, 2 October 1995, paragraph 141; see also ICTY Appeals Chamber, *Prosecutor v Kunarac et al*, Judgement, Case IT-96-23 & 23/1-A, 12 June 2002, paragraph 83. The ICTR and ICC Statutes no longer required such nexus; Genocide Convention, Article 1

21. See Claus Kreß and Stefan Barriga (eds), *The Crime of Aggression: A Commentary*, Volumes 1 & 2 (Cambridge University Press 2017)

evident in the practice of international criminal courts and tribunals, where claims of victor's justice and unequal global application of the law plague the field.

Simpson describes the role of international criminal law as a historical record, stating that '[w]ar crimes trials are historiographical dramas. They enact a tension between the reproduction of conventional images of the past, and the making visible of obscured or disconcerting vectors of history'.[22] We argue that beyond critiquing the representation of victor's justice or the 'drama' represented in war crimes trials, there is a need for an excavation of the gendered contours of the knowledge produced via the institutions of international criminal law. Following Simpson's account of international criminal law as a space of memory and ordering of the armed conflict, we understand international criminal trials as a part of the historiography of armed conflict.[23] We add to Simpson's thesis that this is a recording, an ordering and a telling of the story of 'who did what to whom', which often reflects the dominant gender perceptions of the actors who gain the privilege of scripting and directing post-conflict narratives. International criminal judgements present the world with a written history of the conflict: judgements identify key actors, highlight important geographical locations and speak with a certainty that creates a factual basis for understanding the conflict. Despite the turn towards, and inclusion of, conflict-related sexual violence and other crimes of gender-based violence within the lists of crimes in international statutes and treaties, we argue that this is not sufficiently inclusive of the range of gendered harms that occur during an armed conflict and – when elevated to the dominant narrative of women's experience of war – risks erasing the nuance in gendered experiences of conflict.[24] We also question whether international criminal law has the capacity to be changed for the better by feminist methodologies.

---

22. Gerry Simpson, *Law, War and Crime: War Crimes, Trials and the Reinvention of International Law* (Polity Press 2007) 94

23. Simpson, ibid.

24. Statute of the International Criminal Tribunal for the former Yugoslavia, Security Council Resolution 827 (25 May 1993) UN Doc. S/RES/827 [hereafter ICTY Statute]; Statute of the International Tribunal for Rwanda, Security Council Resolution 955 (8 November 1994) UN Doc. S/RES/955 [hereafter ICTR Statute]; Rome Statute of the International Criminal Court, General Assembly (17 July 1998) UN Doc. A/CONF.183/9 [hereafter Rome Statute]

While international criminal trials, and investigations prior to trials, focus on facts and 'fact finding', the judgements of international criminal courts and tribunals often have a narrow jurisdiction with limited, if any, account of the range of gendered harms that have occurred, beyond sexual violence; or how any specific harm will have specific gendered meanings and effects.[25] Gendered harms, and harms that have distinctly gendered manifestations – including the breakdown of social services, increases in mental illness and domestic violence, a lack of educational opportunities and the destruction of the environment – are often not recognized as losses connected to armed conflict even though they may be the result of conflict and extend beyond the 'official end' of an armed conflict.[26] This raises specific additional concerns when the historical records found within international criminal law are not viewed alongside the work emanating from local transitional justice and reconciliatory spaces. Contemporary feminist scholarship has increasingly highlighted the gender, racial, ethnic and socio-economic tensions that must be addressed in order to facilitate post-conflict peace processes;[27] however, the dominant feminist literature on international criminal law has centred on crimes of sexual violence.[28]

25. Patricia Viseur Sellers, 'Gender Strategy Is Not Luxury for International Courts Symposium: Prosecuting Sexual and Gender-Based Crimes before International/ized Criminal Courts' (2009) 17 (2) Journal of Gender, Social Policy and the Law 301

26. See Catherine O'Rourke, *Gender Politics in Transitional Justice* (Routledge 2013)

27. See Sara E Davies, Nicole George and Jacqui True, 'The Difference That Gender Makes to International Peace and Security' (2017) 19 (1) Special Issue of International Feminist Journal of Politics 1; Nicola Pratt and Sophie Richter-Devroe, 'Critically Examining UNSCR 1325 on Women, Peace and Security' (2011) 13 (4) International Feminist Journal of Politics 489

28. Kelly Dawn Askin, 'Gender Crimes Jurisprudence in the ICTR: Positive Developments' (2005) 3 (4) Journal of International Criminal Justice 1007; Barbara Bedont and Katherine Hall-Martinez, 'Ending Impunity for Gender Crimes under the International Criminal Court' (1999) 6 (1) The Brown Journal of World Affairs 65; Doris Buss, 'Expert Witnesses and International War Crimes Trials: Making Sense of Large-Scale Violence in Rwanda' in Dubravka Zarkov and Marlies Glasius (eds), *Narratives of Justice in and out of the Courtroom: Former Yugoslavia and Beyond* (Springer 2014); Doris Buss, 'Performing Legal

We argue that there is a need to ask uncomfortable questions in response to international criminal law and feminist interventions into international criminal law. Implicit within this analysis is the larger discussion of whether international criminal law should remain a central project within international law and larger transitional justice structures. We revisit this topic later in the chapter when we discuss carceral feminist approaches. Moreover, feminist analysis in international criminal law includes a questioning of the normative values that are placed as self-evident within international criminal legal structures and processes, alongside an enquiry – and asking of – what is lost in the fixing of a narrow binary of heteronormative gendered knowledge as a means to engage and understand an armed conflict.

One area where international criminal law jurisprudence demonstrates the limited gender account within law is in response to female violence. The existence of female actors who participated in leadership crimes during the Second World War is not widely known despite the fact that women played a significant role in the maintenance and operation of concentration camps, as well as contributing to the larger aims of the Nazi ideology. Ilse Koch, along with her husband, ran Buchenwald concentration camp and was known as the 'Queen of Buchenwald', 'Red Witch of Buchenwald', 'Butcher Widow' and 'The Bitch of Buchenwald'. Koch was accused of making household

Order: Some Feminist Thoughts on International Criminal Law' (2011) 11 International Criminal Law Review 409; Doris Buss, 'The Curious Visibility of Wartime Rape: Gender and Ethnicity in International Criminal Law' (2007) 25 Windsor Yearbook of Access to Justice 3; Karen Engle, 'Judging Sex in War' (2008) 106 (6) Michigan Law Review 941; Karen Engle, 'Feminism and Its (Dis)contents: Criminalizing Wartime Rape in Bosnia and Herzegovina' (2005) 99 (4) American Journal of International Law 778; Janet Halley, Prabha Kotiswaran, Hila Shamir and Chantal Thomas, 'From the International to the Local in Feminist Legal Responses to Rape, Prostitution/Sex Work, and Sex Trafficking: Four Studies in Contemporary Governance Feminism' (2006) 29 (2) Harvard Journal of Law & Gender 335; Halley, above note 5; Halley, above note 13; Catharine MacKinnon, 'Rape, Genocide, and Women's Human Rights' (1994) 17 Harvard Women's Law Journal 5; Catharine MacKinnon, 'The ICTR's Legacy on Sexual Violence' (2008) 14 New England Journal of International & Comparative Law 211

objects out of human skin in a US military trial in Germany.[29] Other women were in careers which facilitated their violent conduct. Herta Oberheuser, the doctor who conducted experiments on prisoners in Auschwitz and Ravensbrück concentration camps, was brought before the Nuremberg court in the 'Doctor's trial' conducted by the US military, and was charged with crimes against humanity and common design or conspiracy to commit war crimes or crimes against humanity.[30] While eventually she only served five years in prison, Oberheuser was initially given a sentence of twenty years.[31] There are also the examples of Irma Grese,[32] Erna Petri,[33] Herta Bothe,[34] Maria Mandl,[35] Elisabeth Volkenrath,[36] Juana Boormann,[37] Alice Orlowski,[38] Dorothea Binz,[39] Hildegard Lächert[40] and Hermine Braunsteiner,[41] who were all involved in perpetrating or facilitating violence during the Second World War. However, their existence remains on the fringes of dominant conflict

29. Flint Whitlock, *The Beasts of Buchenwald: Karl & Ilse Koch, Human-Skin Lampshades, and the War-Crimes Trial of the Century (Buchenwald Trilogy)* (Cable Publishing 2011); Isabel Kershner, 'Women's Role in Holocaust May Exceed Old Notions' 17 July 2010, *The New York Times* https://www.nytimes.com/2010/07/18/world/europe/18holocaust.html (accessed December 2019); see Haley A Wodenshek, 'Ordinary Women: Female Perpetrators of the Nazi Final Solution' (2015) *Trinity College Senior Thesis* https://digitalrepository.trincoll.edu/theses/522/ (accessed December 2019)

30. 'Doctors' Trial Transcripts' (1974) *National Archives and Records Administration* https://archive.org/details/DoctorsTrialTranscripts/page/n7 (accessed December 2019)

31. Sentence amended to 10 years and then let out early for good conduct

32. Kershner, above note 29; Wodenshek, above note 29, 110

33. Kershner, above note 29

34. Wendy Adele-Marie Sarti, *Women and Nazis: Perpetrators of Genocide and Other Crimes during Hitler's Regime, 1933–1945* (Academica Press 2011) 85–90

35. Wodenshek, above note 29, 112; Sarti, ibid., 131–40

36. Sarti, ibid., 99–108

37. Sarti, ibid., 76–84

38. Elissa Mailänder, *Female SS Guards and Workaday Violence: The Majdanek Concentration Camp, 1942–1944* (Michigan State University Press 2015)

39. See Mailänder, ibid.; Sarti, above note 34, 71–6

40. Sarti, ibid., 127–30

41. Sarti, ibid., 91–8; Wodenshek, above note 29

accounts, which often underplay women's participation in criminal acts and none of these actors were tried in the international military tribunals. It may seem unnecessary for broader feminist goals to highlight female perpetrators' lack of visibility. Indeed, '[a]cknowledging women's violence or support to violence has been a difficult process for many feminists'.[42] However, we argue that it deserves attention because the erasure of the actions of female perpetrators is underpinned by the same essentialist gendered readings that confine women's accounts of conflict to stories of victimization.

While there is evidence of female perpetrators within the Nazi regime, they have not entered into mainstream historical accounts of the Second World War. Pető argues that the lack of photographs of female perpetrators post-Second World War correlates to the dearth of theoretical analysis on women's participation in the atrocities of Nazi Germany.[43] As a result of the lack of photographic evidence on women's crimes during the Second World War the historical record has been altered and the retellings of women's experiences remain tied only to stories of victims and peacemakers. Furthermore, the process of creating an accurate historical record, said to be an aim of international criminal law, is dismissed when violent acts are forgotten. Lucidly confronting the reality of the conflict is essential in order to prevent such atrocities from happening again. Pető states:

> The question concerns the monopoly of interpretation: who has the right to say what we (should) see in the photo. Thus, returning to the main question, that of the divided memory of the war, we can state that the interpretation of photographs has also contributed to the development of a divided memory.[44]

The privileging of certain historical narratives serves to illustrate the power in both storytelling and knowledge production. If women's

42. Fionnuala Ní Aoláin, Dina Francesca Haynes and Naomi Cahn, *On the Frontlines: Gender, War, and the Post-Conflict Process* (Oxford University Press 2011) 43

43. Andrea Pető, 'Forgotten Perpetrators: Photographs of Female Perpetrators after WWII' in Ayşe Gül Altınay and Andrea Pető (eds), *Gendered Wars, Gendered Memories: Feminist Conversations on War, Genocide and Political Violence* (Routledge 2016) 203–19

44. Pető, ibid., 215

participation in atrocities during the Second World War was integrated into the larger narrative of the conflict, then it might have unearthed nuanced understandings of gender, ethnicity and class, which could have shaped the development of international criminal law.

The International Criminal Tribunal for the former Yugoslavia and the International Criminal Tribunal for Rwanda

Following the increased media attention to human rights violations and the scale of the atrocities committed during the armed conflicts in the former Yugoslavia and Rwanda, the UN Security Council established the International Criminal Tribunal for the former Yugoslavia (ICTY) and the International Criminal Tribunal for Rwanda (ICTR). The Security Council determined that the situation in the territory of the former Yugoslavia constituted 'a threat to international peace and security', as is required to activate Article 41 of the UN Charter, and established the ICTY in 1993.[45] Security Council resolution 827 contained the initial statute for the ICTY, which lists the tribunal's jurisdiction and organizational structure.[46] The ICTY's jurisdiction concerns crimes in 'the territory of the former Socialist Federal Republic of Yugoslavia, including its land surface, airspace and territorial waters' since 1991 and is specifically centred upon four categories: grave breaches of the Geneva Conventions, violations of the laws and customs of war, genocide and crimes against humanity.[47] The Security Council created the ICTR after recognizing that the situation in Rwanda constituted 'a threat to international peace and security' and determining that prosecuting those who violated international humanitarian law would help bring peace and reconciliation to those affected by the conflict.[48] In November 1994, the UN Security Council passed resolution 955, which adopted the statute for the ICTR.[49] The Tribunal was established to prosecute serious violations of international humanitarian law in Rwanda, as well as violations committed by Rwandan citizens

---

45. ICTY Statute, above note 24
46. ICTY Statute, ibid.
47. ICTY Statute, ibid., Articles 2, 3, 4, 5 and 8
48. ICTR Statute, above note 24
49. ICTR Statute, ibid.

in neighbouring states,[50] which included the crimes of genocide, crimes against humanity and violations of Article 3 common to the Geneva Conventions and Additional Protocol II, committed between 1 January 1994 and 31 December 1994.[51]

With the creation of the ICTY and ICTR, the prosecution of crimes that were at one time beyond the reach of international law due to the lack of an 'international criminal code' was able to be pursued.[52] Until the creation of the tribunals, there was not a sufficient legal basis to hold individuals to account for crimes, which was established with the Statutes of the *ad hoc* tribunals. Traditionally, states have been reluctant to cede part of their sovereignty to an international court or tribunal, but the establishment of the tribunals demonstrated that previous barriers to prosecution, such as state sovereignty and the exercise of domestic jurisdiction, could be overcome via the operation of the Security Council's Chapter VII powers. Humphrey describes the tribunals as an attempt to prosecute human rights violations when states were unlikely to do so, and to encourage the application of human rights law in circumstances where states did not protect their people from violence.[53] Both the ICTY and ICTR contributed significantly to international criminal jurisprudence establishing an emergent consensus within international law that an international criminal legal system was desirable. However, Simonovic argues that the establishment

50. ICTR Statute, ibid., Articles 1, 7

51. ICTR Statute, ibid., Articles 2-4, 7; the violations set forth by the Additional Protocol II and Article 3 common to the Geneva Conventions were listed as follows, but not limited to: (a) Violence to life, health and physical or mental well-being of persons, in particular murder as well as cruel treatment such as torture, mutilation or any form of corporal punishment; (b) Collective punishments; (c) Taking of hostages; (d) Acts of terrorism; (e) Outrages upon personal dignity, in particular humiliating and degrading treatment, rape, enforced prostitution and any form of indecent assault; (f) Pillage; (g) The passing of sentences and the carrying out of executions without previous judgment pronounced by a regularly constituted court, affording all the judicial guarantees which are recognized as indispensable by civilized peoples; (h) Threats to commit any of the foregoing acts

52. Ralph Zacklin, 'The Failings of Ad Hoc International Tribunals' (2004) 2 (2) Journal of International Criminal Justice 541

53. Michael Humphrey, 'International Intervention, Justice and National Reconciliation: the Role of the ICTY and ICTR in Bosnia and Rwanda' (2003) 2 (4) Journal of Human Rights 495

of the ICTY and ICTR constituted a selective decision made by the international community, indicative of a selective and partial approach to justice.[54]

Sexual violence had remained largely invisible in the proceedings of the Nuremberg and Tokyo Tribunals and Trials,[55] despite the systematic and widespread existence of sexual abuse and violence.[56] With the creation of the ICTY and ICTR and with the publicity regarding the sexual violence that took place during both conflicts, feminists had an opportunity to ensure crimes of sexual and gender-based violence were not written out of the history of the tribunal proceedings. While initial reports on sexual violence in the former Yugoslavia and Rwanda were ignored, reporting on sexual violence by the media was substantially greater in the former Yugoslavia.[57] Bedont and Hall-Martinez describe the publicity surrounding the 'mass rapes' in both the former Yugoslavia and Rwanda, as the driving force in the creation of the ICTY and ICTR.[58] The role of feminist actors was paramount in the successful prosecution of sexual violence crimes in the ICTY and ICTR. In order to promote adequate prosecution, civil society, NGOs and activists wrote briefs, held seminars, were involved in press work and requested meetings.[59]

54. Ivan Simonovic, 'The Role of the ICTY in the Development of International Criminal Adjudication' (1999) 23 (2) Fordham International Law Journal 446, 453

55. The Tokyo Tribunal recognized the rape of women by military leaders, but this was under the category of war crimes and sexual violence was not recognized in its entirety (IMTFE Judgment)

56. Henry, above note 16; Atina Grossmann, 'A Question of Silence: The Rape of German Women by Occupation Soldiers' (1995) 72 October 42; Regina Mühlhäuser, 'The Historicity of Denial: Sexual Violence against Jewish Women during the War of Annihilation, 1941–1945' in Ayşe Gül Altınay and Andrea Pető (eds), *Gendered Wars, Gendered Memories: Feminist Conversations on War, Genocide and Political Violence* (Routledge 2016); Patricia Viseur Sellers, 'The Prosecution of Sexual Violence in Conflict: The Importance of Human Rights as Means of Interpretation' (2008) Office of the United Nations High Commissioner for Human Rights, Women's Human Rights and Gender Unit

57. Heidi Nichols Haddad, 'Mobilizing the Will to Prosecute: Crimes of Rape at the Yugoslav and Rwandan Tribunals' (2011) 12 Human Rights Review 109, 125, 126

58. See Bedont and Hall-Martinez, above note 28

59. Halley et al., above note 28, 342

Feminists, especially within NGOs, credited themselves with the development of international criminal law through the successful prosecution of sexual and gender-based violence.[60] In the ICTY, the *Tadić* case was the first international criminal trial since Nuremberg and Tokyo, and the first international trial to include indictments for crimes of sexual violence, as well as the first trial to prosecute crimes of sexual violence against men.[61] The *Mucić* case was the first case to affirm that rape, under certain circumstances, could constitute a form of torture under international law.[62] In the ICTR the *Akayesu* case saw the conviction of Jean-Paul Akayesu for rape as a crime against humanity and the inclusion of rape as an act of genocide.[63] The term 'rape' was defined in international criminal law for the first time as, 'a physical invasion of a sexual nature ... under circumstances which are coercive.'[64] Sexual violence was also defined in the *Akayesu* case as 'any act of a sexual nature ... under circumstances which are coercive.'[65] However, despite the jurisprudence on crimes of sexual violence, the ICTR failed to capitalize on the success of the *Akayesu* judgement, and the gender jurisprudence outside of the *Akayesu* case was far from adequate, considering how common sexual violence was during the armed conflict.[66] ICTR judges would often include references to crimes of sexual violence in the judgements of trials even if this had not been included in the original indictment, which can be seen as a way of keeping sexual violence crimes visible within the work of the Tribunal.[67] For example, in the *Kayishema* case, although the indictment did not include sexual violence, the Trial Chamber did make reference to the rapes committed during the armed conflict and the overarching scale of sexual violence in the genocide.[68] Despite these successes, the ICTR in many ways was considered to be an afterthought when compared to the ICTY. Mutua describes the ICTR as 'a sideshow

---

60. Halley et al., ibid.
61. *Prosecutor v Tadić*, above note 6
62. *Prosecutor v Mucić et al*, above note 6
63. *Prosecutor v Akayesu*, above note 5
64. *Prosecutor v Akayesu*, ibid., paragraph 598
65. *Prosecutor v Akayesu*, ibid.
66. Askin, above note 28, 1007, 1008
67. Askin, ibid., 1013
68. ICTR Trial Chamber II, *Prosecutor v Kayishema et al*, Judgement, Case ICTR-95-1-T, 21 May 1999

to the Yugoslav Tribunal' and only in existence because the conflicts in the former Yugoslavia and Rwanda were simultaneously brought into global attention via the media.[69]

Feminist scholars have debated the effectiveness of international criminal trials and in particular prosecutions of conflict-related sexual violence. Engle and Halley have highlighted how the interventions of feminists who shaped the understandings of sexual violence in armed conflict within the ICTY and ICTR in order to promote the criminalization of rape and sexual violence narrowed the focus on women's roles in armed conflict to that of victims.[70] MacKinnon was a prominent advocate of international criminal law's role in prosecuting sexual violence crimes, framed through a perception that law is a form of male power she advocated for writing in of crimes that dealt with violence against women.[71] MacKinnon's mode is akin to the modes of carceral feminism; that is, the focus is on high-profile prosecutions of specific individuals rather than a pursuit of larger structural change. In the debates surrounding the ICTY, MacKinnon vehemently advocated that the rape by Serbian men was genocidal.[72] However, this argument was seen as having the potential to dismiss the sexual violence women experienced on all sides during the conflict in the former Yugoslavia. At the same time, feminists who interacted with the ICTY were said to be frequently frustrated as they tried to elicit stories of sexual violence.[73] This led to the interpretation of women's choice of silence, as acknowledgement of their experience of rape. Many of the advocates who wanted rape to be seen as genocide, in the ICTY, believed that the rapes of Croatian and Bosnian Muslim women by Serbian men constituted genocide. However, as the conflict continued and Croatia began to be seen as an aggressor, these same advocates shifted their broad definition of 'rape as genocide' which was narrowed to only

69. Makau Mutua, 'Never Again: Questioning the Yugoslav and Rwanda Tribunals' (1997) 11 Temple International and Comparative Law Journal 167, 178

70. Engle, 'Feminism and Its (Dis)contents: Criminalizing Wartime Rape in Bosnia and Herzegovina', above note 28, 785–6; Halley, above note 5; Halley, above note 13

71. MacKinnon, 'The ICTR's Legacy on Sexual Violence', above note 28, 214, 215

72. Engle, 'Feminism and Its (Dis)contents: Criminalizing Wartime Rape in Bosnia and Herzegovina', above note 28, 785–6

73. Engle, ibid., 794, 795

the rape of Bosnian Muslim women as genocidal.[74] Consequently, MacKinnon began to favour a definition, which she built on an analogy with anti-Semitism and the Holocaust, that distinguished between 'everyday wartime rape' and the specific wartime rape committed by the Serbian men.[75] This view, Engle states, makes a distinction that rape during armed conflict is considered worse than 'everyday rape'.[76]

Other feminists also disagreed with the focus on genocidal rape. Copelon argued that genocidal rape is horrific as well as obvious; associating rape with genocide creates the possibility of rape becoming invisible and that if rape is elevated to the level of genocide, then when women are raped for reasons other than genocide their experiences will be invisible.[77] Copelon further notes, '[w]omen are targets not simply because they "belong to" the enemy ... They are targets because they, too, *are* the enemy ... because rape embodies male domination and female subordination'.[78] However, only focusing on the rape of women, or a particular group of women, overshadows other issues, such as sexual violence against men and boys as well as other equally horrific forms of gender-based violence. The debates on 'rape as genocide' illustrated the fractures within feminist engagements and highlighted how international feminist interventions into armed conflict remained focused on carceral pursuits. The focus on securing prosecutions of conflict-related sexual violence embeds intersectional power arrangements and risks underplaying the structural biases perpetuated by law.

Furthermore, the *ad hoc* tribunals, through the attention to prosecuting conflict-related sexual violence, contributed to the representation of women as victims and in continual need of protection during armed conflict.[79] Debates around sexual violence, both in and out of the tribunal proceedings, contributed to the hypervisibility of women as victims of sexual violence and in turn aided the creation

74. Engle, ibid., 785–6

75. Engle, ibid.

76. Engle, ibid., 785–803

77. Rhonda Copelon, 'Surfacing Gender: Re-Engraving Crimes against Women in Humanitarian Law' (1994) 5 (2) Hastings Women's Law Journal 243, 246

78. Copelon, ibid., 262, 263 (emphasis in original)

79. Evidence of this is present when shifting through ICTY, ICTR, SCSL, and ICC cases. Engle, 'Judging Sex in War', above note 28, 941

of a victim narrative.[80] Engle states that those who argued for greater legal protection for women from sexual violence often used the argument that rape brings shame on women as well as the community.[81] Engle's argument is that this process of shaming gives power to rape and because rape is not in every war it is not universal or inevitable; therefore, shame is not universal or inevitable.[82] Engle further notes that feminists and advocates who assumed that all raped women are in some way shamed also increased the shame themselves.[83] At the same time, all men, especially Serbian men, were seen as potential sexual perpetrators. This further solidifies both women and men's roles in armed conflict along gender lines. Furthermore, this makes the visibility of female defendants unlikely, as the actions of female defendants are seen as outside the typical parameters of female behaviour in armed conflict. Moreover, the ICTY's jurisprudence 'has functioned to limit' women's stories hence denying their 'sexual, political, and military agency.'[84] While sexual violence was the focus of international feminist study, the work and perspectives of local feminists were not recognized.[85]

From international feminist engagements in the *ad hoc* tribunals to the creation of the ICC, 'women as victims of sexual violence' has been the primary narrative around women's experiences in armed conflict. Throughout this process a victimization rhetoric was bolstered. Feminist scholarship has also highlighted the problematic focus on women's victimhood within feminist interventions into international law and armed conflict, which has diminished women's agency, and narrowed the scope of their experiences in conflict.[86] One experience

---

80. Ratna Kapur, *Erotic Justice: Law and the New Politics of Postcolonialism* (Routledge 2005)

81. Engle, 'Judging Sex in War', above note 28, 953

82. Ibid., 942

83. Ibid., 958

84. Ibid., 942

85. Dubravka Zarkov, 'Feminism and the Disintegration of Yugoslavia: On the Politics of Gender and Ethnicity' (2003) 24 (3) Social Development Issues 1

86. Vasuki Nesiah, 'Introduction: Feminist Interventions: Human Rights, Armed Conflict and International Law' (2009) 103 Proceedings of the Annual Meeting (American Society of International Law) 67; Wendy Brown, *Edgework: Critical Essays on Knowledge and Politics* (Princeton University Press 2006); Wendy Brown, *States of Injury: Power and Freedom in Late Modernity* (Princeton University Press 1995); Kapur, above note 80

that has been given less attention during armed conflict is the role of women as perpetrators, defendants and accused. Female defendants, just as male defendants, can be tried under international criminal law.[87] Nevertheless, this is not evident in the jurisprudence of the *ad hoc* tribunals given that Biljana Plavšić was the only woman tried by the ICTY,[88] and Pauline Nyiramasuhuko was the only woman brought before the ICTR.[89] Having so few women brought before international courts and tribunals may give the impression that equally few women have participated as aggressors during these conflicts.

Biljana Plavšić was the 'Serbian representative to the collective Presidency of Bosnia and Herzegovina; member of the collective and expanded Presidencies of the Bosnian Serb Republic [and] had *de facto* control and authority over members of the Bosnian Serb armed forces'.[90] At her trial in the ICTY, Plavšić pleaded guilty to crimes against humanity.[91] The Trial Chamber gave weight to Plavšić's guilty plea as well as the statement of remorse she made in court.[92] In her plea she admitted that she 'victimised countless innocent people', and said that a mix of fear and obsession led her to dismiss the allegations of criminal acts being committed.[93] Plavšić admitted that she did not seek to investigate the crimes against non-Serbs, but rather focused on 'innocent Serb victims'.[94] Nevertheless, Plavšić's guilty plea did not include any reference to specific crimes; both Del Ponte and Subotić have noted that the guilty plea was extremely general and therefore

87. This statement refers to the 'gender-neutral' language in the definitions of crimes in the statutes of the International Courts and Tribunals

88. ICTY Prosecutor, *Prosecutor v Plavšić*, Initial Indictment, Case IT-00-39 & 40/1, 3 April 2000

89. ICTR Prosecutor, *Prosecutor v Nyiramasuhuko and Ntahobali*, Amended Indictment, Case ICTR-97-21-I, 1 March 2001; ICTR Trial Chamber II, *Prosecutor v Nyiramasuhuko et al*, Judgement and Sentence, Case ICTR-98-42-T, 24 June 2011

90. Plavšić, Case Sheet https://www.icty.org/x/cases/plavsic/cis/en/cis_plavsic_en.pdf (accessed December 2019); see further ICTY Trial Chamber, *Prosecutor v Plavšić*, Sentencing Judgement, Case IT-00-39 & 40/1-S, 27 February 2003

91. *Prosecutor v Plavšić*, ibid., Section 2

92. *Prosecutor v Plavšić*, ibid.

93. Statement of Guilt: Biljana Plavšić (2002) *ICTY Website* https://www.icty.org/en/content/statement-guilt-biljana-plavšić (accessed December 2019)

94. Statement of Guilt: Biljana Plavšić, ibid.

carried little meaning for Plavšić's victims.[95] Plavšić was eventually sentenced to eleven years imprisonment, but only served two-thirds of the sentence before being released.[96]

Pauline Nyiramasuhuko was the Minister of Family and Women's Development in the Interim Government of Rwanda, a member of the National Republican Movement for Democracy and Development, and a political figure in the Butare prefecture.[97] She was tried in conjunction with her son Arsène Shalom Ntahobali before the ICTR. Nyiramasuhuko's indictment accused her of using a roadblock that was set up near her home to identify, abduct and kill Tutsi.[98] Nyiramasuhuko, accompanied by her son and other militia, was also said to have entered the prefecture offices to abduct Tutsi refugees.[99] Nyiramasuhuko was accused of encouraging the killing of Tutsi on multiple occasions, and being responsible for crimes of a sexual nature and rape.[100] Nyiramasuhuko was indicted with conspiracy to commit genocide, genocide, complicity in genocide, crimes against humanity and violations of Article 3 common to the Geneva Conventions and Additional Protocol II.[101] Specifically, she was charged with rape as a crime against humanity, and a war crime (outrages upon personal dignity).[102] The other charges of crimes against humanity included: murder, extermination, inhumane acts, and persecution on political, racial, or religious grounds.[103] Nyiramasuhuko was initially convicted

---

95. Jelena Subotić, 'The Cruelty of False Remorse: Biljana Plavšić at The Hague' (2012) 36 *Southeastern Europe* 39, 46; Carla Del Ponte and Chuck Sudetic, *Madame Prosecutor: Confrontations with Humanity's Worst Criminals and the Culture of Impunity* (Other Press 2009)

96. Subotić, ibid.; Del Ponte and Sudetic, ibid.

97. *Prosecutor v Nyiramasuhuko and Ntahobali*, above note 89, section 4.2

98. *Prosecutor v Nyiramasuhuko and Ntahobali*, ibid., sections 5.1, 6.15, 6.27

99. *Prosecutor v Nyiramasuhuko and Ntahobali*, ibid., sections 6.29–6.31

100. *Prosecutor v Nyiramasuhuko and Ntahobali*, ibid., sections 6.31, 6.38, 6.52–6.56, 7

101. *Prosecutor v Nyiramasuhuko and Ntahobali*, ibid., section 7

102. *Prosecutor v Nyiramasuhuko and Ntahobali*, ibid., section 7 (counts 7 and 11)

103. Nyiramasuhuko was also charged for killing and causing violence to health and to the physical or mental well-being of civilians as part of an internal armed conflict and, as such committing serious violations of Article 3 common to the Geneva Conventions and of Additional Protocol II

on seven of the eleven charges. She was found guilty of conspiracy to commit genocide and genocide; extermination, rape and persecution as crimes against humanity; as well as violence to life and outrages upon personal dignity as war crimes. Nyiramasuhuko was sentenced to life in prison, which was later reduced to forty-seven years and her conviction for persecution was reversed. Nyiramasuhuko was the first woman to be indicted by an international court and was the first woman to be convicted for rape as a crime against humanity. Nyiramasuhuko was considered by Prime Minister Kambanda as one of the 'inner circle', which was said to have been responsible for organizing the genocide and was the main instigator of the genocide in Butare.[104]

Domestic prosecutions have tried far more women for their roles in the conflicts of Rwanda and the former Yugoslavia.[105] Conversely, Plavšić

104. Carrie Sperling, 'Mother of Atrocities: Pauline Nyiramasuhuko's Role in the Rwandan Genocide' (2006) 33 (2) Fordham Urban Law Journal 101, 110–11

105. See, for example, Kieth B Richburg, 'Rwandan Nuns Jailed in Genocide' 9 June 2001, *The Washington Post* https://www.washingtonpost.com/archive/politics/2001/06/09/rwandan-nuns-jailed-in-genocide/fce3308b-3e6e-4784-8490-0887f69c7a39/ (accessed December 2019); Edecio Martinez, 'Kentucky Woman Indicted for Bosnian War Crimes' 18 March 2011, *CBS News* https://www.cbsnews.com/news/kentucky-woman-indicted-for-bosnian-war-crimes/ (accessed December 2019); 'Dutch Yvonne Basebya Jailed for Rwanda Crimes' 1 March 2013, *BBC News* https://www.bbc.co.uk/news/world-africa-21632819 (accessed December 2019); Aida Cerkez, 'US Extradites War Crimes Suspect to Bosnia' 27 December 2011, *NBC News* http://www.nbcnews.com/id/45799565/ns/world_news-europe/t/us-extradites-war-crimes-suspect-bosnia/#.Xf5i-_KTL-0 (accessed December 2019); Kristina Sgueglia, 'Woman Lied about Role in Rwanda Genocide, U.S. Jury Says' 22 February 2013, *CNN* https://edition.cnn.com/2013/02/21/us/new-hampshire-rwanda-genocide/index.html (accessed December 2019); Mirror Online, 'Bosnia Arrests "Female Monster"– Wife of Warlord "Serb Adolf"' 22 December 2011, *The Mirror* https://www.mirror.co.uk/news/uk-news/bosnia-arrests-female-monster---98517 (accessed December 2019); Amy Oliver, 'The US Single Mother Who Was Actually a War Criminal: Killer Becomes First Woman to Be Convicted of Bosnian War Crimes' 1 May 2012, *The Daily Mail* https://www.dailymail.co.uk/news/article-2137411/Rasema-Handanovic-guilty-war-crimes-Bosnia.html (accessed December 2019); 'Rwanda Jails Journalist Valerie Bemeriki for Genocide' 14 December

and Nyiramasuhuko are currently the only two women to have been tried before an international criminal tribunal. This means that despite the active participation of women in the conflicts, their existence has not entered into the mainstream international conflict narrative. While present-day international criminal law is supposed to also support and develop the principle of complementarity,[106] the *ad hoc* tribunals were in many ways privileged via funding and resources, which further contributed to the gendered binary of international/domestic where the domestic is othered to the international domain.

By situating the international tribunals as the main source of post-conflict justice in the former Yugoslavia and Rwanda, domestic processes were viewed as less significant or, in the case of the Rwandan courts, less legal, entrenching divisions between the international and domestic prosecutions and modes of transitional justice. For the Gacaca courts in Rwanda the local hearings drew on traditional justice modes but were mostly not regarded as adequate legal alternatives.[107] Although still subject to gender critique, the Gacaca focused on community cohesion and repair with opportunities for confessions to ameliorate sentences and with the aim of providing answers to those

2009, *BBC News* http://news.bbc.co.uk/1/hi/world/africa/8412014.stm (accessed December 2019); see also Elizabeth Becker, 'Khieu Ponnary, 83, First Wife of Pol Pot, Cambodian Despot' 3 July 2003, *The New York Times* https://www.nytimes.com/2003/07/03/world/khieu-ponnary-83-first-wife-of-pol-pot-cambodian-despot.html (accessed December 2019); 'Ieng Thirith: "First Lady" of Cambodia's Khmer Rouge Dies While Facing Charges of Genocide, Crimes against Humanity' 22 August 2015, *ABC News Australia* https://www.abc.net.au/news/2015-08-22/ieng-thirith-dies-while-facing-charges-of-genocide-cambodia/6717644 (accessed December 2019)

106. Rome Statute, above note 24, Article 17

107. Phil Clark, 'Hybridity, Holism, and "Traditional" Justice: The Case of the Gacaca Courts in Post-Genocide Rwanda' (2007) 39 George Washington International Law Review 765, 803–7; Phil Clark, *The Gacaca Courts, Post-Genocide Justice and Reconciliation in Rwanda: Justice without Lawyers* (Cambridge University Press 2010); Paul Christoph Bornkamm, *Rwanda's Gacaca Courts: Between Retribution and Reparation* (Oxford University Press 2012)

seeking understanding of what happened to loved ones.[108] The Gacaca courts have also been accused of being biased and of being dominated by the agenda of the post-conflict government rather than sufficiently impartial.[109] While biases in national jurisdictions within post-conflict environments are a serious concern, taking primacy away from national legal processes does little to facilitate reconciliation amongst local communities, who do not remain in control of post-conflict justice processes or narratives that are removed to international settings. One response to these criticisms has been the development of hybrid courts, drawing in local justice processes that work with international actors to prosecute conflict-related crimes.

The two *ad hoc* tribunals mark an important shift in the 1990s where the international community responded to the armed conflict in the former Yugoslavia and the genocide in Rwanda through the creation of spaces for prosecuting crimes. These institutions then paved the way for the creation of the ICC at the end of the decade. With the ICTY, the ICTR and the ICC, gender-based crimes have emerged as an important element of the international prosecutions undertaken. Key prosecutions have centred conflict-related sexual violence and produced a quite specific account of women's experiences of these conflicts that is not necessarily representative of the diversity of gendered harms – or gendered violence. Within this discourse the histories of female violence, including the crimes committed and prosecuted, have drawn minimal attention creating a skewed understanding that prioritizes women as victims while emphasizing female vulnerability. Within these accounts the space between domestic and international processes remains significant for the gendered construction and assumptions about law

---

108. Clark, 'Hybridity, Holism, and "Traditional" Justice', above note 107, 787, 817; Fionnuala Ní Aoláin, Dina Francesca Haynes and Naomi Cahn, *On the Frontlines: Gender, War, and the Post-Conflict Process* (Oxford University Press 2011) 170–2; Karen Brounéus, 'Truth-Telling as Talking Cure? Insecurity and Retraumatization in the Rwandan Gacaca Courts' (2008) 39 (1) Security Dialogue 55

109. Bert Ingelaere, 'The Gacaca Courts in Rwanda' in Luc Huyse and Mark Salter (eds), *Traditional Justice and Reconciliation after Violent Conflict: Learning from African Experiences* (International Institute for Democracy and Electoral Assistance 2008) 54 but see Phil Clark, 'Bringing the Peasants Back In, Again: State Power and Local Agency in Rwanda's Gacaca Courts' (2014) 8 (2) Journal of Eastern African Studies 193

and its effectiveness. Central to a redistribution of post-conflict justice processes are questions not only with regard to how gendered stories of agency and victimhood emerge in conflict, but equally how they manifest in the construction of peace.

Hybrid courts and tribunals

In contrast to the *ad hoc* tribunals, hybrid courts are designed to embrace both local and international criminal justice systems. Moving away from the assumption of a one-size-fits-all approach to post-conflict justice, hybrid courts can, in theory, better adapt to the needs of local populations and methods of justice as well as also local gender arrangements. Hybrid courts incorporate elements of existing domestic legal structures together with the presence and participation of international actors, often as judges and court officials. Hybrid courts are often charged with strengthening local justice structures alongside creating a credible and accessible space for post-conflict prosecutions. Linton notes that the hybrid systems of international justice represent a reversal in the thinking that inclusion of the domestic legal systems, as well as the nationals from the affected states, impacted negatively on impartiality.[110] Local courts have the benefit of trying the accused within the state in which the crimes were committed. This is thought to promote adherence to local legal principles and reinforce the domestic rule of law. Nevertheless, in the Cambodian context, questions remain as to whether the Extraordinary Chambers in the Courts of Cambodia (ECCC) has actually benefited the Cambodian legal system.[111] The ECCC was established decades after the atrocities of the Cambodian

---

110. Suzannah Linton, 'Cambodia, East Timor and Sierra Leone: Experiments in International Justice' (2001) 12 (2) Criminal Law Forum 185; Suzannah Linton, 'Rising from the Ashes: The Creation of a Viable Criminal Justice System in East Timor' (2001) 25 (1) Melbourne University Law Review 122

111. Kirsten Ainley, 'Justifying Justice: Verdicts at the ECCC' (2014) *Justice in Conflict Blog* https://justiceinconflict.org/2014/09/16/justifying-justice-verdicts-at-the-eccc/ (accessed December 2019); Jane Stromseth, 'Justice on the Ground: Can International Criminal Courts Strengthen Domestic Rule of Law in Post-Conflict Societies?' (2009) 1 (1) Hague Journal on the Rule of Law 87

genocide took place and, as a result, failed to indict the vast majority of leaders responsible, with only minimal cases brought before the court. Similar hybrid models include the first hybrid court, the Special Court for Sierra Leone (SCSL) and the Special Panels for Serious Crimes in East Timor, as well as the Iraqi High Tribunal and the Special Tribunal for Lebanon (STL).[112] The STL was created in order to prosecute those involved in the assassination of Prime Minister Hariri. The STL faced obstacles including: the jurisdiction being limited to the prosecution of the assassination of former Prime Minister Hariri, the location of proceedings in the Netherlands rather than in Lebanon, the legality of trials *in absentia*, and the multifaceted political landscape in Lebanon, which was not given sufficient attention within the construction of the Tribunal.[113] Burgis-Kasthala argues that Hariri's murder was turned into an international terrorist incident marking the first time an international criminal tribunal would prosecute acts that occurred in 'peacetime'.[114] Burgis-Kasthala uses the construction of the STL in order to highlight the role international criminal lawyers have in producing narratives:

When trying to make sense of our role in the world, international lawyers not only participate in esoteric exercises explicable to the elect; they (re)construct the world through particular linguistic

112. Lindsey Raub, 'Positioning Hybrid Tribunals in International Criminal Justice' (2009) 41 New York University Journal of International Law and Politics 1013; Kevin Jon Heller, 'A Poisoned Chalice: The Substantive and Procedural Defects of the Iraqi High Tribunal' (2006–2007) 39 Case Western Reserve Journal of International Law 261
113. Amal Alamuddin, Nidal Nabil Jurdi and David Tolbert, *The Special Tribunal for Lebanon: Law and Practice* (Oxford University Press 2014); Wayne Jordash and Tim Parker, 'Trials in Absentia at the Special Tribunal for Lebanon: Incompatibility with International Human Rights Law' (2010) 8 (2) Journal of International Criminal Justice 487; Nidal Nabil Jurdi, 'The Subject-Matter Jurisdiction of the Special Tribunal for Lebanon' (2007) 5 (5) Journal of International Criminal Justice 1125
114. Michelle Burgis-Kasthala, 'An Arresting Event: Assassination within the Purview of International Criminal Law' in Christine Schwöbel (ed), *Critical Approaches to International Criminal Law: An Introduction* (Routledge 2014) 246

devices that then enable members of their community to see only certain aspects of a given event.[115]

This understanding of an international criminal lawyer's ability to create conflict narratives links to our argument that gender narratives promoted within international criminal law, which focus on women as victims, have the power to make certain experiences visible and render other experiences hidden.

The Iraqi High Tribunal was established in order to try Saddam Hussein as well as other Iraqi officials. However, there have been several concerns raised in relation to the Iraqi hybrid court. The Iraqi High Tribunal suffered from an unstable structure which was the result of assassinations, boycotts and resignations.[116] It also sentenced Saddam Hussein to death, drawing criticism due to the use of capital punishment as well as the spectacle of his televised execution.[117] With these types of structural and foundational concerns plaguing hybrid tribunals the advent of any gender analysis has been limited. Furthermore, the focus on political leaders draws attention away from the structural gendered harms of armed conflict and state repression, re-inscribing political transitions and legal justice as the (assumed) domain of men. Moreover, the production of knowledge within the confines of international criminal law has remained limited within the hybrid courts. Drumbl questions, 'to what extent might the narrow truth and artificial reductionism of the criminal trial (i.e., binary categories of guilt or innocence) shield much deeper inquiries?'[118] We argue that

115. Schwöbel, ibid., 252, 259

116. See Jennifer Trahan, 'A Critical Guide to the Iraqi High Tribunal's Anfal Judgement: Genocide against the Kurds' (2009) 30 (2) Michigan Journal of International Law 305; Michael P Scharf, 'The Iraqi High Tribunal: A Viable Experiment in International Justice?' (2007) 5 (2) Journal of International Criminal Justice 258

117. M Cherif Bassiouni and Michael Wahid Hanna, 'Ceding the High Ground: The Iraqi High Criminal Court Statute and the Trial of Saddam Hussein' (2006–2007) 39 (1) Case Western Reserve Journal of International Law 21; Michael A Newton, 'The Iraqi High Criminal Court: Controversy and Contributions' (2006) 88 (862) International Review of the Red Cross 399

118. Mark A Drumbl, 'The Iraqi High Tribunal and Rule of Law: Challenges' (2006) 100 Proceedings of the ASIL Annual Meeting, Cambridge University Press 79, 82

there is a tendency for international criminal legal proceedings to focus on a narrow jurisdiction and highlight the acts of a small group of people, while ignoring wider structural gender inequalities and the involvement of other international actors. The range of experiences women face during armed conflict, as both perpetrators and victims, have the potential to be dismissed when international criminal legal narratives fail to consider gender at a structural level, informing the foundations of the justice mechanisms and the local expectations, legal arrangements and legacies from the conflict.

Limited jurisprudence on female perpetrators has emerged from the SCSL with the case against Margaret Fomba Brima, Neneh Binta Bah Jalloh, Ester Kamara and Anifa Kamara.[119] However, this case was brought against the defendants not due to their participation in the armed conflict, but rather for contempt of court, in particular for threatening witnesses who were to testify against their husbands. Despite this, Coulter notes that 10 to 30 per cent of all fighters in the Sierra Leone War were women.[120] Coulter also highlights the presence of female fighters throughout the various regions of Africa and the consistent failure to recognize women's roles in armed conflict beyond victims. This not only limits women's reintegration into society after the cessation of hostilities, but also the meaning of 'gender' in post-conflict communities, where gender is used as shorthand for references to conflict-related sexual violence. The crime of forced marriage was prosecuted at the SCSL and adds to the discourse of gendered harms identified within international criminal processes.[121] In this discourse, the complexity of gender arrangements within the various factions across the conflict, and in the post-conflict space, is reduced to an additional account of female vulnerability and male military brutality.

In the ECCC, two women were indicted, Ieng Thirith and Im Chaem. However, neither indictment resulted in a trial before the

---

119. SCSL Trial Chamber I, *Independent Counsel v Brima et al*, Sentencing Judgement in Contempt Proceedings, Case SCSL-2005-02 and Case SCSL-2005-03, 21 September 2005

120. Chris Coulter, 'Female Fighters in the Sierra Leone War: Challenging the Assumptions?' (2008) 88 Feminist Review 54, 55

121. SCSL Appeals Chamber, *Prosecutor v Alex Tamba Brima, Brima Bazzy Kamara and Santigie Borbor Kanu*, Judgment, Case SCSL-04-16-A, 22 February 2008

court.[122] The existence of four women, who were part of the leadership of the Khmer Rouge – Ieng Thirith, Khieu Ponnary, Yun Yat and Im Chaem – offers an example of women in power accused of committing criminal acts.[123] While some women attained high levels of leadership in the Khmer Rouge, other women inhabited lower-level positions as cadres.[124] However, wider accounts of the genocide fail to acknowledge women in positions of power who committed crimes and limit the stories of female experiences during this period. Ieng Thirith's case before the ECCC was dismissed due to her being deemed unfit to stand trial, and Im Chaem was initially charged *in absentia* and her case was later dismissed. Khieu Ponnary had previously been given amnesty by the Cambodian government and died in 2003.[125]

The silences within the histories around the genocide are evident not only within the ECCC, but in the lack of interrogation around the experiences within the Khmer Rouge as well. Linton's work finds that Im Chaem's position as a female cadre of the Khmer Rouge is not an anomaly of the Cambodian genocide. Linton highlights female participation in the atrocities of the Khmer Rouge.[126] Those individuals involved in committing violent acts in the conflict included women and despite knowledge of the involvement of women in the atrocities during this period, their existence has been downplayed in official records.[127] Within the ruling elite, women were promoted to positions of power. For example, Ieng Sary's daughter was appointed head of

122. ECCC Trial Chamber, *Co-Prosecutors v Ieng Thirith*, Decision on Reassessment of Accused Ieng Thirith's Fitness to Stand Trial Following Supreme Court Chamber Decision of 13 December 2011, Case 002/19-09-2007/ECCC/TC, 13 September 2012; ECCC Office of the Co-Investigating Judges, *Co-Prosecutors v Im Chaem*, Closing Order Disposition, Case 004/1/07-09-2009-ECCC/OCIJ, 22 February 2017

123. *Co-Prosecutors v Ieng Thirith*, ibid.

124. Suzannah Linton, 'Women Accused of International Crimes: A Trans-Disciplinary Inquiry and Methodology' (2016) 27 Criminal Law Forum 159, 171

125. Becker, above note 105

126. Linton, above note 124

127. Brent Crane, 'Female Cadres of the Khmer Rouge' 1 August 2015, *Phnom Penh Post* https://www.phnompenhpost.com/post-weekend/female-cadres-khmer-rouge (accessed December 2019)

the Calmette Hospital although she was still in secondary school.[128] Ieng Sary's niece was given a job as an English translator for Radio Phnom Penh.[129] Linton's focus on female cadres in the Khmer Rouge has uncovered evidence that women participated in all levels of the regime. Initially civilian women were in low level, low publicity roles that stayed in line with strict gender ideals around what is considered 'women's work'.[130]

Female perpetrators, defendants and accused exist within armed conflicts despite their relative absence from international criminal trials. It is necessary to be cautious about assuming that a factual historical record can be found only by looking at international criminal proceedings. A gender analysis that accounts for women as victims must also ask about women's participation in international crimes. This research is a means to unsettle expectations around agency and victims and has the capacity to illuminate how international criminal law prosecutions reproduce a status quo of men as political and military agents settling the agenda for change, as well as the record that criminal law prosecutions produce. Despite the lack of female defendants in international courts and tribunals, as compared with the total number of accused persons, women have been documented to have been involved in every aspect of the hostilities in the former Yugoslavia, Rwanda, Cambodia and Sierra Leone.[131] These tensions within international law demonstrate a series of underlying gendered assumptions that inform the discipline. In the following section we explore how the placement of gender within international courts and tribunals might be reconsidered to develop jurisprudence beyond the prosecution of conflict-related sexual violence, beyond the limitations of 'victor's justice' and narrow accounts of the conflict, towards a multi-faceted set of agendas that reach towards peace rather than looking back at violence. Perhaps the lack of female prosecutions simply demonstrates the ways in which dominant gender norms deprive communities, including the international community, of alternative conceptions of war and peace in law.

---

128. Timothy Dylan Wood, 'Tracing the Last Breath: Movements in Anlong Veng' (2009) (PhD Dissertation Rice University) 347
129. Wood, ibid.
130. Crane, above note 127
131. Coulter, above note 120; Nicole Hogg, '"I Never Poured Blood": Women Accused of Genocide in Rwanda' (2001) (LLM thesis McGill University) on file with authors; for a limited list of examples, above note 105

Beyond carceral modes

The intrepid Congressional participants risked being branded as traitors by sending delegations to speak with European governments. They were hoping to bring the conflict to a quick conclusion by giving neutral governments information on what politicians were thinking in the warring countries. Their efforts failed because ... making the first move towards negotiations would be seen as a sign of "weakness" on the part of the warring country and would put them at a disadvantage when it came to settling the terms of peace.[132]

In this section we draw together the concept of complementarity and anti-carceral feminist scholarship to critique international criminal law, to expose gaps and to articulate feminist projects beyond the current courts and tribunal structures.[133] Through opening the analysis of the international law on war and peace to different perspectives on feminist engagement, we conclude the book with a glimpse into Volume Two, where we consider further the histories of feminist peace activism and the complicity of international law in the production of everyday violence. Following Otto, we seek to interrogate the ways in which acts of agency and statehood are implicitly (and explicitly) gendered. That is, to identify how the choice to prosecute international crimes can contribute to gendered narratives around state behaviours. The double gendering of agency thus lies in the production of gendered states and the assumption that political and military leaders, as with perpetrators of international crimes, are predominantly men. This gendered reality leaves the relationship between law and violence intact. A crisis mode, preferred over, say, consensus thinking, leads to an inevitability of violence that

132. Dianne Otto, 'A Sign of "Weakness"? Disrupting Gender Certainties in the Implementation of Security Council Resolution 1325' (2006) 13 Michigan Journal of Gender & Law 113, 114

133. Janet Halley, Prabha Kotiswaran, Rachel Rebouché and Hila Shamir (eds), *Governance Feminism: An Introduction* (University of Minnesota Press 2018); Halley et al., above note 28; Anette Bringedal Houge and Kjersti Lohne, 'End Impunity! Reducing Conflict-Related Sexual Violence to a Problem of Law' (2017) 51 (4) Law & Society Review 755; Angela Davis, *Are Prisons Obsolete?* (Seven Stories Press 2003); Grady, above note 13

prioritizes military solutions. In Volume Two we explore this further noting that, in contrast to international criminal law processes, alternative transitional justice models often shift away from carceral outcomes. The retention of carceral modes for leadership crimes, in contrast, increasingly retains the prominence of the military-industrial complex where private security companies benefit from the need for secure facilities in the space between local and international courts.[134] Beyond international courts and tribunals and the emergence of hybrid courts, the concept of complementarity must be discussed alongside conceptions of state power, as an additional legal space where local and international jurisdictions are negotiated. Complementarity is a key principle of international criminal law, enshrined in Article 17 of the Rome Statute establishing the ICC. Article 17 requires that the ICC only undertakes investigation and prosecution where the national courts have demonstrated an unwillingness or inability to proceed with cases.[135] There are a range of debates around the topic of complementarity within the ICC. Burke-White has argued that instead of the Office of the Prosecutor (OTP) demonstrating 'passive complementarity' (where the ICC only steps in when states fail to prosecute individuals themselves), the OTP should adopt a policy of 'active complementarity' (working with and assisting national jurisdictions to encourage accountability).[136] With reference to the crime of aggression, Trahan has instead suggested that the concept of complementarity may need to be rethought, with primacy to prosecute resting with the ICC, due to the fact that national courts may be biased and decide to prosecute solely based on the desire to keep prosecution out of the ICC.[137] Chappell, Grey and Waller argue that the principle of complementarity retains a 'gender justice complementarity shadow', as the sexual and gender-

---

134. Grady, above note 13

135. Rome Statute, above note 24

136. William W Burke-White, 'Proactive Complementarity: The International Criminal Court and National Courts in the Rome System of International Justice' (2008) 49 (1) Harvard International Law Journal 53

137. See Jennifer Trahan, 'Is Complementarity the Right Approach for the International Criminal Court's Crime of Aggression? Considering the Problem of "Overzealous" National Court Prosecutions' (2012) 45 (3) Cornell International Law Journal 569

based crimes in the Rome Statute have not required parallel local developments for complementarity to be achieved.[138]

Simone Gbagbo's case, tried before local Côte d'Ivoire courts in 2015, has been argued by Heller to be an example where 'radical complementarity' should have been accepted within the ICC. That is, an understanding that regardless of the outcome, or processes, of domestic state prosecutions the international court should not proceed once a case is progressing via local means.[139] Gbagbo was charged with domestic crimes of disturbing the peace, organizing armed gangs and undermining state security, and was sentenced to twenty years' imprisonment, although she was eventually given amnesty by the state.[140] However, the ICC stated that while Gbagbo was sentenced to prison, her charges did not reflect the status of crimes against humanity for which she was indicted by the ICC and therefore the local prosecution of Gbagbo, which resulted in twenty years' imprisonment, was not a successful example of complementarity. As such the ICC charges of crimes against humanity, including crimes of rape and sexual violence, remain in place against Gbagbo. Heller has stated that despite the deference to sovereignty found in Article 17 of the Rome Statute, the article also includes the 'same conduct' requirement, which was the reason why the ICC did not find the 2015 Côte d'Ivoire trial to be sufficient. The OTP stated that the charges were not of 'substantially the same conduct' as the ones in the ICC indictment. Heller argues that the ICC's reluctance to consider the 2015 Côte d'Ivoire's prosecution of Gbagbo was too restrictive and inconsistent with the ICC Statute.[141] Heller concludes that until the ICC re-evaluates its relationship with local courts it will not fulfil its mandate.[142] However,

138. Louise Chappell, Rosemary Grey and Emily Waller, 'The Gender Justice Shadow of Complementarity: Lessons from the International Criminal Court's Preliminary Examinations in Guinea and Colombia' (2013) 7 (3) The International Journal of Transitional Justice 455

139. Kevin Heller, 'Radical Complementarity' (2016) 14 Journal of International Criminal Justice 1

140. ICC Pre-Trial Chamber III, *Prosecutor v Simone Gbagbo*, Warrant of Arrest, Case ICC-02/11-01/12, 29 February 2012; in 2015, Gbagbo was sentenced via a domestic court to twenty years for her role in the violence that followed the 2010 elections in which more than 3,000 people died; in 2018, Gbagbo was granted amnesty

141. Heller, above note 139, 2

142. Ibid., 38

this discussion is somewhat of a hypothetical debate, as Gbagbo was granted amnesty by Côte d'Ivoire in 2018.

As a female defendant Gbagbo presents an interesting story of agency and denial in relation to female violence: at once charged and given prominence yet also, always, tied to the acts of her husband and ultimately given amnesty at the state level. Importantly, her case reveals the limitations of complementarity in an institution that assumes local prosecutions as otherwise inferior to the ICC processes. While Heller's argument identifies a significant lack of recognition of the potential for domestic prosecutions, following Chappell, Grey and Waller it is significant that the gender-based crimes on the international charge sheet did not appear in the domestic prosecutions. Similarly, Kapur argues that the ICC can play an important role in filtering prosecutions for gender- and sexual-based crimes downwards, into states, via the principle of complementarity.[143] An analysis of complementarity that holds the wider gendered contours of how conflict-related sexual violence has emerged as an agenda within international criminal law, the curious prosecutions of some female accused and the overarching discourse on gender remains one that prioritizes re-telling women's vulnerability over stories of survival, agency and participation. At the centre of these accounts is the persistence of the gender binary, assumed uniform in its lived realities, despite evidence that challenges the neutrality of gender difference when female violence and male victims are positioned within understandings and the record of armed conflict. The reproduction of the gender binary in international criminal law reduces the capacity for gender to be understood as an intersectional tool or for the international institutions to be understood as embedding knowledge histories that over themselves have very specific gendered expectations. Juxtaposing Gbagbo's domestic prosecution, and subsequent amnesty, with the retention of the international arrest warrant, also demonstrates the manner in which gendered expectations are imposed as a means to 'read' state behaviour, interlocking with accounts of civilized states versus states that are lagging behind in their application of the rule of law.

143. Amrita Kapur, 'Complementarity as a Catalyst for Gender Justice in National Prosecutions' in Fionnuala Ní Aoláin, Naomi Cahn, Dina Francesca Haynes and Nahla Valji (eds), *The Oxford Handbook of Gender and Conflict* (Oxford University Press 2018) 225

International criminal law has developed through different forms (the *ad hoc* tribunals, hybrid courts and a permanent criminal court), yet each example has brought about its own set of problems that move international focus away from the victims themselves and towards international trials that draw international attention. Many states, including the US, are not within the jurisdiction of the ICC and other states have recently left the court over claims of bias. Thus, if the ICC were to focus on complementarity it may see less need for an international incarnation of post-conflict justice. However, if the ICC positioned itself as a champion of alternative justice processes, it could maintain its role as a key participant in post-conflict justice.

Moreover, a focus on an expansive understanding of complementarity might also encourage the inclusion of anti-carceral modes of post-conflict justice. Minow asks the question: 'should the international institution treat truth commissions, grants of amnesty, and other alternatives to prosecution as satisfying the predicate of national action that in turn deprives the ICC of authority to proceed?'[144] Minow argues that 'restorative justice processes' have the potential to satisfy the principles laid out in the Rome Statute. Alternative approaches that lead to the 'repair of relationships, restitution, community harmony, and the future more than the past' invite discussions that step away from the primacy of carceral approaches to armed conflict justice.[145] While Minow warns of the potential for domestic approaches to ignore the range of gendered harms, the opportunity to include alternative justice models, which are founded upon feminist practices, holds future potential. Indeed, these feminist spaces have existed in the form of women's hearings and truth telling,[146] and the challenge will be to see these justice projects gain primacy in domestic post-conflict justice decisions. In Volume Two we analyse feminist and indigenous justice models as alternatives to international criminal law institutions that pivot around the pursuit of prosecutions and carceral outcomes. This is an important aspect of the focus on a different understanding of the relationship between peace and conflict that informs our overarching

144. Martha Minow, 'Do Alternative Justice Mechanisms Deserve Recognition in International Criminal Law? Truth Commissions, Amnesties, and Complementarity at the International Criminal Court' (2019) 60 (1) Harvard International Law Journal 1, 5
145. Minow, ibid., 44
146. See Volume Two for a discussion of alternative justice models

theme and arguments. Through feminist and indigenous justice frames, we interrogate knowledge frames beyond the dominant structures that inform contemporary international law, institutions and the framing of the laws of war and peace.

This chapter has outlined the development of international criminal law beginning with the work of the Nuremberg and Tokyo Tribunals and continuing to the present status of the ICC. Throughout international criminal law's expansion, narratives of justice have been founded on criminal prosecutions. Not only has this promoted international criminal law as a source of knowledge when deciphering the history of armed conflict, it has also connected notions of truth to the outcomes of international trials. The process of reconciliation has been seen as synonymous with establishing international courts or tribunals, which ties post-conflict reconciliation to *successful* international prosecutions.[147] However, international courts are often plagued by difficulties between international and national conceptions of justice as well as structural issues, which have the potential to derail effective prosecutions.

The Nuremberg and Tokyo Tribunals created prosecutions based on individual responsibility for the first time in international law but focused only on the crimes committed by Germany and Japan, ignoring the crimes committed by the Allies. Moreover, the tribunals and subsequent trials did not address the systematic gender abuse found within the war. Female perpetrators in the Second World War were recognized by courts, but their actions did not remain a part of the consciousness of the Second World War history. In the 1990s international criminal law expanded, establishing the *ad hoc* tribunals and effectively developing jurisprudence in the areas of sexual and gender-based violence. The successful prosecution of sexual violence was rooted in feminist demands and a much-needed development of international criminal

147. Chidi Anselm Odinkalu, 'International Criminal Justice, Peace and Reconciliation in Africa: Re-imagining an Agenda Beyond the ICC' (2015) 40 (2) Africa Development 257; Catherine Gegout, 'The International Criminal Court: Limits, Potential and Conditions for the Promotion of Justice and Peace' (2013) 34 (5) Third World Quarterly 800; Juan Méndez, 'National Reconciliation, Transnational Justice, and the International Criminal Court' (2001) 15 (1) Ethics & International Affairs 25; Payam Akhavan, 'Are International Criminal Tribunals a Disincentive to Peace?: Reconciling Judicial Romanticism with Political Realism' (2009) 31 (3) Human Rights Quarterly 624

law. However, because of the legal discourse and procedures, as well as the media coverage around the conflicts in the former Yugoslavia and Rwanda, women were portrayed primarily as victims. Feminist interventions into international criminal law by way of both scholarship and activism contributed to a hyperfocus on sexual violence crimes within the conflicts, and likewise contributed to the narrative of women's victimhood in armed conflict. Law – and in particular, the criminal trial through its emphasis on monolithic categories – lends itself to this kind of intervention as opposed to the development and promotion of a fuller analysis of gender and war. If a history of the conflict is constructed merely on an examination of criminal trials, then it will likely deliver a narrative of women's victimhood. Indeed, as mentioned above, this is facilitated by the fact that international criminal law should be understood not only as a branch of international law, but as a space of memory and ordering of the conflict.[148] It is the task of feminist legal scholars to insist on the insufficiency of this narrative to fully understand the role of gender, conflict and law.

International hybrid courts have included domestic legal perspectives in their creation and function in order to address the notion that international criminal law remains ignorant of local post-conflict justice perspectives. However, the existence of the hybrid courts has also contributed to the fragmentation of international criminal law. Contrary to what linear accounts of the development of international criminal law might suggest, the project of an international criminal court as the authoritative single voice on international justice has not materialized. Moreover, without all five permanent members of the Security Council under the court's jurisdiction, the ICC remains an institution with limited scope and embedded unequal power structures.

The current system of international criminal law is not sufficient in order to address the magnitude of harms experienced by individuals during armed conflict. This is why local justice processes are so important for attending to victims' needs as well as assessing the best way to address what are often deep-seated tensions. There is a need for transnational feminist networks, whose scholarship and activism draw closer the link between international and domestic post-conflict justice. Transnational feminists recognize the fluidity of the peace/conflict continuum. This perspective also highlights the importance of publicly acknowledging the crimes committed during armed conflict

148. Simpson, above note 22, 94

while respecting the wishes of a community regarding post-conflict justice. By applying transnational feminist approaches to international criminal law, the gaps between current narratives of armed conflict and the realities of individual experiences are made visible.

As critiques of carceral feminism have noted, incarceration presumes that justice is somehow achieved merely by putting offenders behind bars. Many victims feel a sense of justice when perpetrators are convicted with custodial sentences. Still, there is also a need to consider the various other mechanisms and methods, which are required under models of transitional justice, in order to ensure that a peaceful, more equal, and just society can be obtained. Importantly, jail sentences do not *per se* address the structural causes which fostered the conflict in the first place, such as ethnic tensions or class and wealth inequality. While international criminal law has, indeed, provided a sense of justice for some, and while some tribunals, such as the ECCC, have focused on alternative means of providing remedy,[149] much of international criminal law and most feminist interventions into international criminal law have largely focused on punishing sexual violence and subsequent imprisonment.[150] This carceral feminist project ignores the wider factors which are needed to provide structural justice and wider peace, with alternative measures such as the redistribution of wealth and property or educational programmes which seek to dismantle gender stereotypes, for example, being sidelined by the international criminal law project.[151] Models for transitional justice beyond incarceration hold the power to challenge binary understandings of peace and conflict, noting the need to constantly build towards peace in all countries globally. This conversation, which features in Volume Two, looks towards alternative feminist futures, which take seriously structural bias, intersectional and transnational feminisms as well as the implications of queer theory, while also seeking to promote posthuman feminist justice.

149. Maria Elander, *Figuring Victims in International Criminal Justice: The case of the Khmer Rouge Tribunal* (Routledge 2018)

150. Engle, above note 13; Bernstein, above note 13, Halley, above note 13

151. Emily Jones, 'Gender and Reparations: Seeking Transformative Justice' in Carla Ferstman and Mariana Goetz (eds), *Reparations for Victims of Genocide, War Crimes and Crimes against Humanity: Systems in Place and Systems in the Making* (Brill 2020)

Looking ahead to Volume Two

To conclude, mainstream international legal approaches place international criminal law as a pivot between war and peace. However, in this chapter we have interrogated the role courts and tribunals have played in representing conflict, the victims of conflict and the gendered contours of law. Throughout the book we have argued for an understanding of gender as fluid and as interconnected to wider discourses of power and privilege. In working to dismantle, or challenge, the gender binary we have also developed an argument about the nature of the relations between war and peace, armed conflict and peacetime. In Volume Two we enlarge this argument through analysing the presence and persistence of militarism in post-conflict spaces, including the formation of peace agreements, the deployment of peacekeeping and the contours of peacebuilding. Following Otto, we regard the peace-war relation not merely as a continuum, but as fluid, and multiple, like gender.[152]

In Volume Two, the text commences with an account of feminist methodologies, reflecting on the different frames articulated in this book, alongside the role of the politics of the everyday, feminist anti-militarism and histories of peace activism. The methodology outlined in this volume is thus developed to further exemplify the impact of a structural bias feminist analysis. This is done through deepening our theoretical engagements, drawing, for example, on intersectional theory once again to further complicate gendered narratives of war and peace while enlarging the focus to apply critical disability studies and crip theories. In addition, we will consider further the challenge of postcolonial feminisms, expanding upon our analysis in this volume to seek new ways of knowing and understanding the law through a focus on indigenous epistemologies of law and justice. Our starting point of understanding war and peace as intertwined realities, rather than distinct modes, is thus expanded to develop a contribution to feminist methodologies beyond the accounts of either the laws on resorting to war (*jus ad bellum*) or the laws of war (*jus in bello*) to analysis of post-conflict legal structures.

The analysis of post-conflict legal structures commences with what has been titled the *lex pacificatoria*, or law of the peacemakers, and its influence on the making of peace agreements and international

---

152. Otto, above note 4

law.[153] As peace agreements mark the end of an armed conflict and the commencement of the post-conflict period, they are often important blueprints for the imagined peace after war. We analyse the space between the projected (radical) potentials of peace agreements and the liberal constraints on the design and implementation of peace processes. This analysis returns us to the relationship between law and violence, as discussed in Chapter 1 of this volume, and drawing in the feminist methodologies described above, we caution against the limits of contemporary readings of peace agreements as simply requiring increased female participants, noting the need for a more in-depth and sustained feminist analysis of peace agreements.

Volume Two also provides an analysis of both peacekeeping and peacebuilding operations, and their reliance on military personnel, military leadership and military organization for their mobilization. Drawing in feminist understandings of feminist alternatives, focused on unarmed civilian protection models, on political economy agendas and indigenous forms of justice, the two chapters on peacekeeping and peacebuilding provide an account of the long reach of war into peacetime and of the gendered impact of the current design of peacekeeping and peacebuilding. A feminist postcolonial approach draws attention to who is least well off in post-conflict communities, and how peripheral subjects might be re-framed as experts in the design, possibilities and futures of post-conflict missions. We offer a study of the move towards the use of protection of civilians mandates as a tool for increasing authorization of force for peacekeepers and the role of the language of exception as used to characterize specific spaces as needing new and novel forms of peacekeeping interventions, that ultimately look like a continuance of war rather than a shift towards peace. Local feminist iterations and their nexus to regional and transnational feminisms are used to further question dominant modes of international interventions, through peacekeeping and peacebuilding missions.

153. Christine Bell, 'Of Jus Post Bellum and Lex Pacificatoria: What's in a Name?' in Carsten Stahn, Jennifer S Easterday and Jens Iverson (eds), *Jus Post Bellum: Mapping the Normative Foundations* (Oxford University Press 2014) 185; Christine Bell, *On the Law of Peace: Peace Agreements and the Lex Pacificatoria* (Oxford University Press 2008); Christine Bell, 'Peace Agreements: Their Nature and Legal Status' (2006) 100 American Journal of International Law 373

EQ0HPQ08UkVZ

The final two chapters of Volume Two look at transitional justice and military technologies, respectively. Through both studies, we open up the texts to an exploration and understanding of security and insecurity and the gendered knowledge that directs international legal responses to insecurity towards militarism. The study of transitional justice, building on the account of international criminal law in this chapter, looks at non-legal and quasi-legal structures that incorporate alternative epistemologies and knowledge frames to remember and to rebuild community. The final chapter of Volume Two picks up the study of posthumanism and subjectivity in Chapter 4 of this volume, to consider the contours of feminist approaches that interrogate the structures of foundational knowledge on subjectivity, humanness and the prevalence of military-capitalist modes of power. Across Volume Two our study of war and peace highlights and frames the role of international law alongside the potential for gender analysis to transform the status quo of the law of war and peace.

To develop a gender analysis of war and peace in this volume, we have centred in each chapter a different set of laws, each of which has benefited from gender analysis. We have teased out, developed and re-imagined feminist approaches through a multi-faceted understanding of gender approaches that include intersectional, postcolonial, transnational, posthuman, queer and accounts of the relationship between law and violence. This has given us a means to analyse the persistence of militarism; tropes of imperialism; the interconnectedness of gender with race, sexuality, class, ableism and religion; articulations of human-nonhuman relationships; and an account of how feminist projects have approached the international from armed conflict to post-conflict. Many of these themes emerge in Volume Two, some with greater emphasis and others as part of a matrix of feminist and gender theories that assist new ways of understanding the laws of war and peace.

BIBLIOGRAPHY

Aditya Adhikari, *The Bullet and the Ballot Box: The Story of Nepal's Maoist Revolution* (Verso 2014)

Giorgio Agamben, *State of Exception*, (trans. Kevin Attell, University of Chicago Press 2005)

Kirsten Ainley, 'Justifying Justice: Verdicts at the ECCC' (2014) *Justice in Conflict Blog* https://justiceinconflict.org/2014/09/16/justifying-justice-verdicts-at-the-eccc/ (accessed December 2019)

Nadje Al-Ali, 'Women, Gender Relations, and Sanctions in Iraq' in Shams Inati (ed), *Iraq: Its History, People and Politics* (Humanity Books 2003)

Nadje Al-Ali and Nicola Pratt, *What Kind of Liberation? Women and the Occupation of Iraq* (University of California Press 2009)

Suleiman Al-Khalidi, 'Russian-backed Forces Gain Ground in Rebel-held Northwest Syria' 22 December 2019, *Reuters* https://www.reuters.com/article/us-syria-security-idlib/russian-backed-forces-gain-ground-in-rebel-held-northwest-syria-idUSKBN1YQ0DB (accessed December 2019)

Dapo Akande and Marko Milanovic, 'The Constructive Ambiguity of the Security Council's ISIS Resolution' (2015) *EJIL: Talk!* https://www.ejiltalk.org/the-constructive-ambiguity-of-the-security-councils-isis-resolution (accessed December 2019)

Payam Akhavan, 'Are International Criminal Tribunals a Disincentive to Peace?: Reconciling Judicial Romanticism with Political Realism' (2009) 31 (3) Human Rights Quarterly 624

Amal Alamuddin, Nidal Nabil Jurdi and David Tolbert, *The Special Tribunal for Lebanon: Law and Practice* (Oxford University Press 2014)

Miranda Alison, *Women and Political Violence: Female Combatants in Ethno-National Conflict* (Routledge 2009)

Miranda Alison, 'Women as Agents of Political Violence: Gendering Security' (2004) 35 (4) Security Dialogue 447

Jamie Allinson, 'The Necropolitics of Drones' (2015) 9 International Political Sociology 113

Roy Allison, 'The Russian Case for Military Intervention in Georgia: International Law, Norms and Political Calculation' (2009) 18 (2) European Security 173

Laila Alodaat, 'No Women, No Peace in Syria' 9 December 2016, *The Huffington Post* https://www.huffpost.com/entry/no-women-no-peace-in-syri_b_8762904 (accessed December 2019)

Laila Alodaat, 'The Armed Conflict in Syria and Its Disproportionate Impact on Women' (2014) *Focus Gender InfoBrief*, on file with authors

Ayşe Gul Altınay and Andrea Pető (eds), *Gendered Wars, Gendered Memories: Feminist Conversations on War, Genocide and Political Violence* (Routledge 2016)

Amnesty International, 'Upturned Lives: The Disproportionate Impact of France's State of Emergency' (2016) *Amnesty International* https://www. amnesty.org/download/Documents/EUR2133642016ENGLISH.pdf (accessed December 2019)

Antony Anghie, 'Finding the Peripheries: Sovereignty and Colonialism in Nineteenth-Century International Law' (1999) 40 (1) Harvard International Law Journal 1

Antony Anghie, *Imperialism, Sovereignty and the Making of International Law* (Cambridge University Press 2007)

Kwadwo Appiagyei-Atua, 'United Nations Security Council Resolution 1325 on Women, Peace, and Security – Is It Binding?' (2011) 18 (3) Human Rights Brief 2 https://digitalcommons.wcl.american.edu/hrbrief/vol18/iss3/1 (accessed December 2019)

Associated Press, 'Syrian Peace Talks in Geneva Reach Impasse after Five Days of Sparring' 14 February 2014, *The Guardian* https://www.theguardian.com/world/2014/feb/14/syrian-peace-talks-impasse-five-days-sparring (accessed December 2019)

Article 36, 'Effects of Explosive Weapons: Working Paper on Explosive Weapons in Populated Areas' (2019) *Article 36* http://www.article36.org/wp-content/uploads/2019/12/Working-paper-Article-36.pdf (accessed December 2019)

Article 36, 'Science, Technology and Weaponization: Preliminary Observations' (2017) *Article 36* http://www.article36.org/wp-content/uploads/2017/11/Science-tech-and-weaponisation-preliminary-observations-FINAL-Nov17.pdf (accessed December 2019)

Matilda Arvidsson, 'Targeting, Gender, and International *Posthuman*itarian Law and Practice: Framing the Question of the Human in International Humanitarian Law' (2018) 44 (1) Australian Feminist Law Journal 9

Kelly Dawn Askin, 'Gender Crimes Jurisprudence in the ICTR: Positive Developments' (2005) 3 (4) Journal of International Criminal Justice 1007

Nazli Avdan, *Visas and Walls: Border Security in the Age of Terrorism* (University of Pennsylvania Press 2019)

Shamel Azmeh, 'Syria's Passage to Conflict: The End of the "Developmental Rentier Fix" and the Consolidation of New Elite Rule' (2016) 44 (4) Politics and Society 499

Anne Barnard and Nick Cumming-Bruce, 'After Second Round of Syria Talks, No Agreement Even on How to Negotiate' 15 February 2014, *The New York Times* https://www.nytimes.com/2014/02/16/world/middleeast/after-second-round-of-syria-talks-no-agreement-even-on-how-to-negotiate.html (accessed December 2019)

Amy Barrow, 'UN Security Council Resolutions 1325 and 1820: Constructing Gender in Armed Conflict and International Humanitarian Law' (2010) 92 International Review of the Red Cross 221

Katharine T Bartlett, 'Feminist Legal Methods' (1990) 103 (4) Harvard Law Review 829

Rebecca Barber, 'Uniting for Peace Not Aggression: Responding to Chemical Weapons in Syria without Breaking the Law' (2019) 24 (1) Journal of Conflict and Security Law 71

M Cherif Bassiouni and Michael Wahid Hanna, 'Ceding the High Ground: The Iraqi High Criminal Court Statute and the Trial of Saddam Hussein' (2006–2007) 39 (1) Case Western Reserve Journal of International Law 21

BBC News Online, 'Syria Air Strikes: US and Allies Attack "Chemical Weapons Sites"' 14 April 2018, *BBC News* https://www.bbc.co.uk/news/world-middle-east-43762251 (accessed December 2019)

BBC News Online, 'Dutch Yvonne Basebya Jailed for Rwanda Crimes' 1 March 2013, *BBC News* https://www.bbc.co.uk/news/world-africa-21632819 (accessed December 2019)

BBC News Online, 'Rwanda Jails Journalist Valerie Bemeriki for Genocide' 14 December 2009, *BBC News* http://news.bbc.co.uk/1/hi/world/africa/8412014.stm (accessed December 2019)

Elizabeth Becker, 'Khieu Ponnary, 83, First Wife of Pol Pot, Cambodian Despot' 3 July 2003, *The New York Times* https://www.nytimes.com/2003/07/03/world/khieu-ponnary-83-first-wife-of-pol-pot-cambodian-despot.html (accessed December 2019)

Mohammed Bedjaoui, *Towards a New International Economic Order* (Holmes & Meier 1979)

Barbara Bedont and Katherine Hall-Martinez, 'Ending Impunity for Gender Crimes under the International Criminal Court' (1999) 6 (1) The Brown Journal of World Affairs 65

Andrew Bell, 'Syria, Chemical Weapons, and a Qualitative Threshold for Humanitarian Intervention' (2018) *Just Security* https://www.justsecurity.org/54665/syria-chemical-weapons-international-law-developing-qualitative-threshold-humanitarian-intervention/ (accessed December 2019)

Christine Bell, 'Of Jus Post Bellum and Lex Pacificatoria: What's in a Name?' in Carsten Stahn, Jennifer S Easterday and Jens Iverson (eds), *Jus Post Bellum: Mapping the Normative Foundations* (Oxford University Press 2014)

Christine Bell, *On the Law of Peace: Peace Agreements and the Lex Pacificatoria* (Oxford University Press 2008)

Christine Bell, 'Peace Agreements: Their Nature and Legal Status' (2006) 100 American Journal of International Law 373

Ofra Bengio, 'Game Changers: Kurdish Women in Peace and War' (2016) 70 (1) The Middle East Journal 30

Isaline Bergamaschi, 'French Military Intervention in Mali: Inevitable, Consensual Yet Insufficient' (2013) 2 (2) Stability: International Journal of Security and Development 20

Elizabeth Bernstein, 'Militarized Humanitarianism Meets Carceral Feminism: The Politics of Sex, Rights, and Freedom in Contemporary Antitrafficking Campaigns' (2010) 36 (1) Signs: Journal of Women in Culture and Society 45

Eileen Berrington and Päivi Honkatukia, 'An Evil Monster and a Poor Thing: Female Violence in the Media' (2002) 3 (1) Journal of Scandinavian Studies in Criminology and Crime Prevention 50

Sara Bertotti, 'Separate or Inseparable? How Discourse Interpreting Law and Politics as Separable Categories Shaped the Formation of the UN Human Rights Council's Universal Periodic Review' (2019) 23 (7) The International Journal of Human Rights 1140

John Biersack and Shannon O'Lear, 'The Geopolitics of Russia's Annexation of Crimea: Narratives, Identities, Silences, and Energy' (2014) 55 (3) Eurasian Geography and Economics 247

Jamille Bigio and Rachel Vogelstein, 'Women and Terrorism: Hidden Threats, Forgotten Partners' (2019) *Council on Foreign Relations* https://cdn.cfr. org/sites/default/files/report_pdf/Discussion_Paper_Bigio_Vogelstein_ Terrorism_OR.pdf (accessed December 2019)

Ruth Blakeley, 'Drones, State Terrorism and International Law' (2018) 11 Critical Studies on Terrorism 321

Jennifer Bond and Laurel Sherret, 'Mapping Gender and the Responsibility to Protect: Seeking Intersections, Finding Parallels' (2012) 4 (2) Global Responsibility to Protect 133

Paul Christoph Bornkamm, *Rwanda's Gacaca Courts: Between Retribution and Reparation* (Oxford University Press 2012)

RJB Bosworth, *Claretta: Mussolini's Last Lover* (Yale University Press 2017)

Avtar Brah, *Cartographies of Diaspora: Contesting Identities* (Routledge 1996)

Karen Brounéus, 'Truth-Telling as Talking Cure? Insecurity and Retraumatization in the Rwandan Gacaca Courts' (2008) 39 (1) Security Dialogue 55

Wendy Brown, *Edgework: Critical Essays on Knowledge and Politics* (Princeton University Press 2006)

Wendy Brown, *States of Injury: Power and Freedom in Late Modernity* (Princeton University Press 1995)

Anna Maria Bruzzone and Rachele Farina, *La Resistenza Taciuta: Dodici Vite di Partigiane Piemontesi* (2nd edn, Bollati Boringhieri 2016)

Hedley Bull, Benedict Kingsbury and Adam Roberts (eds), *Hugo Grotius and International Relations* (Clarendon Press 1992)

Michelle Burgis-Kasthala, 'An Arresting Event: Assassination within the Purview of International Criminal Law' in Christine Schwöbel (ed), *Critical Approaches to International Criminal Law: An Introduction* (Routledge 2014)

William W Burke-White, 'Proactive Complementarity: The International Criminal Court and National Courts in the Rome System of International Justice' (2008) 49 (1) Harvard International Law Journal 53

Doris Buss, 'Expert Witnesses and International War Crimes Trials: Making Sense of Large-Scale Violence in Rwanda' in Dubravka Zarkov and Marlies Glasius (eds), *Narratives of Justice in and out of the Courtroom: Former Yugoslavia and Beyond* (Springer 2014)

Doris Buss, 'Performing Legal Order: Some Feminist Thoughts on International Criminal Law' (2011) 11 International Criminal Law Review 409

Doris Buss, 'Queering International Legal Authority' (2007) 101 Proceedings of the Annual Meeting of the American Society of International Law 122

Doris Buss, 'The Curious Visibility of Wartime Rape: Gender and Ethnicity in International Criminal Law' (2007) 25 Windsor Yearbook of Access to Justice 3

Doris Buss and Ambreena Manji (eds), *International Law: Modern Feminist Approaches* (Hart Publishing 2005)

Judith Butler, *Frames of War: When Is Life Grievable?* (Verso 2010)

Judith Butler, *Gender Trouble: Feminism and the Subversion of Identity* (Routledge 1990)

Laurie Calhoun, *We Kill because We Can: From Soldiering to Assassination in the Drone Age* (Zed Books 2016)

Meghan Campbell, 'CEDAW and Women's Intersecting Identities: A Pioneering New Approach to Intersectional Discrimination' (2015) 11 (2) Direito GV Law Review 479

R Charli Carpenter, '*Innocent Women and Children*': Gender, Norms and the Protection of Civilians (Routledge 2006)

Becky Carter, 'Women and Violent Extremism' (Governance, Social Development, Humanitarian, Conflict - Applied Knowledge Services, 13 March 2013) http://gsdrc.org/docs/open/hdq898.pdf (accessed December 2019)

Antonio Cassese, *International Law* (2nd edn, Oxford University Press 2005)

Antonio Cassese and Paola Gaeta, *Cassese's International Criminal Law* (Oxford University Press 2013)

Aida Cerkez, 'US Extradites War Crimes Suspect to Bosnia' 27 December 2011, *NBC News* http://www.nbcnews.com/id/45799565/ns/world_news-europe/t/us-extradites-war-crimes-suspect-bosnia/#.Xf5i-_KTL-0 (accessed December 2019)

Grégoire Chamayou, *A Theory of the Drone*, (trans. Janet Lloyd, The New Press 2015)

Louise Chappell, *The Politics of Gender Justice at the International Criminal Court: Legacies and Legitimacy* (Oxford University Press 2016)

Louise Chappell and Andrea Durbach (eds), 'The International Criminal Court - a Site of Gender Justice' (2014) Special Issue of International Feminist Journal of Politics

Louise Chappell, Rosemary Grey and Emily Waller, 'The Gender Justice Shadow of Complementarity: Lessons from the International Criminal Court's Preliminary Examinations in Guinea and Colombia' (2013) 7 (3) The International Journal of Transitional Justice 455

Hilary Charlesworth, 'The Women Question in International Law' (2011) 1 (1) Asian Journal of International Law 33

Hilary Charlesworth, 'Feminist Reflections on the Responsibility to Protect' (2010) 2 (3) Global Responsibility to Protect 232

Hilary Charlesworth, 'International Law: A Discipline of Crisis' (2002) 65 (3) Modern Law Review 377

Hilary Charlesworth and Christine Chinkin, *The Boundaries of International Law: A Feminist Analysis* (Manchester University Press 2000)

Hilary Charlesworth and Emma Larking, 'Introduction: The Regulatory Power of the Universal Periodic Review' in Hilary Charlesworth and Emma Larking (eds), *Human Rights and the Universal Periodic Review: Rituals and Ritualism* (Cambridge University Press 2015)

Christine Chinkin, 'Rethinking Legality/Legitimacy after the Iraq War' in Richard Falk, Mark Juergensmeyer and Vesselin Popovski (eds), *Legality and Legitimacy in Global Affairs* (Oxford University Press 2012)

Christine Chinkin, 'The State That Acts Alone: Bully, Good Samaritan or Iconoclast?' (2000) 11 European Journal of International Law 31

Christine Chinkin, 'Kosovo: A "Good" or "Bad" War?' (1999) 93 (4) American Journal of International Law 841

Christine Chinkin, 'A Gendered Perspective to the International Use of Force' (1992) 12 Australian Yearbook of International Law 279

Christine Chinkin and Mary Kaldor, *International Law and New Wars* (Cambridge University Press 2017)

Martin Chulov, '40,000 Iraqis Stranded on Mountain as Isis Jihadists Threaten Death' 7 August 2014, *The Guardian* https://www.theguardian.com/world/2014/aug/07/40000-iraqis-stranded-mountain-isis-death-threat;

Martin Chulov, Mona Mahmood and Ian Sample, 'Syria Conflict: Chemical Weapons Blamed as Hundreds Reported Killed' 22 August 2013, *The Guardian* https://www.theguardian.com/world/2013/aug/21/syria-conflcit-chemical-weapons-hundreds-killed (accessed December 2019)

Chien-peng Chung, 'China's Uyghur Problem after the 2009 Urumqi Riot: Repression, Recompense, Readiness, Resistance' (2018) 13 Journal of Policing, Intelligence and Counter Terrorism 185

Chien-peng Chung, 'China's "War on Terror": September 11 and Uighur [sic] Separatism' (2002) 81 (4) Foreign Affairs 8

Phil Clark, 'Bringing the Peasants Back in, Again: State Power and Local Agency in Rwanda's Gacaca Courts' (2014) 8 (2) Journal of Eastern African Studies 193

Phil Clark, *The Gacaca Courts, Post-Genocide Justice and Reconciliation in Rwanda: Justice without Lawyers* (Cambridge University Press 2010)

Phil Clark, 'Hybridity, Holism, and "Traditional" Justice: The Case of the Gacaca Courts in Post-Genocide Rwanda' (2007) 39 George Washington International Law Review 765

Dana L Cloud, '"To Veil the Threat of Terror": Afghan Women and the <Clash of Civilizations> in the Imagery of the U.S. War on Terrorism' (2004) 90 (3) Quarterly Journal of Speech 285

Cynthia Cockburn, 'The Continuum of Violence: A Gender Perspective on War and Peace' in Wenona Giles and Jennifer Hyndman (eds), *Sites of Violence: Gender and Conflict Zones* (University of California Press 2004)

Cynthia Cockburn, *The Space between Us: Negotiating Gender and National Identities in Conflict* (Zed Books 1998)

Cynthia Cockburn and Dubravka Zarkov (eds), *The Postwar Moment: Militaries, Masculinities and International Peacekeeping* (Lawrence and Wishart 2002)

Carol Cohn (ed), *Women and Wars: Contested Histories, Uncertain Futures* (Polity Press 2013)

Carol Cohn, 'Mainstreaming Gender in UN Security Policy: A Path to Political Transformation?' in Shirin M Rai and Georgina Waylen (eds), *Global Governance: Feminist Perspectives* (Palgrave Macmillan 2008)

Carol Cohn, 'Wars, Wimps, and Women: Talking Gender and Thinking War' in Miriam Cooke and Angela Woollacott (eds), *Gendering War Talk* (Princeton University Press 1993)

Carol Cohn, 'Sex and Death in the Rational World of Defense Intellectuals' (1987) 12 (4) Signs: A Journal of Women in Culture and Society 687

Carol Cohn, Helen Kinsella and Sheri Gibbings, 'Women, Peace and Security Resolution 1325' (2004) 6 (1) International Feminist Journal of Politics 130

Ryan Conrad (ed), *Against Equality: Queer Critiques of Gay Marriage* (AK Press 2010)

Radhika Coomaraswamy, 'Preventing Conflict Transforming Justice Securing the Peace: A Global Study on the Implementation of United Nations Security Council Resolution 1325' (2015) *UN Women* https://reliefweb.int/sites/reliefweb.int/files/resources/UNW-GLOBAL-STUDY-1325-2015.pdf (accessed December 2019)

Neil Cooper, 'Race, Sovereignty, and Free Trade: Arms Trade Regulation and Humanitarian Arms Control in the Age of Empire' (2018) 3 (4) Journal of Global Security Studies 444

Rhonda Copelon, 'Surfacing Gender: Re-engraving Crimes against Women in Humanitarian Law' (1994) 5 (2) Hastings Women's Law Journal 243

Chris Coulter, 'Female Fighters in the Sierra Leone War: Challenging the Assumptions?' (2008) 88 Feminist Review 54

Counter Extremism Project, 'ISIS's Persecution of Women' (2017) *Counter Extremism Project* https://www.counterextremism.com/sites/default/files/ISIS%20Persecution%20of%20Women_071117.pdf (accessed December 2019)

Robert Cover, 'The Supreme Court 1982 Term; Foreword: Nomos and Narrative' (1983) 97 Harvard Law Review 4

Brent Crane, 'Female Cadres of the Khmer Rouge' 1 August 2015, *Phnom Penh Post* https://www.phnompenhpost.com/post-weekend/female-cadres-khmer-rouge (accessed December 2019)

Matthew Craven, 'What Happened to Unequal Treaties? The Continuities of Informal Empire' (2005) 74 Nordic Journal of International Law 335

Emily Crawford and Alison Pert, *International Humanitarian Law* (Cambridge University Press 2015)

James Crawford and Martti Koskenniemi (eds), *The Cambridge Companion to International Law* (Cambridge University Press 2012)

Kimberlé Crenshaw, 'Demarginalizing the Intersection of Race and Sex: A Black Feminist Critique of Antidiscrimination Doctrine, Feminist Theory and Antiracist Politics' (1989) 1 The University of Chicago Legal Forum 139

Cara Daggett, 'Drone Disorientations: How "Unmanned" Weapons Queer the Experience of Killing in War' (2015) 17 (3) International Feminist Journal of Politics 361

Margaret Davies, 'Feminism and the Flat Law Theory' (2008) 16 (3) Feminist Legal Studies 281

Margaret Davies and Vanessa Munro (eds), *The Ashgate Research Companion to Feminist Legal Theory* (Ashgate 2013)

Sara E Davies and Jacqui True (eds), *The Oxford Handbook of Women, Peace, and Security* (Oxford University Press 2019)

Sara E Davies and Jacqui True, 'Reframing Conflict-related Sexual and Gender-based Violence: Bringing Gender Analysis Back In' (2015) 46 (6) Security Dialogue 495

Sara E Davies, Nicole George and Jacqui True, 'The Difference That Gender Makes to International Peace and Security' (2017) 19 (1) Special Issue of International Feminist Journal of Politics 1

Sara E Davies, Zim Nwokora, Eli Stamnes and Sarah Teitt (eds), *Responsibility to Protect and Women, Peace and Security: Aligning the Protection Agendas* (Martinus Nijhoff Publishers 2013)

Angela Davis, *Are Prisons Obsolete?* (Seven Stories Press 2003)

Erika de Wet, 'The Invocation of the Right to Self-defence in Response to Armed Attacks Conducted by Armed Groups: Implications for Attribution' (2019) 32 Leiden Journal of International Law 91

Ashley Deeks, '"Unwilling or Unable": Toward a Normative Framework for Extraterritorial Self-defense' (2012) 52 Virginia Journal International Law 483

Carla Del Ponte and Chuck Sudetic, *Madame Prosecutor: Confrontations with Humanity's Worst Criminals and the Culture of Impunity* (Other Press 2009)

Jacques Derrida, 'Force of Law: The "Mystical Foundation of Authority"' (1990) 11 Cardozo Law Review 920

Sophia Dingli and Navtej Purewal (eds), 'Special Issue: Gendering (In) Security' (2018) 3 (2) Third World Thematics

Yoram Dinstein, *War, Aggression and Self-defence* (6th edn, Cambridge University Press 2017)

Lucie Drechselová and Adnan Çelik (eds), *Kurds in Turkey: Ethnographies of Heterogenous Experiences* (Lexington Books 2019)

Mark A Drumbl, 'The Iraqi High Tribunal and Rule of Law: Challenges' (2006) 100 Proceedings of the ASIL Annual Meeting, Cambridge University Press 79

Claire Duncanson, 'Anti-militarist Feminist Approaches to Researching Gender and the Military' in Rachel Woodward and Claire Duncanson (eds), *The Palgrave International Handbook of Gender and the Military* (Palgrave 2017)

Claire Duncanson, *Gender and Peacebuilding* (Polity Press 2016)

Meral Düzgün, 'Jineology: The Kurdish Women's Movement' (2016) 12 (2) Journal of Middle East Women's Studies 284

Patricia L Easteal, Lorana Bartels, Kate Holland and Noni Nelson, 'How Are Women Who Kill Portrayed in Newspaper Media? Connections with Social Values and the Legal System' (2015) 51 Women's Studies International Forum 31

Maria Elander, *Figuring Victims in International Criminal Justice: The Case of the Khmer Rouge Tribunal* (Routledge 2018)

Maria Elander, 'The Victim's Address: Expressivism and the Victim at the Extraordinary Chambers in the Courts of Cambodia' (2013) 7 The International Journal of Transitional Justice 95

Karen Engle, 'Judging Sex in War' (2008) 106 (6) Michigan Law Review 941

Karen Engle, '"Calling in the Troops": The Uneasy Relationship among Women's Rights, Human Rights and Humanitarian Intervention' (2007) 20 Harvard Human Rights Journal 189

Karen Engle, 'Feminism and Its (Dis)contents: Criminalizing Wartime Rape in Bosnia and Herzegovina' (2005) 99 (4) American Journal of International Law 778

Cynthia Enloe, *Nimo's War, Emma's War: Making Feminist Sense of the Iraq War* (University of California Press 2010)

Cynthia Enloe, 'Wielding Masculinity inside Abu Ghraib: Making Feminist Sense of an American Military Scandal' (2004) 10 (3) Asian Journal of Women's Studies 89

Cynthia Enloe, *Maneuvers: The International Politics of Militarizing Women's Lives* (University of California Press 2000)

Cynthia Enloe, *Bananas, Beaches and Bases: Making Feminist Sense of International Politics* (2nd edn, University of California Press 2014)

Pınar Gözen Ercan, 'UN General Assembly Dialogues on the Responsibility to Protect and the Use of Force for Humanitarian Purposes' (2019) 11 (3) Global Responsibility to Protect 313

Kathryn Ann Farr, 'Defeminizing and Dehumanizing Female Murderers' (2000) 11 (1) Women and Criminal Justice 49

Lucy Ferguson, '"This Is Our Gender Person": The Messy Business of Working as a Gender Expert in International Development' (2015) 17 International Feminist Journal of Politics 380

Martha Albertson Fineman, Jack E Jackson and Aman P Romero (eds), *Feminist and Queer Legal Theory: Intimate Encounters, Uncomfortable Conversations* (Ashgate 2009)

Michel Foucault, *Histoire de la Sexualité I: La Volonté de Savoir* (Éditions Gallimard 1976)

France 24, 'France Ready to "Punish" Those behind Syria Gas Attack' 27 August 2013, *France 24* https://www.france24.com/en/20130827-france-punish-syrian-chemical-attack-hollande (accessed December 2019)

Thomas Franck, 'Humanitarian and Other Interventions' (2005) 43 Columbia Journal of Transnational Law 321

Nancy Fraser, 'Feminism, Capitalism and the Cunning of History' (2009) 56 New Left Review 97

Marilyn Friedman, 'Female Terrorists: What Difference Does Gender Make?' (2007) 23 Social Philosophy Today 189

Judith Gardam, 'War, Law, Terror, Nothing New for Women' (2010) 32 Australian Feminist Law Journal 61

Judith Gardam, *Necessity, Proportionality and the Use of Force by States* (Cambridge University Press 2009)

Judith Gardam, 'A Role for Proportionality in the War on Terror' (2005) 74 (1) Nordic Journal of International Law 3

Judith Gardam, 'Proportionality as a Restraint on the Use of Force' (1999) 20 Australian Yearbook of International Law 9

Judith Gardam, 'Women, Human Rights and International Humanitarian Law' (1998) 38 (324) International Review of the Red Cross 421

Judith Gardam, 'Gender and Non-combatant Immunity' (1993) 3 Transnational Law and Contemporary Problems 345

Judith Gardam and Hilary Charlesworth, 'Protection of Women in Armed Conflict' (2000) 22 Human Rights Quarterly 148

Judith Gardam and Michelle Jarvis, *Women, Armed Conflict and International Law* (Kluwer Law International 2001)

Judith Gardam and Michelle Jarvis, 'Women and Armed Conflict: The International Response to the Beijing Platform for Action' (2000) 32 Columbia Human Rights Law Review 1

Caron E Gentry, 'Epistemological Failures: Everyday Terrorism in the West' (2015) 8 (3) Critical Studies on Terrorism 362

Caron E Gentry and Laura Sjoberg, *Beyond Mothers, Monsters, Whores: Thinking about Women's Violence in Global Politics* (Zed Books 2015)

Catherine Gegout, 'The International Criminal Court: Limits, Potential and Conditions for the Promotion of Justice and Peace' (2013) 34 (5) Third World Quarterly 800

Nazila Ghanea, 'Intersectionality and the Spectrum of Racist Hate Speech: Proposals to the UN Committee on the Elimination of Racial Discrimination' (2013) 35 (4) Human Rights Quarterly 935

Sophie Giscard d'Estaing, 'Engaging Women in Countering Violent Extremism: Avoiding Instrumentalisation and Furthering Agency' (2017) 25 (1) Gender and Development 103

Peter H Gleick, 'Water, Drought, Climate Change, and Conflict in Syria' (2014) 6 Weather, Climate, and Society 331

Global Justice Center, 'UN Security Council Adopts Resolution 2467' (2019) *Global Justice Center* http://globaljusticecenter.net/press-center/press-releases/1117-un-security-council-adopts-resolution-2467 (accessed December 2019)

Samantha Godec, 'Between Rhetoric and Reality: Exploring the Impact of
Military Humanitarian Intervention upon Sexual Violence – Post-conflict
Sex Trafficking in Kosovo' (2010) 92 (877) International Review of the Red
Cross 235

Beth Goldblatt, 'Intersectionality in International Anti-discrimination Law:
Addressing Poverty in Its Complexity' (2015) 21 (1) Australian Journal of
Human Rights 47

Kate Grady, 'Towards a Carceral Geography of International Law' in Sundhya
Pahuja and Shane Chalmers (eds), *The Routledge Handbook of International
Law and the Humanities* (Routledge 2020)

Robbie Gramer and Colum Lynch, 'How a U.N. Bid to Prevent Sexual
Violence Turned into a Spat over Abortion' 23 April 2019, *Foreign Policy*
https://foreignpolicy.com/2019/04/23/united-nations-bid-end-sexual-
violence-rape-support-survivors-spat-trump-administration-sexual-
reproductive-health-dispute-abortion-internal-state-department-cable/
(accessed December 2019)

Christine Gray, *International Law and the Use of Force* (4th edn, Oxford
University Press 2018)

James Green, 'Questioning the Peremptory Status of the Prohibition on the
Use of Force' (2011) 32 Michigan Journal of International Law 215

Derek Gregory, 'Drone Geographies' (2014) 183 Radical Philosophy 7

Thomas Gregory, 'Potential Lives, Impossible Deaths: Afghanistan, Civilian
Casualties and the Politics of Intelligibility' (2012) 14 (3) International
Feminist Journal of Politics 327

Christopher Greenwood, 'The Concept of War in Modern International Law'
(1987) 36 International and Comparative Law Quarterly 283

Aeyal Gross, 'Queer Theory and International Human Rights Law: Does Each
Person Have a Sexual Orientation?' (2007) Proceedings of the Annual
Meeting of the American Society of International Law 129

Oren Gross, 'Unresolved Legal Questions Concerning Operation Inherent
Resolve' (2017) 52 (2) Texas International Law Journal 221

Atina Grossmann, 'A Question of Silence: The Rape of German Women by
Occupation Soldiers' (1995) 72 October 42

Hugo Grotius, *On the Law of War and Peace*, (trans. Archibald Colin
Campbell, Anodos Books 2019)

Group of Eight, 'Declaration on Preventing Sexual Violence in Conflict'
11 April 2013 https://www.gov.uk/government/uploads/system/uploads/
attachment_data/file/185008/G8_PSVI_Declaration_-_FINAL.pdf
(accessed December 2019)

Iain Guest, 'Rape in Congo Is Not a Myth – If Anything, It Is Under-
reported' 21 November 2012, *The Guardian* https://www.theguardian.
com/commentisfree/2012/nov/21/rape-congo-not-myth-under-reported
(accessed December 2019)

Onur Güven and Olivier Ribbelink, 'The Protection of Nationals Abroad: A
Return to Old Practice?' in Christophe Paulussen, Tamara Takács, Vesna

Lazić and Ben Van Rompuy (eds), *Fundamental Rights in International and European Law* (T.M.C. Asser Press 2016)

Jamie J Hagen, 'Queering Women, Peace and Security' (2016) 92 (2) International Affairs 313

Monica Hakimi, 'Defensive Force against Non-state Actors: The State of Play' (2015) 91 International Law Studies 1

Jack Halberstam, *The Queer Art of Failure* (Duke University Press 2011)

Janet Halley, 'Rape at Rome: Feminist Interventions in the Criminalisation of Sex-related Violence in Positive International Criminal Law' (2008) 30 (1) Michigan Journal of International Law 1

Janet Halley, 'Rape in Berlin: Reconsidering the Criminalisation of Rape in the International Law of Armed Conflict' (2008) 9 (1) Melbourne Journal of International Law 78

Janet Halley, *Split Decisions: How and Why to Take a Break from Feminism* (Princeton University Press 2006)

Janet Halley, Prabha Kotiswaran, Rachel Rebouché and Hila Shamir (eds), *Governance Feminism: Notes from the Field* (University of Minnesota Press 2019)

Janet Halley, Prabha Kotiswaran, Rachel Rebouché and Hila Shamir (eds), *Governance Feminism: An Introduction* (University of Minnesota Press 2018)

Janet Halley, Prabha Kotiswaran, Hila Shamir and Chantal Thomas, 'From the International to the Local in Feminist Legal Responses to Rape, Prostitution/ Sex Work, and Sex Trafficking: Four Studies in Contemporary Governance Feminism' (2006) 29 (2) Harvard Journal of Law and Gender 335

Nancy Hartsock, 'Feminist Theory and the Development of Revolutionary Strategy' in Zillah R Eisenstein (ed), *Capitalist Patriarchy and the Case for Socialist Feminism* (Monthly Review Press 1978)

Anders Henriksen, *International Law* (2nd edn, Oxford University Press 2019)

Gina Heathcote, *Feminist Dialogues on International Law: Successes, Tensions, Futures* (Oxford University Press 2019)

Gina Heathcote, 'Security Council Resolution 2242 on Women, Peace and Security: Progressive Gains or Dangerous Development?' (2018) 32 (4) Global Society 374

Gina Heathcote, 'War's Perpetuity: Disabled Bodies of War and the Exoskeleton of Equality' (2018) 44 (1) Australian Feminist Law Journal 71

Gina Heathcote, 'Women and Children and Elephants as Justification for Force' (2017) 4 (1) Journal on the Use of Force and International Law 66

Gina Heathcote, 'LAWs, UFOs and UAVs: Feminist Encounters with the Law of Armed Conflict' in Dale Stephens and Paul Babie (eds), *Imagining Law: Essays in Conversation with Judith Gardam* (University of Adelaide Press 2016)

Gina Heathcote, 'Robust Peacekeeping, Gender and the Protection of Civilians' in Jeremy Farrall and Hilary Charlesworth (eds), *Strengthening the Rule of Law through the UN Security Council* (Routledge 2016)

Gina Heathcote, 'Naming and Shaming: Human Rights Accountability in Security Council Resolution 1960 (2010) on Women, Peace and Security' (2012) 4 (1) Journal of Human Rights Practice 82

Gina Heathcote, *The Law on the Use of Force: A Feminist Analysis* (Routledge 2012)

Gina Heathcote, 'Feminist Politics and the Use of Force: Theorising Feminist Action and Security Council Resolution 1325' (2011) 7 Socio-Legal Review 23

Gina Heathcote and Dianne Otto (eds), *Rethinking Peacekeeping, Gender Equality and Collective Security* (Palgrave Macmillan 2014)

Kevin Jon Heller, 'Radical Complementarity' (2016) 14 Journal of International Criminal Justice 1

Kevin Jon Heller, 'A Poisoned Chalice: The Substantive and Procedural Defects of the Iraqi High Tribunal' (2006–2007) 39 Case Western Reserve Journal of International Law 261

Jean-Marie Henckaerts and Louise Doswald-Beck (eds), *Customary International Humanitarian Law: Volume I: Rules* (International Committee of the Red Cross 2005)

Nicola Henry, 'Theorizing Wartime Rape: Deconstructing Gender, Sexuality, and Violence' (2016) 30 (1) Gender and Society 44

Nicola Henry, 'Memory of an Injustice: The "Comfort Women" and the Legacy of the Tokyo Trial' (2013) 37 (3) Asian Studies Review 362

Rosalyn Higgins, 'The Advisory Opinion on Namibia: Which UN Resolutions Are Binding under Article 25 of the Charter?' (1972) 21 (2) International and Comparative Law Quarterly 270

Loveday Hodson, 'Women's Rights and the Periphery: CEDAW's Optional Protocol' (2014) 25 (2) European Journal of International Law 561

Loveday Hodson and Troy Lavers (eds), *Feminist Judgments in International Law* (Hart Publishing 2019)

Nicole Hogg, '"I Never Poured Blood": Women Accused of Genocide in Rwanda' (2001) (LLM thesis McGill University) on file with authors

Maria Holt, 'The Unlikely Terrorist: Women and Islamic Resistance in Lebanon and the Palestinian Territories' (2010) 3 (3) Critical Studies on Terrorism 365

Home Office (UK), 'Immigration Directorate Instruction Family Migration: Appendix FM Section 1.7, Appendix Armed Forces, Financial Requirement' (2017) *Home Office* https://assets.publishing.service.gov.uk/government/uploads/system/uploads/attachment_data/file/826340/Appendix-FM-1-7-Financial-Requirement-ext_1.pdf (accessed December 2019)

Anette Bringedal Houge and Kjersti Lohne, 'End Impunity! Reducing Conflict-related Sexual Violence to a Problem of Law' (2017) 51 (4) Law and Society Review 755

Karen Hulme, *War Torn Environment: Interpreting the Legal Threshold* (Brill 2004)

Human Rights Watch, 'France: Prolonged Emergency State Threatens Rights' 22 July 2016 https://www.hrw.org/news/2016/07/22/france-prolonged-emergency-state-threatens-rights (accessed December 2019)

Michael Humphrey, 'International Intervention, Justice and National Reconciliation: The Role of the ICTY and ICTR in Bosnia and Rwanda' (2003) 2 (4) Journal of Human Rights 495

Bert Ingelaere, 'The Gacaca Courts in Rwanda' in Luc Huyse and Mark Salter (eds), *Traditional Justice and Reconciliation after Violent Conflict: Learning from African Experiences* (International Institute for Democracy and Electoral Assistance 2008)

Alexandria J Innes and Brent J Steele, 'Spousal Visa Law and Structural Violence: Fear, Anxiety and Terror of the Everyday' (2015) 8 (3) Critical Studies on Terrorism 401

Intelligence and Security Committee of Parliament, 'UK Lethal Drone Strikes in Syria' (2017) *Intelligence and Security Committee of Parliament* http://isc.independent.gov.uk/news-archive/26april2017 (accessed December 2019)

International Crisis Group, 'Nigeria: Women and the Boko Haram Insurgency' (2016) *International Crisis Group* https://d2071andvip0wj.cloudfront.net/242-nigeria-women-and-the-boko-haram%20Insurgency.pdf (accessed December 2019)

International Development Research Centre, 'The Responsibility to Protect: Report of the International Commission on Intervention and State Sovereignty' (2001) *ICISS* http://responsibilitytoprotect.org/ICISS%20Report.pdf (accessed December 2019)

Annamarie Jagose, 'The Trouble with Antinormativity' (2015) 26 (1) Differences 26

Gregory D Johnsen, *The Last Refuge: Yemen, Al-Qaeda, and the Battle for Arabia* (Oneworld 2013)

Emily Jones, 'Gender and Reparations: Seeking Transformative Justice' in Carla Ferstman and Mariana Goetz (eds), *Reparations for Victims of Genocide, War Crimes and Crimes against Humanity: Systems in Place and Systems in the Making* (Brill 2020)

Emily Jones, 'Review of Dianne Otto (ed), Queering International Law: Possibilities, Alliances, Complicities, Risks' (2019) 27 (1) Feminist Legal Studies 115

Emily Jones, 'A Posthuman-Xenofeminist Analysis of the Discourse on Autonomous Weapons Systems and Other Killing Machines' (2018) 44 (1) Australian Feminist Law Journal 93

Emily Jones, Sara Kendall and Yoriko Otomo, 'Gender, War and Technology: Peace and Armed Conflict in the 21st Century' (2018) 44 (1) Australian Feminist Law Journal 1

Wayne Jordash and Tim Parker, 'Trials in Absentia at the Special Tribunal for Lebanon: Incompatibility with International Human Rights Law' (2010) 8 (2) Journal of International Criminal Justice 487

Nidal Nabil Jurdi, 'The Subject-Matter Jurisdiction of the Special Tribunal for Lebanon' (2007) 5 (5) Journal of International Criminal Justice 1125

Mary Kaldor, 'Old Wars, Cold Wars, New Wars, and the War on Terror' (2005) 42 International Politics 491

Mary Kaldor, *New and Old Wars: Organized Violence in a Global Era* (Polity Press 1999)

Ratna Kapur, 'On Gender, Alterity and Human Rights: Freedom in a Fishbowl' (2019) 122 Feminist Review 167

Ratna Kapur, *Gender, Alterity and Human Rights: Freedom in a Fishbowl* (Edward Elgar 2018)

Ratna Kapur, *Erotic Justice: Law and the New Politics of Postcolonialism* (Routledge 2005)

Helene Kazan, 'The Architecture of Slow, Structural, and Spectacular Violence and the Poetic Testimony of War' (2018) 44 (1) Australian Feminist Law Journal 119

Pardiss Kebriaei, 'The Distance between Principle and Practice in the Obama Administration's Targeted Killing Program: A Response to Jeh Johnson' (2012) 31 Yale Law and Policy Review 151

Hans Kelsen, 'Collective Security and Collective Self-Defense under the Charter of the United Nations' (1948) 42 (4) American Journal of International Law 783

Conor Kennedy, 'The Struggle for Blue Territory: Chinese Maritime Militia Grey-Zone Operations' (2018) 163 (5) The RUSI Journal 8

David Kennedy, *Of War and Law* (Princeton University Press 2006)

Isabel Kershner, 'Women's Role in Holocaust May Exceed Old Notions' 17 July 2010, *The New York Times* https://www.nytimes.com/2010/07/18/world/europe/18holocaust.html (accessed December 2019)

Maryam Khalid, 'Gender, Orientalism and Representations of the "Other" in the War on Terror' (2011) 23 (1) Global Change, Peace and Security 15

As'ad AbuKhalil, 'Sex and the Suicide Bomber' 13 November 2001, *Salon.com* https://www.salon.com/2001/11/07/islam_2/ (accessed December 2019)

Laleh Khalili, 'Gendered Practices of Counterinsurgency' (2011) 37 Review of International Studies 1471

Helen Kinsella, *The Image before the Weapon: A Critical History of the Distinction between Combatant and Civilian* (Cornell University Press 2011)

Helen Kinsella, 'Gendering Grotius: Sex and Sex Difference in the Laws of War' (2006) 34 (2) Political Theory 161

Robert Kolb, 'The Main Epochs of Modern International Humanitarian Law since 1864 and Their Related Dominant Legal Constructions' in Kjetil Mujezinović Larsen, Camilla Guldahl Cooper and Gro Nystuen (eds), *Searching for a 'Principle of Humanity' in International Humanitarian Law* (Cambridge University Press 2012)

Sari Kouvo, 'Feminism, Gender and International (Criminal) Law: From Asking the "Woman Question" in Law to Moving beyond Law' (2014) 16 (4) International Feminist Journal of Politics 666

Sari Kouvo and Zoe Pearson, *Feminist Perspectives on Contemporary International Law: Between Resistance and Compliance?* (Hart Publishing 2011)

Claus Kreß and Stefan Barriga (eds), *The Crime of Aggression: A Commentary, Volumes 1 & 2* (Cambridge University Press 2017)

Sheri Labenski, *Female Defendants in International Criminal Law: Feminist Dialogues* (Routledge 2021, forthcoming)

Nicola Lacey, 'Feminist Legal Theory and the Rights of Women' in Karen Knop (ed), *Gender and Human Rights* (Oxford University Press 2004)

May-Len Skilbrei, 'Sisters in Crime: Representations of Gender and Class in the Media Coverage and Court Proceedings of the Triple Homicide at Orderud Farm' (2013) 9 (2) Crime Media Culture 136

Gail Lewis, 'Questions of Presence' (2017) 117 (1) Feminist Review 1

Paul Lewis and Spencer Ackerman, 'US Set for Syria Strikes after Kerry Says Evidence of Chemical Attack Is "Clear"' 31 August 2013, *The Guardian* https://www.theguardian.com/world/2013/aug/30/john-kerry-syria-attack-clear-evidence (accessed December 2019)

Suzannah Linton, 'Women Accused of International Crimes: A Trans-Disciplinary Inquiry and Methodology' (2016) 27 Criminal Law Forum 159

Suzannah Linton, 'Cambodia, East Timor and Sierra Leone: Experiments in International Justice' (2001) 12 (2) Criminal Law Forum 185

Suzannah Linton, 'Rising from the Ashes: The Creation of a Viable Criminal Justice System in East Timor' (2001) 25 (1) Melbourne University Law Review 122

Catharine MacKinnon, 'The ICTR's Legacy on Sexual Violence' (2008) 14 New England Journal of International and Comparative Law 211

Catharine MacKinnon, 'Women's September 11th: Rethinking the International Law of Conflict' (2006) 47 Harvard International Law Journal 1

Catharine MacKinnon, 'Rape, Genocide, and Women's Human Rights' (1994) 17 Harvard Women's Law Journal 5

MADRE, The International Human Rights Clinic at City University of New York School of Law, and WILPF, 'Seeking Accountability and Demanding Change: A Report on Women's Human Rights Violations in Syria before and during the Conflict' *United Nations Committee to End All Forms of Discrimination against Women*, 58th Session (2014)

Elissa Mailänder, *Female SS Guards and Workaday Violence: The Majdanek Concentration Camp, 1942–1944* (Michigan State University Press 2015)

Nikita Malik, 'Trafficking Terror: How Modern Slavery and Sexual Violence Fund Terrorism' (2017) *Henry Jackson Society* http://henryjacksonsociety.org/wp-content/uploads/2017/10/HJS-Trafficking-Terror-Report-web.pdf (accessed December 2019)

Edecio Martinez, 'Kentucky Woman Indicted for Bosnian War Crimes' 18 March 2011, *CBS News* https://www.cbsnews.com/news/kentucky-woman-indicted-for-bosnian-war-crimes/ (accessed December 2019)

Christian Marxsen, 'The Crimea Crisis – An International Law Perspective' (2014) 74 (2) Heidelberg Journal of International Law 367

Achille Mbembe, 'Necropolitics' (2003) 15 (1) Public Culture 39

Anne McClintock, *Imperial Leather: Race, Gender and Sexuality in the Colonial Contest* (Routledge 1995)

Lorna Mcgregor, Daragh Murray and Vivian Ng, 'International Human Rights Law as a Framework for Algorithmic Accountability' (2019) 68 (2) International and Comparative Law Quarterly 309

Akanksha Mehta, 'The Aesthetics of "Everyday" Violence: Narratives of Violence and Hindu Right-wing Women' (2015) 8 (3) Critical Studies on Terrorism 416

Mary Jo Melone, 'You've Come a Long Way Baby; Was It for This?' 7 May 2004, *St. Petersburg Times*, on file with authors

Juan Méndez, 'National Reconciliation, Transnational Justice, and the International Criminal Court' (2001) 15 (1) Ethics & International Affairs 25

Ikechi Mgbeoji, *Collective Insecurity: The Liberian Crisis, Unilateralism, and Global Order* (UBC Press 2003)

Martha Minow, 'Do Alternative Justice Mechanisms Deserve Recognition in International Criminal Law? Truth Commissions, Amnesties, and Complementarity at the International Criminal Court' (2019) 60 (1) Harvard International Law Journal 1

Mirror Online, 'Bosnia Arrests "Female Monster"– Wife of Warlord "Serb Adolf"' 22 December 2011, *The Mirror* https://www.mirror.co.uk/news/uk-news/bosnia-arrests-female-monster---98517 (accessed December 2019)

Chandra Talpade Mohanty, 'Under Western Eyes: Feminist Scholarship and Colonial Discourses' (1988) 30 Feminist Review 61

Robin Morgan, *The Demon Lover: The Roots of Terrorism* (2nd edn, Pocket Books 2001)

Caroline Moser and Fiona Clark (eds), *Victims, Perpetrators or Actors? Gender, Armed Conflict and Political Violence* (Zed Books 2001)

Makau Mutua, 'Never Again: Questioning the Yugoslav and Rwanda Tribunals' (1997) 11 Temple International and Comparative Law Journal 167

Ngaire Naffine and Rosemary Owens (eds), *Sexing the Subject of Law* (Law Book Company 1997)

Jennifer Nash, *Black Feminism Reimagined: After Intersectionality* (Duke University Press 2019)

Jennifer Nash, 'Re-thinking Intersectionality' (2008) 89 Feminist Review 1

Vasuki Nesiah, 'Introduction: Feminist Interventions: Human Rights, Armed Conflict and International Law' (2009) 103 Proceedings of the Annual Meeting (American Society of International Law) 67

Vasuki Nesiah, 'Resistance in the Age of Empire: Occupied Discourse Pending Investigation' (2006) 27 (5) Third World Quarterly 903

Vasuki Nesiah, 'From Berlin to Bonn to Baghdad: A Space for Infinite Justice' (2004) 17 Harvard Human Rights Journal 75

Vasuki Nesiah, 'The Ground Beneath Her Feet: "Third World" Feminisms' (2003) 4 (3) Journal of International Women's Studies 30

Michael A Newton, 'The Iraqi High Criminal Court: Controversy and Contributions' (2006) 88 (862) International Review of the Red Cross 399

Fionnuala Ní Aoláin, 'The "War on Terror" and Extremism: Assessing the Relevance of the Women, Peace and Security Agenda' (2016) 92 (2) International Affairs 275

Fionnuala Ní Aoláin and Oren Gross, 'A Skeptical View of Deference to the Executive in Times of Crisis' (2008) 41 Israel Law Review 545

Fionnuala Ní Aoláin, Dina Francesca Haynes and Naomi Cahn, *On the Frontlines: Gender, War, and the Post-Conflict Process* (Oxford University Press 2011)

Fionnuala Ní Aolain, Naomi Cahn, Dina Francesca Haynes and Nahla Valji (eds), *The Oxford Handbook of Gender and Conflict* (Oxford University Press 2018)

Michelle Nichols, 'U.S. Pitted against Britain, France, South Africa, Others at UN over Abortion' 29 October 2019, *Reuters* https://www.reuters.com/article/us-women-rights-usa-un/us-pitted-against-britain-france-south-africa-others-at-un-over-abortion-idUSKBN1X829K (accessed December 2019)

Heidi Nichols Haddad, 'Mobilizing the Will to Prosecute: Crimes of Rape at the Yugoslav and Rwandan Tribunals' (2011) 12 Human Rights Review 109

Marianne S Noh, Matthew T Lee and Kathryn M Feltey, 'Mad, Bad, or Reasonable? Newspaper Portrayals of the Battered Woman Who Kills' (2010) 27 Gender Issues 110

Megan A O'Branski, '"The Savage Reduction of the Flesh": Violence, Gender and Bodily Weaponisation in the 1981 Irish Republican Hunger Strike Protest' (2014) 7 (1) Critical Studies on Terrorism 97

Catherine O'Rourke, 'Feminist Strategy in International Law: Understanding Its Legal, Normative and Political Dimensions' (2017) 28 European Journal of International Law 1019

Catherine O'Rourke, *Gender Politics in Transitional Justice* (Routledge 2013)

Catherine O'Rourke and Aisling Swaine, 'CEDAW and the Security Council: Enhancing Women's Rights in Conflict' (2018) 67 International and Comparative Law Quarterly 167

Abdullah Öcalan, *The Political Thought of Abdullah Öcalan: Kurdistan, Woman's Revolution and Democratic Confederalism* (Pluto Press 2017)

Chidi Anselm Odinkalu, 'International Criminal Justice, Peace and Reconciliation in Africa: Re-imagining an Agenda beyond the ICC' (2015) 40 (2) Africa Development 257

Office of the Prime Minister, 'Chemical Weapon Use by Syrian Regime: UK Government Legal Position' 29 August 2013, *Office of the Prime Minister* http://www.gov.uk/government/publications/chemical-weapon-use-by-syrian-regime-uk-government-legal-position (accessed December 2019)

Awino Okech, 'Asymmetrical Conflict and Human Security: Reflections from Kenya' (2015) 37 (1) Strategic Review for Southern Africa 53

Lola Okolosie, 'Beyond "Talking" and "Owning" Intersectionality' (2014) 108 Feminist Review 90

Amy Oliver, 'The US Single Mother Who Was Actually a War Criminal: Killer Becomes First Woman to Be Convicted of Bosnian War Crimes' 1 May 2012, *The Daily Mail* https://www.dailymail.co.uk/news/article-2137411/Rasema-Handanovic-guilty-war-crimes-Bosnia.html (accessed December 2019)

Eki Omorogbe, 'The African Union, the Boko Haram Crisis and Violence against Women' (2017) 2 Ragion Pratica 437

Anne Orford, *Reading Humanitarian Intervention: Human Rights and the Use of Force in International Law* (Cambridge University Press 2003)

Anne Orford, 'Feminism, Imperialism and the Mission of International Law' (2002) 71 Nordic Journal of International Law 275

Anne Orford, 'Muscular Humanitarianism: Reading Narratives of the New Interventionism' (1999) 10 (4) European Journal of International Law 679

Anne Orford, 'The Politics of Collective Security' (1996) 17 Michigan Journal of International Law 373

Yoriko Otomo, 'Of Mimicry and Madness: Speculations on the State' (2008) 28 Australian Feminist Law Journal 53

Dianne Otto, *Rethinking Peace from a Queer Feminist Perspective*, 26 September 2019, Public Lecture at LSE Centre for Women, Peace and Security, London

Dianne Otto (ed), *Queering International Law: Possibilities, Alliances, Complicities, Risks* (Routledge 2018)

Dianne Otto, 'Queering Gender [Identity] in International Law' (2015) 33 (4) Nordic Journal of Human Rights 299

Dianne Otto, 'Transnational Homo-assemblages: Reading "Gender" in Counter-terrorism Discourses' (2013) 4 (2) Jindal Global Law Review 79

Dianne Otto, 'Power and Danger: Feminist Engagement with International Law through the UN Security Council' (2010) 32 Australian Feminist Law Journal 97

Dianne Otto, 'The Security Council's Alliance of Gender Legitimacy: The Symbolic Capital of Resolution 1325' in Hilary Charlesworth and Jean-Marc Coicaud (eds), *Fault Lines of International Legitimacy* (Cambridge University Press 2010)

Dianne Otto, 'Making Sense of Zero Tolerance Policies in Peacekeeping Sexual Economies' in Vanessa Munro and Carl Stychin (eds), *Sexuality and the Law: Feminist Engagements* (Routledge 2007)

Dianne Otto, '"Taking a Break" from "Normal": Thinking Queer in the Context of International Law' (2007) Proceedings of the Annual Meeting of the American Society of International Law 119

Dianne Otto, 'A Sign of "Weakness"? Disrupting Gender Certainties in the Implementation of Security Council Resolution 1325' (2006) 13 Michigan Journal of Gender and Law 113

Dianne Otto, 'Integrating Questions of Gender into Discussion of the Use of Force in the International Law Curriculum' (1995) 14 Legal Education Review 219

Khaled Yacoub Oweis, 'Syria Adds Opposition Peace Talks Delegates to "Terrorist List"' 15 February 2014, *Reuters* https://www.reuters.com/article/us-syria-crisis-blacklist/syria-adds-opposition-peace-talks-delegates-to-terrorist-list-idUSBREA1E0QI20140215 (accessed December 2019)

Oxfam International, 'Now, the World Is without Me. An Investigation of Sexual Violence in Eastern Democratic Republic of Congo' (2010) *Oxfam International* https://www.oxfam.org/en/research/now-world-without-me (accessed December 2019)

Swati Parashar, 'Feminist International Relations and Women Militants: Case Studies from Sri Lanka and Kashmir' (2009) 22 (2) Cambridge Review of International Affairs 235

Rose Parfitt, 'Theorizing Recognition and International Personality' in Anne Orford and Florian Hoffmann (eds), *The Oxford Handbook of the Theory of International Law* (Oxford University Press 2016)

Peace Women Alliance, PEWA Nepal, 'Open Letter from Women Peace Alliance, PEWA to Mr. Ian Martin, Personal Envoy of the UN Secretary General to Nepal for Inclusive, Proportionate Representation and Women Sensitive Peace Process' (2006) *Peace Women Alliance, PEWA Nepal* https://www.nepalresearch.com/crisis_solution/papers/pewa_061212.pdf (accessed December 2019)

V Spike Peterson (ed), *Gendered States: Feminist (Re)Visions of International Relations Theory* (Lynne Rienner Publishers 1992)

Catherine Powell, 'How Women Could Save the World, If Only We Would Let Them: From Gender Essentialism to Inclusive Security' (2017) 28 Yale Journal of Law & Feminism 271

Nicola Pratt and Sophie Richter-Devroe, 'Critically Examining UNSCR 1325 on Women, Peace and Security' (2011) 13 (4) International Feminist Journal of Politics 489

Jasbir K Puar, 'Rethinking Homonationalism' (2013) 45 International Journal of Middle East Studies 336

Jasbir K Puar, 'Abu Ghraib and U.S. Sexual Exceptionalism' (2011) 29 (57/58) Works and Days 115

Jasbir K Puar, *Terrorist Assemblages: Homonationalism in Queer Times* (Duke University Press 2007)

Jasbir K Puar and Amit S Rai, 'Monster, Terrorist, Fag: The War on Terrorism and the Production of Docile Patriots' (2002) 20 (3(72)) Social Text 117

Joseph Pugliese, *State Violence and the Execution of Law: Biopolitical Caesurae of Torture, Black Sites, Drones* (Routledge 2013)

Lindsey Raub, 'Positioning Hybrid Tribunals in International Criminal Justice' (2009) 41 New York University Journal of International Law and Politics 1013

Diana Rayes, Miriam Orcutt, Aula Abbara and Wasim Maziak, 'Systematic Destruction of Healthcare in Eastern Ghouta, Syria' (2018) 360 British Medical Journal 1368

Madeleine Rees, 'Syrian Women Demand to Take Part in the Peace Talks in Geneva' (2014) *Open Democracy* https://www.opendemocracy.net/ en/5050/syrian-women-demand-to-take-part-in-peace-talks-in-geneva/ (accessed December 2019)

Kieth B Richburg, 'Rwandan Nuns Jailed in Genocide' 9 June 2001, *The Washington Post* https://www.washingtonpost.com/archive/ politics/2001/06/09/rwandan-nuns-jailed-in-genocide/fce3308b-3e6e-4784-8490-0887f69c7a39/ (accessed December 2019)

Tom Ruys, *'Armed Attack' and Article 51 of the UN Charter: Evolutions in Customary Law and Practice* (Cambridge University Press 2010)

Kristin Sandvik, 'Technology, Dead Male Bodies, and Feminist Recognition: Gendering ICT Harm Theory' (2018) 44 (1) Australian Feminist Law Journal 49

Austin Sarat and Thomas R Kearns (eds), *Law's Violence* (University of Michigan Press 1992)

Wendy Adele-Marie Sarti, *Women and Nazis: Perpetrators of Genocide and Other Crimes during Hitler's Regime, 1933–1945* (Academica Press 2011)

Marco Sassòli, *International Humanitarian Law: Rules, Controversies, and Solutions to Problems Arising in Warfare* (Edward Elgar 2019)

Michael P Scharf, 'The Iraqi High Tribunal: A Viable Experiment in International Justice?' (2007) 5 (2) Journal of International Criminal Justice 258

Michael N Schmitt and Christopher M Ford, 'Assessing U.S. Justifications for Using Force in Response to Syria's Chemical Attacks: An International Law Perspective' (2017) 9 Journal of National Security Law and Policy 283

Security Council Report, 'Monthly Forecast: January 2020' (2019) *Security Council Report* https://www.securitycouncilreport.org/monthly_ forecast/2020-01 (accessed December 2019)

Security Council Report, 'Monthly Forecast: May 2014' (2014) *Security Council Report* https://www.securitycouncilreport.org/monthly_ forecast/2014-05 (accessed December 2019)

Security Council Report, 'Monthly Forecast: April 2014' (2014) *Security Council Report* https://www.securitycouncilreport.org/monthly_ forecast/2014-04 (accessed December 2019)

Security Council Report, 'Monthly Forecast: March 2014' (2014) *Security Council Report* https://www.securitycouncilreport.org/monthly_ forecast/2014-03 (accessed December 2019)

Security Council Report, 'Monthly Forecast: February 2014' (2014) *Security Council Report* https://www.securitycouncilreport.org/monthly_ forecast/2014-02 (accessed December 2019)

Security Council Report, 'Monthly Forecast: September 2011' (2011) *Security Council Report* https://www.securitycouncilreport.org/monthly_forecast/2011-09 (accessed December 2019)

Lara Seligman and Colum Lynch, 'As Assad Gains Ground, New Syria Talks Offer Little Hope of Peace' 12 November 2019, *Foreign Policy* https://foreignpolicy.com/2019/11/12/as-assad-gains-ground-new-syria-talks-offer-little-hope-of-peace/ (accessed December 2019)

Patricia Viseur Sellers, 'Gender Strategy Is Not Luxury for International Courts Symposium: Prosecuting Sexual and Gender-based Crimes before International/ized Criminal Courts' (2009) 17 (2) Journal of Gender, Social Policy and the Law 301

Kristina Sgueglia, 'Woman Lied about Role in Rwanda Genocide, U.S. Jury Says' 22 February 2013, *CNN* https://edition.cnn.com/2013/02/21/us/new-hampshire-rwanda-genocide/index.html (accessed December 2019)

Amr Shalakany, 'On a Certain Queer Discomfort with *Orientalism*' (2007) 101 Proceedings of the Annual Meeting of the American Society of International Law 125

Malcolm N Shaw, *International Law* (8th edn, Cambridge University Press 2017)

Laura Shepherd, 'The Women, Peace, and Security Agenda at the United Nations' in Anthony Burke and Rita Parker (eds), *Global Insecurity: Futures of Global Chaos and Governance* (Palgrave Macmillan 2017)

Laura Shepherd, 'Making War Safe for Women? National Action Plans and the Militarisation of the Women, Peace and Security Agenda' (2016) 37 (3) International Political Science Review 324

Laura Shepherd, *Gender, Violence and Security: Discourse as Practice* (Zed Books 2008)

Ivan Simonovic, 'The Role of the ICTY in the Development of International Criminal Adjudication' (1999) 23 (2) Fordham International Law Journal 440

Gerry Simpson, *Law, War and Crime: War Crimes, Trials and the Reinvention of International Law* (Polity Press 2007)

Gerry Simpson, *Great Powers and Outlaw States: Unequal Sovereigns in the International Legal Order* (Cambridge University Press 2004)

Laura Sjoberg, 'The Terror of Everyday Counterterrorism' (2015) 8 (3) Critical Studies on Terrorism 383

Laura Sjoberg, 'Gendered Realities of the Immunity Principle: Why Gender Analysis Needs Feminism' (2006) 50 (4) International Studies Quarterly 889

Laura Sjoberg and Caron E Gentry, 'It's Complicated: Looking Closely at Women in Violent Extremism' (2016) 17 (2) Georgetown Journal of International Affairs 23

Laura Sjoberg and Caron E Gentry (eds), *Women, Gender, and Terrorism* (University of Georgia Press 2011)

Laura Sjoberg and Caron E Gentry, *Mothers, Monsters, Whores: Women's Violence in Global Politics* (Zed Books 2007)

Dean Spade and Craig Willse, 'Marriage Will Never Set Us Free' 6 September 2013, *Organising Upgrade* http://archive.organizingupgrade.com/index.php/modules-menu/beyond-capitalism/item/1002-marriage-will-never-set-us-free (accessed December 2019)

Carrie Sperling, 'Mother of Atrocities: Pauline Nyiramasuhuko's Role in the Rwandan Genocide' (2006) 33 (2) Fordham Urban Law Journal 101

Eli Stamnes, 'The Responsibility to Protect: Integrating Gender Perspectives into Policies and Practices' (2012) 4 (2) Global Responsibility to Protect 172

Stanford International Human Rights & Conflict Resolution Clinic, 'Living under Drones: Death, Injury, and Trauma to Civilians from US Drone Practices in Pakistan' (2012) *Stanford International Human Rights & Conflict Resolution Clinic* https://www-cdn.law.stanford.edu/wp-content/uploads/2015/07/Stanford-NYU-LIVING-UNDER-DRONES.pdf (accessed December 2019)

Anna Stavrianakis, 'Legitimising Liberal Militarism: Politics, Law and War in the Arms Trade Treaty' (2016) 37 (5) Third World Quarterly 840

Brian Stelter, 'James Foley Remembered as "Brave and Tireless" Journalist' 21 August 2014, *CNN* https://edition.cnn.com/2014/08/20/us/james-foley-life/index.html (accessed December 2019)

Lorina Sthapit and Philippe Doneys, 'Female Maoist Combatants during and after the People's War' in Åshild Kolås (ed), *Women, Peace and Security in Nepal: From Civil War to Post-conflict Reconstruction* (Special Nepal Edition, Routledge 2018)

Dan E Stigall, 'The French Military Intervention in Mali, Counter-Terrorism, and the Law of Armed Conflict' (2015) 223 Military Law Review 1

Will Storr, 'The Rape of Men: The Darkest Secret of War' 17 July 2011, *The Observer* https://www.theguardian.com/society/2011/jul/17/the-rape-of-men (accessed December 2019)

Elisabeth Storrs, '"Our Scapegoat": An Exploration of Media Representations of Myra Hindley and Rosemary West' (2004) 11 (1) Theology & Sexuality 9

Jane Stromseth, 'Justice on the Ground: Can International Criminal Courts Strengthen Domestic Rule of Law in Post-conflict Societies?' (2009) 1 (1) Hague Journal on the Rule of Law 87

Jelena Subotić, 'The Cruelty of False Remorse: Biljana Plavšić at the Hague' (2012) 36 Southeastern Europe 39

Nikki Sullivan, *A Critical Introduction to Queer Theory* (New York University Press 2003)

Seira Tamang, 'Historicizing State "Fragility" in Nepal' (2012) 17 (2) Studies in Nepali History and Society 263

Seira Tamang, 'The Politics of Conflict and Difference or the Difference of Conflict in Politics: The Women's Movement in Nepal' (2009) 91 Feminist Review 61

J Ann Tickner, *Gender in International Relations: Feminist Perspectives on Achieving Global Security* (Columbia University Press 1992)

Jennifer Trahan, 'Is Complementarity the Right Approach for the International Criminal Court's Crime of Aggression? Considering the Problem of "Overzealous" National Court Prosecutions' (2012) 45 (3) Cornell International Law Journal 569

Jennifer Trahan, 'A Critical Guide to the Iraqi High Tribunal's Anfal Judgement: Genocide against the Kurds' (2009) 30 (2) Michigan Journal of International Law 305

Torunn L Tryggestad, 'Trick or Treat? The UN and Implementation of Security Council Resolution 1325 on Women, Peace, and Security' (2009) 15 Global Governance 539

Nicholas Tsagourias, 'Self-defence against Non-state Actors: The Interaction between Self-defence as a Primary Rule and Self-defence as a Secondary Rule' (2016) 29 (3) Leiden Journal of International Law 801

Nicholas Tsagourias and Nigel White, *Collective Security: Theory, Law and Practice* (Cambridge University Press 2013)

David Turns, 'The Law of Armed Conflict (International Humanitarian Law)' in Malcom D Evans (ed), *International Law* (5th edn, Oxford University Press 2018)

Leila Ullrich, '"But What about Men?": Gender Disquiet in International Criminal Justice' (published online 28 November 2019) Theoretical Criminology https://doi.org/10.1177/1362480619887164 (accessed December 2019)

UN News, 'UN-Arab League Envoy Apologizes to Syrian People over Stalemate in Peace Talks' 15 February 2014, *UN News* https://news.un.org/en/story/2014/02/461922-un-arab-league-envoy-apologizes-syrian-people-over-stalemate-peace-talks (accessed December 2019)

US Department of Justice, 'Lawfulness of a Lethal Operation Directed against a US Citizen Who Is a Senior Operational Leader of Al-Qa'ida or an Associated Force' (2011) *US Department of Justice* https://fas.org/irp/eprint/doj-lethal.pdf (accessed December 2019)

USAID, 'People, not Pawns: Women's Participation in Violent Extremism across MENA' (2015) *USAID*

Marguerite Waller and Jennifer Rycenga (eds), *Frontline Feminisms: Women, War, and Resistance* (Routledge 2001)

Eyal Weizman, 'Legislative Attack' (2010) 27 (6) Theory, Culture and Society 11

Marc Weller (ed), *The Oxford Handbook of the Use of Force in International Law* (Oxford University Press 2015)

What's in Blue, 'In Hindsight: Negotiations on Resolution 2467 on Sexual Violence in Conflict' 2 May 2019, *What's in Blue* https://www.whatsinblue. org/2019/05/in-hindsight-negotiations-on-resolution-2467-on-sexual-violence-in-conflict.php (accessed December 2019)

Flint Whitlock, *The Beasts of Buchenwald: Karl & Ilse Koch, Human-skin Lampshades, and the War-crimes Trial of the Century (Buchenwald Trilogy)* (Cable Publishing 2011)

Robyn Wiegman, *Object Lessons* (Duke University Press 2012)

Lauren Wilcox, 'Embodying Algorithmic War: Gender, Race, and the Posthuman in Drone Warfare' (2017) 48 (1) Security Dialogue 11

Lauren Wilcox, 'Drones, Swarms and Becoming-insect: Feminist Utopias and Posthuman Politics' (2017) 116 Feminist Review 25

Lauren Wilcox, 'Drone Warfare and the Making of Bodies Out of Place' (2015) 3 (1) Critical Studies on Security 127

Haidi Willmot, Ralph Mamiya, Scott Sheeran and Marc Weller (eds), *Protection of Civilians* (Oxford University Press 2016)

Patrick Wintour, '"Golden Opportunity" Lost as Syrian Peace Talks Collapse' 14 December 2017, *The Guardian* https://www.theguardian.com/ world/2017/dec/14/golden-opportunity-lost-as-syrian-peace-talks-collapse (accessed December 2019)

Haley A Wodenshek, 'Ordinary Women: Female Perpetrators of the Nazi Final Solution' (2015) (Senior Thesis Trinity College) https://digitalrepository. trincoll.edu/theses/522/ (accessed December 2019)

Elisabeth Jean Wood, 'Conflict-related Sexual Violence and the Policy Implications of Recent Research' (2014) 96 (894) International Review of the Red Cross 457

Timothy Dylan Wood, 'Tracing the Last Breath: Movements in Anlong Veng' (2009) (PhD Dissertation Rice University)

Oliver Wright, 'The Heir to Blair: PM Makes "Moral Case" for Attack on Syria' 28 August 2013, *The Independent* https://www.independent.co.uk/ news/uk/politics/the-heir-to-blair-pm-makes-moral-case-for-attack-on-syria-8786783.html (accessed December 2019)

Shelley Wright, 'The Horizon of Becoming: Culture, Gender and History after September 11' (2002) 71 Nordic Journal of International Law 215

Rola Yasmine and Catherine Moughalian, 'Systemic Violence against Syrian Refugee Women and the Myth of Effective Intrapersonal Interventions' (2016) 24 (47) Reproductive Health Matters 27

Nira Yuval-Davis, 'Intersectionality and Feminist Politics' (2006) 13 (3) European Journal of Women's Studies 193

Ralph Zacklin, 'The Failings of Ad Hoc International Tribunals' (2004) 2 (2) Journal of International Criminal Justice 541

Dubravka Zarkov, 'Feminism and the Disintegration of Yugoslavia: On the Politics of Gender and Ethnicity' (2003) 24 (3) Social Development Issues 1

UN AND OTHER DOCUMENTS

Convention on Prohibitions or Restrictions on the Use of Certain Conventional Weapons

Additional Protocol to the Convention on Prohibitions or Restrictions on the Use of Certain Conventional Weapons Which May Be Deemed to Be Excessively Injurious or to Have Indiscriminate Effects (Protocol IV, entitled Protocol on Blinding Laser Weapons) (13 October 1995) 2024 UNTS 163

Convention on Prohibitions or Restrictions on the Use of Certain Conventional Weapons Which May Be Deemed to Be Excessively Injurious or to Have Indiscriminate Effects (10 October 1980) 1342 UNTS 137

Report of the 2016 Informal Meeting of Experts on Lethal Autonomous Weapons Systems (LAWS), Geneva (12–16 December 2016) UN Doc. CCW/CONF.V/2

Committee on the Elimination of Discrimination against Women

Committee on the Elimination of Discrimination against Women, 'General Recommendation No. 18 – Tenth Session, 1991 Disabled Women' (30 January 1992) UN Doc. A/46/38

Committee on the Elimination of Discrimination against Women, 'General Recommendation No. 26 on Women Migrant Workers' (5 December 2008) UN Doc. CEDAW/C/2009/WP.1/R

Committee on the Elimination of Discrimination against Women, 'General Recommendation No. 30 on Women in Conflict Prevention, Conflict and Post-conflict Situations' (1 November 2013) UN Doc. CEDAW/C/GC/30

Committee on the Elimination of Discrimination against Women, 'Concluding Observations on the Second Periodic Report of the Syrian Arab Republic' (24 July 2014) UN Doc. CEDAW/C/SYR/CO/2

Committee on the Elimination of Discrimination against Women, 'General Recommendation No. 32 on the Gender-related Dimensions of Refugee Status, Asylum, Nationality and Statelessness of Women' (14 November 2014) UN Doc. CEDAW/C/GC/32

Committee on the Elimination of Discrimination against Women, 'General Recommendation No. 34 on the Rights of Rural Women' (7 March 2016) UN Doc. CEDAW/C/GC/34

Committee on the Elimination of Discrimination against Women, 'General Recommendation No. 35 on Gender-based Violence against Women, Updating General Recommendation No. 19' (26 July 2017) UN Doc. CEDAW/C/GC/35

General Assembly and Security Council

UN General Assembly and Security Council, 'United Nations Mission to Investigate Allegations of the Use of Chemical Weapons in the Syrian Arab Republic: Final Report' (13 December 2013) UN Doc. A/68/663–S/2013/735

The Geneva Conventions and Their Additional Protocols

Geneva Convention for the Amelioration of the Condition of the Wounded and Sick in Armed Forces in the Field (12 August 1949) 75 UNTS 31
Geneva Convention for the Amelioration of the Condition of the Wounded, Sick and Shipwrecked Members of Armed Forces at Sea (12 August 1949) 75 UNTS 85
Geneva Convention Relative to the Protection of Civilian Persons in Time of War (12 August 1949) 75 UNTS 287
Geneva Convention Relative to the Treatment of Prisoners of War (12 August 1949) 75 UNTS 135
Protocol Additional to the Geneva Conventions of 12 August 1949, and Relating to the Protection of Victims of International Armed Conflicts (Protocol I) (8 June 1977) 1125 UNTS 3
Protocol Additional to the Geneva Conventions of 12 August 1949, and Relating to the Protection of Victims of Non-International Armed Conflicts (Protocol II) (8 June 1977) 1125 UNTS 609

The Hague Peace Conference 1899

Convention for the Pacific Settlement of International Disputes (29 July 1899) 1 Bevans 230
Convention with Respect to the Laws and Customs of War on Land (29 July 1899) 1 Bevans 247
Declaration Concerning Asphyxiating Gases (29 July 1899) 187 CTS 453
Declaration Concerning Expanding Bullets (29 July 1899) 187 CTS 459
Declaration to Prohibit for the Term of Five Years the Launching of Projectiles and Explosives from Balloons, and Other Methods of a Similar Nature (29 July 1899) 1 Bevans 270
Final Act of the International Peace Conference, 29 July 1899 https://ihl-databases.icrc.org/ihl/INTRO/145 (accessed December 2019)

The Hague Peace Conference 1907

Convention Relating to the Status of Enemy Merchant Ships at the Outbreak of Hostilities (18 October 1907) in Carnegie Endowment for International Peace, Pamphlet No 14 (The Endowment 1915)

Convention Relative to the Laying of Automatic Submarine Contact Mines (18 October 1907) 1 Bevans 669

Convention Respecting the Rights and Duties of Neutral Powers and Persons in Case of War on Land (18 October 1907) 1 Bevans 654

Convention Respecting the Laws and Customs of War on Land (18 October 1907) 1 Bevans 631

Declaration Prohibiting the Discharge of Projectiles and Explosives from Balloons (18 October 1907) 1 Bevans 739

Final Act of the Second Peace Conference, 18 October 1907 https://ihl-databases.icrc.org/applic/ihl/ihl.nsf/INTRO/185 (accessed December 2019)

Human Rights Committee

Human Rights Committee, CCPR General Comment no. 29, Article 4: Derogations during a State of Emergency (31 August 2001) CCPR/C/21/Rev.1/Add.11, adopted at the 1950th meeting on 24 July 2001

Human Rights Council

Human Rights Council, 'Report of the Human Rights Council on Its Seventeenth Special Session' (18 October 2011) UN Doc. A/HRC/S-17/2

Human Rights Council, 'Report of the Independent International Commission of Inquiry on the Syrian Arab Republic' (23 November 2011) UN Doc. A/HRC/S-17/2/Add.1

Human Rights Council Resolution 22/24 'Situation of Human Rights in the Syrian Arab Republic' (12 April 2013) UN Doc. A/HRC/RES/22/24

Human Rights Council Resolution 23/26 'The Deterioration of the Situation of Human Rights in the Syrian Arab Republic, and the Need to Grant Immediate Access to the Commission of Inquiry' (25 June 2013) UN Doc. A/HRC/RES/23/26

Human Rights Council, 'Report of the Independent International Commission of Inquiry on the Syrian Arab Republic' (18 July 2013) UN Doc. A/HRC/23/58

Human Rights Council, 'Report of the Independent International Commission of Inquiry on the Syrian Arab Republic' (16 August 2013) UN Doc. A/HRC/24/46

Human Rights Council Resolution 25/23 'The Continuing Grave Deterioration of the Human Rights and Humanitarian Situation in the Syrian Arab Republic' (9 April 2014) UN Doc. A/HRC/RES/25/23

Human Rights Council Resolution 26/23 'The Continuing Grave Deterioration in the Human Rights and Humanitarian Situation in the Syrian Arab Republic' (17 July 2014) UN Doc. A/HRC/RES/26/23

Human Rights Council Resolution 27/16 'The Continuing Grave Deterioration in the Human Rights and Humanitarian Situation in the Syrian Arab Republic' (3 October 2014) UN Doc. A/HRC/RES/27/16

Human Rights Council, 'Report of the Independent International Commission of Inquiry on the Syrian Arab Republic' (2 February 2017) UN Doc. A/HRC/34/64

Human Rights Council, 'Report of the Independent International Commission of Inquiry on the Syrian Arab Republic' (8 August 2017) UN Doc. A/HRC/36/55

International Criminal Court

Rome Statute of the International Criminal Court, General Assembly (17 July 1998) UN Doc. A/CONF.183/9

International Law Commission

International Law Commission, 'The Charter and Judgement of the Nürnberg Tribunal: History and Analysis' (1949) UN Doc. A/CN.4/5

'Report of the International Law Commission on the Work of Its Eighteenth Session' (4 May–19 July 1966) UN Doc. A/6309/Rev.1

International Treaties (Other)

Convention on the Prevention and Punishment of the Crime of Genocide (9 December 1948) 78 UNTS 277

Convention on the Elimination of All Forms of Discrimination against Women (18 December 1979) 1249 UNTS 13

International Covenant on Civil and Political Rights (16 December 1966) 999 UNTS 171

Convention on Cluster Munitions (30 May 2008) 2688 UNTS 39

Letters

'Identical Letters Dated 14 June 1997 from the Permanent Representative of Iraq to the United Nations Addressed to the Secretary-General and to the President of the Security Council' UN Doc. S/1997/461 (16 June 1997)

'Letter Dated 14 January 2013 from the Chargé d'affaires a.i. of the Permanent Mission of Switzerland to the United Nations Addressed to the Secretary-General' (16 January 2013) UN Doc. A/67/694-S/2013/19

'Letter Dated 20 September 2014 from the Permanent Representative of Iraq to the United Nations Addressed to the President of the Security Council' (22 September 2014) UN Doc. S/2014/691

'Letter Dated 23 September 2014 from the Permanent Representative of the United States of America to the United Nations Addressed to the Secretary-General' (23 September 2014) UN Doc. S/2014/695

'Letter Dated 9 October 2019 from the Permanent Representative of Turkey to the United Nations Addressed to the President of the Security Council' (9 October 2019) UN Doc. S/2019/804

Office of the United Nations High Commissioner for Human Rights

Office of the United Nations High Commissioner for Human Rights, 'Nepal Conflict Report' October 2012 https://www.ohchr.org/Documents/Countries/NP/OHCHR_Nepal_Conflict_Report2012.pdf (accessed December 2019)

Office of the United Nations High Commissioner for Human Rights, 'UN rights Experts Urge France to Protect Fundamental Freedoms while Countering Terrorism' 19 January 2016 http://www.ohchr.org/EN/NewsEvents/Pages/DisplayNews.aspx?NewsID=16966&LangID=E (accessed December 2019)

Patricia Viseur Sellers, 'The Prosecution of Sexual Violence in Conflict: The Importance of Human Rights as Means of Interpretation' (2008) Office of the United Nations High Commissioner for Human Rights, Women's Human Rights and Gender Unit

Security Council

Statement by the President of the Security Council (2 October 2013) UN Doc. S/PRST/2013/15

Security Council, 'Report of the Secretary-General on the Implementation of Security Council Resolution 2139' (20 June 2014) UN Doc. S/2014/427

Statement by the President of the Security Council (28 July 2014) Un Doc. S/PRST/2014/14

Record of the 8649th Meeting of the UN Security Council (29 October 2019) UN Doc. S/PV.8649

Security Council Resolutions

Security Council Resolution 50 (29 May 1948) UN Doc. S/RES/50
Security Council Resolution 788 (19 November 1992) UN Doc. S/RES/788
Security Council Resolution 827 (25 May 1993) UN Doc. S/RES/827
Security Council Resolution 955 (8 November 1994) UN Doc. S/RES/955
Security Council Resolution 1306 (5 July 2000) UN Doc. S/RES/1306
Security Council Resolution 1325 (31 October 2000) UN Doc. S/RES/1325
Security Council Resolution 1373 (28 September 2001) UN Doc. S/RES/1373
Security Council Resolution 1542 (30 April 2004) UN Doc. S/RES/1542

Security Council Resolution 1624 (14 September 2005) UN Doc. S/RES/1624
Security Council Resolution 1718 (14 October 2006) UN Doc. S/RES/1718
Security Council Resolution 1820 (19 June 2008) UN Doc. S/RES/1820
Security Council Resolution 1888 (30 September 2009) UN Doc. S/RES/1888
Security Council Resolution 1889 (5 October 2009) UN Doc. S/RES/1889
Security Council Resolution 1960 (16 December 2010) UN Doc. S/RES/1960
Security Council Resolution 1970 (26 February 2011) UN Doc. S/RES/1970
Security Council Resolution 1973 (17 March 2011) UN Doc. S/RES/1973
Security Council Resolution 2106 (24 June 2013) UN Doc. S/RES/2106
Security Council Resolution 2118 (27 September 2013) UN Doc. S/RES/2118
Security Council Resolution 2122 (18 October 2013) UN Doc. S/RES/2122
Security Council Resolution 2129 (17 December 2013) UN Doc. S/RES/2129
Security Council Resolution 2139 (22 February 2014) UN Doc. S/RES/2139
Security Council Resolution 2165 (14 July 2014) UN Doc. S/RES/2165
Security Council Resolution 2170 (15 August 2014) UN Doc. S/RES/2170
Security Council Resolution 2199 (12 February 2015) UN Doc. S/RES/2199
Security Council Resolution 2242 (13 October 2015) UN Doc. S/RES/2242
Security Council Resolution 2249 (20 November 2015) UN Doc. S/RES/2249
Security Council Resolution 2254 (18 December 2015) UN Doc. S/RES/2254
Security Council Resolution 2449 (13 December 2018) UN Doc. S/RES/2449
Security Council Resolution 2467 (23 April 2019) UN Doc. S/RES/2467
Security Council Resolution 2493 (29 October 2019) UN Doc. S/RES/2493

Security Council Counter-Terrorism Committee

Security Council Counter-Terrorism Committee, 'In a First for the Counter-terrorism Committee, the Security Council Body Holds Open Briefing on the Role of Women in Countering Terrorism and Violent Extremism' 9 September 2015 https://www.un.org/sc/ctc/news/2015/09/09/in-a-first-for-the-counter-terrorism-committee-the-security-council-body-holds-open-briefing-on-the-role-of-women-in-countering-terrorism-and-violent-extremism/ (accessed December 2019)
Security Council Counter-Terrorism Committee, 'The Role of Women in Countering Terrorism and Violent Extremism' Open Briefing of the Counter-terrorism Committee 9 September 2015 http://webtv.un.org/meetings-events/watch/the-role-of-women-in-countering-terrorism-and-violent-extremism-open-briefing-of-the-counter-terrorism-committee/4474290840001 (accessed December 2019)

INDEX

www.ingramcontent.com/pod-product-compliance
Lightning Source LLC
Chambersburg PA
CBHW050411280326
41932CB00013BA/1815